I0148414

Breckinridge Long

American Eichmann???

Also by Neil Rolde

Real Political Tales: Short Stories by a Veteran Politician
York Is Living History
O. Murray Carr: A Novel
Maine in the World: Stories of Some of Those From Here Who
Went Away
Continental Liar From the State of Maine: James G. Blaine
Maine: Downeast and Different, an Illustrated History
Unsettled Past, Unsettled Future: The Story of Maine Indians
The Baxters of Maine: Downeast Visionaries
The Interrupted Forest: A History of Maine's Wildlands
Your Money or Your Health
So You Think You Know Maine
Rio Grande Do Norte: The Story of Maine's Partner State in Brazil
Sir William Pepperrell of Colonial New England

BRECKINRIDGE LONG

AMERICAN EICHMANN???

An Enquiry Into the Character
of the
Man Who Denied Visas to the Jews

Neil Rolde

Polar Bear & Company
An imprint of the
Solon Center for Research and Publishing
Solon & Rockland, Maine

Polar Bear & Company™
info@soloncenter.org
Polarbearandco.org, Soloncenter.org
PO Box 311, Solon, Maine 04979 U.S.A.
Solon Center for Research and Publishing

Copyright © 2013 by Neil Rolde. All rights reserved. No part of this
book may be reproduced in any form without permission in writing
from the author's assignees or from the publisher, except for brief
quotations for critical articles and reviews. One or more names in the
text have been changed for anonymity.

First edition 2013
Library of Congress Control Number: 2013934237
Retailers may order via Ingram: ISBN 978-1-882190-13-3

Cover by Ramona du Houx
Manufactured on durable, acid-free paper in more than one country.

Contents

Foreword

Students of mid-twentieth-century American political and diplomatic history remember Breckinridge Long as a well-connected and influential force, particularly during the Roosevelt years. Those with a particular concern for the tragically inadequate American efforts to rescue victims of the Holocaust point to Long as a central figure in resisting and obstructing those efforts. He has been characterized as an anti-Semite, a xenophobe, and alternatively as an anti-communist who opposed immigration out of fear of communist infiltration. Interesting historical figures are, regretfully, often reduced to single dimensions, and the complexity of their lives and motivations are lost. In this erudite, thoughtful and well-written biography, Neil Rolde has fleshed out a multidimensional portrait of this gifted, influential and flawed public figure, traced his extraordinary career, and explored a range of theories as to Long's motivations. In so doing, Rolde has provided a wealth of information not only about Long but also about this critical and troubled chapter in modern American political and diplomatic history.

David M. Gordis, PhD
President Emeritus
Hebrew College

Introduction

St. Louis

In St. Louis, the locals like to boast that Forest Park, the swath of wooded greenery traversing the middle of the Missouri city, is larger than Manhattan's celebrated Central Park. Along its north side runs Lindell Boulevard, definitely a high-rent district, where quasi-mansions side by side occupy the grounds of the original site for the famous *Meet Me In St. Louis, Louie* World's Fair of 1904. Near the north end sits 5145 Lindell, a stately neo-Greek Revival residence still talked about in awe because of the actual art gallery its one-time owners built inside to house their private collection. Those owners were the Longs—Breckinridge Long and his wife, the former Christine Alexander Graham.

Mrs. Long, born to significant wealth, had the St. Louis pedigree. Her maternal grandfather was Francis Preston Blair Jr., a seminal hero in Missouri history, credited with having kept the state out of Confederate hands during the Civil War. Muckraking Washington, DC columnist Drew Pearson once wrote that Mr. Long was famous "for his St. Louis mansion in which he entertained Marshal Joffre (the commander of French forces in World War I) and the Count de Chambrun" (a descendant of Lafayette) and "for his gracious millionaire wife . . . whose greatest passion in life is bridge." This heiress's money had come to her, an only child, through her father, Benjamin Brown Graham, founder and owner of the largest paper distributing company west of the Mississippi.

The Breckinridge pedigree was far more distinguished on a national scale. Samuel Miller Breckinridge Long, to give him his literal birth name (he preferred *Breck*) had a heritage as Brahmin as any Beacon Hill Bostonian, although in the Southern aristocracy. His forebear John Cabell Breckinridge was vice president of the United States under James Buchanan and ran for president as the pro-slavery candidate in that famous four-way 1860 election won by Lincoln. Breck Long's own father served as a Confederate officer, a major with the 44th North Carolina regiment.

So it could be said that two great sectional strains had merged through the Long-Graham marriage and, indeed, there were even genealogical connections between the Breckinridge and Blair families, since both were of Scots-Irish Presbyterian descent.

Breckinridge Long, to give him the name he is most known by, has taken a hammering from writers who hold him responsible for the "paper walls" he erected to keep Jews out of the U.S., while serving as an assistant secretary of state during the period 1940-44. Here are some sample opinions:

Eran Lerman, executive director of the American Jewish Committee's Israel Middle East Office in Jerusalem: "What happened to Jews here and to Jews in Europe at the hands of the likes of Breckinridge Long—which most people have forgotten—but in my mind he ranks with the worst offenders."[1]

Robert S. Wistrich's book, *Anti-Semitism, The Longest Hatred*, states,

> The attitude of the chief State Department official responsible for refugees in the Roosevelt Administration, Breckinridge Long Jr. [*sic*], a paranoid anti-Semite who regarded all Jews as Communists, demonstrates the extent of American responsibility when it came to the Jewish immigration issue. Nor was this merely isolationist protectionism. After reading "Mein Kampf," Long, for example, he called it "eloquent in opposition to Jewry and to Jews as exponents of Communism and chaos."[2]

Ian Henzel, "stylemaker," from a review of the Internet's "The American Experience: America and the Holocaust. Deceit and Indifference": "Pity that we did not treat Breckinridge Long as a war criminal."[3]

Saul Friedlander's exhaustive study of the Holocaust, *The Years of Extermination*, contains this estimation of Long:

> His attitude, openly expressed in his diary, derived from an unmistakable hostility to Jews. Long's anti-Semitism was neither shrill nor rabid; yet there is little doubt that the assistant secretary spared no effort to limit immigration to the utmost while it was still possible to scuttle any rescue projects during the crucial 1942–43 period.[4]

And Alan M. Dershowitz, well-known lawyer and Harvard law professor, has written: "Roosevelt's failure to fire Breckinridge Long who was instrumental in delaying visas and causing the deaths of so many Jews seems inexcusable to me, even in retrospect."[5]

Anger against such a prejudiced bureaucrat boils up automatically when reading these assertions—and has led, indeed, to my subtitle for what I believe is the first full-scale biography of Breckinridge Long: *An American Eichmann???*, but with question marks added. Therein lies the motivation behind a wholesale look at the life of someone I first immediately began thinking of as an *unsung villain*. In the Library of Congress, there is a voluminous collection of Long's papers, left by him to the Manuscript Division. The World War II years have been heavily used by scholars. The rest seems untouched, with his diaries starting in 1916 and family letters traced back to the eighteenth century. What goes into the making of an unsung villain is there in mind-boggling profusion.

In the interests of full disclosure, I am Jewish, second-generation American, born in Boston, whose oft-despised ancestors dwelt in the Eastern European communities wiped out by the Holocaust. Dozens of relatives I never knew, nor even heard of, presumably perished. Moreover, my wife, née Carlotta Florsheim in Munich, Germany, in 1933, escaped, as she so nicely puts it, "from becoming a bar of soap," when her parents managed to leave Germany in 1938 and—pre-Breckinridge Long—gained visas to the U.S. in 1939.

Still, I intend to write about this Breckinridge Long, this courtly gentleman, this Princeton grad and Princeton trustee, this Wilsonian and Rooseveltian Democrat, with as much scrupulous objectivity as possible, in an attempt to understand the mechanisms of his alleged villainy. Besides, his story is played out against a backdrop of the twentieth century's most dramatic events—World War I and World War II—and their aftermaths, which included the creation of the United Nations and subsequently, because of a UN decision, the State of Israel—all relevant to the tragedy of the Holocaust.

Now, briefly, back to St. Louis. I have sketched the mansion at 5145 Lindell Boulevard in which Breckinridge Long lived with his heiress bride. Not much more than a stone's throw across the street is a statue in Forest Park of Christine Long's distinguished grandfather, Francis Preston Blair Jr., hailed on its pedestal's plaque as "the indomitable Free-Soil Leader of the West, the Herald and Standard Bearer of Freedom in Missouri." Yet there is another commemorative sculpture nearby that also draws attention. Upon examination, one wonders: Was it put there deliberately to mock Breckinridge Long, the oft-labeled anti-Semite? For this elaborate monument, with its various bas-reliefs, honors "The 300th Anniversary of the first Jewish settlement in America." Its initial dedication, dated November 1956, reads:

> THE LUCY AND STANLEY LOPATA PLAZA COMMEMORATING THE 300TH ANNIVERSARY OF THE FIRST JEWISH SETTLEMENT OF AMERICA WAS THE INSPIRATION OF RABBI FERDINAND ISSERMAN.

That is the first paragraph. The impulse behind it, if one sees the set of carved stones as a symbolic finger poked in Breckinridge Long's eye in his own hometown, within sight of his former home, has to be the second paragraph:

> THOUGH MARKING A JEWISH HISTORICAL EVENT, IT CELEBRATES AMERICA AS A HAVEN FOR ALL PEOPLE SEEKING FREEDOM OF LIFE, WORSHIP, SPEECH AND OPPORTUNITY.

"America as a haven for all people," a concept that the assistant secretary of state, despite his distinguished lineage with its deep roots in our nation's history, seems to have found distasteful, whether he was an anti-Semite or not.

Breckinridge Long died two years after the memorial's installation.

Chapter One

A Special Sunday
at the
White House

ORDINARILY, BUSINESS WASN'T CONDUCTED ON Sundays at Franklin Delano Roosevelt's World War II White House. But on Sunday afternoon January 16, 1944, FDR sat behind his desk in the Oval Office facing three visibly agitated members of his administration. The trio was led by his long-time friend and Dutchess County, New York, neighbor, Henry Morgenthau Jr., secretary of the Treasury, and with him were two top Treasury aides, General Counsel Randolph Paul and head of the Foreign Funds Control Unit, John Pehle. Another Funds Control Unit staffer, Josian DuBois, apparently wasn't there, but he had spent all of Christmas Day, on his own time, writing the document that was handed to the president.

From many years of experience, FDR knew it was not out of character for his old pal Henry to be downright pushy at times. *A Jewish trait*, he may have thought automatically if benignly. However, those other fellows in the chairs opposite him, the younger guys, they didn't look at all Jewish and still they had the same fierce, determined, stubborn expressions on their faces as did their boss. They had brought an eighteen-page paper to present. The president couldn't know that its original inflammatory title, "Report to the Secretary on the Acquiescence of this Government to the Murder of the Jews" had been softened by the Treasury Secretary to a bland "Personal Report to the President." Nevertheless, Morgenthau had included a preamble in which he emphasized the potentially explosive "nasty scandal" should the story of our State Department's willful obstruction in saving Jewish victims of Nazism be made public. Obviously, he didn't add that the report's prime author, "Joe" DuBois, had threatened to resign and go to the press if nothing were done.

Here it might be well to discuss a question—even an accusation—not infrequently raised about Franklin Roosevelt. Was he a closet anti-Semite? Aside from the fact he undoubtedly had put more Jews into the upper echelons of his government than all other U.S. presidents before or since, his slipshod handling of the Holocaust and its victims has been taken by some writers to show an active if well-disguised bias on his part. He has been charged with cracking jokes when Jewish leaders pleading for their co-religionists came to beseech him. He was said to have slipped out the back door of the White House when a delegation of 400 Orthodox rabbis arrived at the front entrance to lobby him for a rescue plan. A story is told that once in a facetious mood he claimed the Roosevelts had Jewish blood and, as if to prove his point, touched a forefinger to the side of his nose in a Shylock-type gesture.

On the other hand, FDR's style lent itself to all sorts of suppositions. One of the best characterizations of what it seemed like to meet with him was later penned by Congressman Emanuel Celler—a strong New Dealer.

Wrote Celler in his 1958 autobiography, *You Never Leave Brooklyn:*[1]

> Whenever I visited Roosevelt on official business, I found a man adroit, voluble, assured and smiling . . . Mostly he talked. He talked with seeming frankness and when I left, I found that he committed himself to no point of view. At the end of each visit, I realized that I had been hypnotized. His humor was broad, his manner friendly without condescension . . . What did he possess? Intuition, yes. Inspiration, yes. Love of adventure, the curiosity of the experimental . . . I believe his magic lay in one facet of his personality. He could say and he did say, 'Let's try it.'

Another picture of FDR comes from one of his appointees, Robert H. Jackson, whom he made attorney general, then a Supreme Court justice, and who served as chief prosecutor of the Nazi war criminals at the Nuremberg Trials. Jackson was a close friend of Roosevelt's but always regarded him in an objectively critical light, despite the man's "magic." In his biography of FDR, *That Man*, he offered the following observation concerning the president's role at cabinet meetings:

> If a distasteful subject or one in which ill feeling was apparent

between members was brought up, he was likely to end the discussion with a joke or some light comment. It did not solve the issue but postponed it. He was a difficult man to force into a discussion of any subject toward which he wanted to close his eyes.[2]

Assuredly, the problem of the Nazi persecution of the Jews was one of those to which FDR would have preferred to maintain a blind eye. It had been dogging him ever since 1933, and he had "tried" a few things, most notably the Evian Conference of 1938 in France, which had turned out to be worse than a dud. Hopes of finding sanctuaries just for the German and Austrian Jews the Nazis were evicting from their countries—turning to places like Latin America or European colonies in Africa—proved wills of the wisp, and the need swelled to greater proportions with each new German conquest. After 1940, FDR seemed content to leave the whole matter for the most part in the hands of Breckinridge Long, whom he had known ever since both of them were young men working in the Wilson Administration—FDR as assistant secretary of the navy and Breck Long, an assistant secretary of state.

A second FDR trait Robert Jackson revealed was his loyalty to subordinates.

He didn't like to dismiss people from his service. He thought dismissals involved some element of injustice to a man, particularly if he had tried and failed through causes other than disloyalty. It was just easier, and the path of least resistance, to set up overriding authority.[3]

Two elements were at work in this Sunday afternoon confrontation. The Treasury men had planned not only to blast the State Department's handling of the rescue issue, primarily zeroing in on FDR's friend Breck Long, but also to strip away Long's authority to deal with refugees and bestow it upon an *entirely new body outside of the State Department* that would take immediate action.

Resolutions had been introduced in Congress to do just that—set up an "overriding authority," to use Justice Jackson's term.

In fact, the storm had been gathering throughout 1943. Early on, finding homes and help for now stateless Jews whom the Nazis were robbing and deporting had been difficult enough. Then, in 1942, it was learned that those deportations had a different direction—straight to special concentration camps where the inmates would be worked to death or gassed upon arrival. But no recognition of this dire fact had been acknowledged by the State Department.

As the man in charge, Long insisted upon clinging to outworn bureaucratic procedures. For example, at the joint British-American Conference on Refugees, held at his insistence in wartime Bermuda far from the intruding eyes of the American press, the only action taken was a recommendation to revive an almost moribund world body created six years previously at Evian. This organization was the Intergovernmental Committee on Political Refugees (IGC) and had a skeleton crew chaired by Lord Herbert Emerson of England. Henry L. Feingold, in his hallmark book, *The Politics of Rescue*,[4] cynically suggested: "It appeared as if the State Department planned to use the IGC to rid itself of the rescue problem in much the same way the Roosevelt Administration used the Department [and Breckinridge Long] to absorb the pressure of the rescue advocates."[5]

Following the do-nothing Bermuda Conference in April 1943, such pressure had begun to reach a boiling point. The arrival in the U.S. of a Lithuanian-born young Palestinian Jew had produced a galvanizing spark. His name was Hillel Kook but he used the pseudonym Peter Bergson to avoid embarrassing his family, particularly his uncle, the Grand Rabbi of Palestine. A disciple of Vladimir Jabotinsky, the militant Zionist underground leader in the Holy Land, Bergson soon began developing a "radical" approach in America to the refugee problem. The "Bergson group" formed an Emergency Rescue Committee, which placed a full-page ad in *The New York Times*, lambasting the Bermuda Conference, and followed up with a gathering of 1,000 delegates to a six-day meeting in New York City's Commodore Hotel. Out of these deliberations, an eight-point platform emerged, and a key demand was the call for a separate U.S. government agency devoted to the rescue of Hitler's victims.

Next, Bergson proceeded to open a lobbying office in Washington, DC One helpful official was Oscar Cox, a high-ranking lawyer with the Lend Lease program, and meetings organized by Bergson would be held at Cox's home. Converts to the cause were made and included, ominously for the Democrats, prominent Republicans like Wendell Willkie, Herbert Hoover, Senator Robert Taft, and Thomas Dewey. Unable to see FDR, Bergson did manage to meet with Secretary of State Cordell Hull and even with Breckinridge Long, who was enraged by Bergson's visit to the State Department but in his smooth Princetonian manner, concealed his ire. He did, nevertheless, try to convince this "rabble rouser" that it would be more advantageous for the Jews to keep quiet rather than further intensify the ruckus they were raising. Peter Bergson wasn't impressed.

By November of 1943, Bergson's efforts were achieving results in Congress. In both the House and Senate, resolutions were put forward asking for an independent rescue agency. Senator Guy Gillette (D-Iowa) and Congressmen Will Rogers Jr. (D-California) (son of the famed humorist) and Joseph Baldwin (R-New York) were sponsors of proposed legislation, and support was growing fast in a body that previously had been actively hostile to helping these poor persecuted people overseas.

As always, FDR had keen political antennae. Crisis time, as he could intuit, especially after Breck Long had been publicly exposed using false figures to oppose any Congressional action. Thus his willingness to meet at Morgenthau's request. No one had to tell him 1944 was a presidential election year and, most likely, he would be heading the ballot yet again. Cool and in command, jaunty although recovering from the flu, he asked that Henry summarize the Treasury Department's report, and later he would read it in its entirety. Morgenthau then had John Pehle make the truncated presentation.

In this quiet, elegant setting, there was high drama. A comparison, brought to mind by DuBois's French surname and the Jewish subject matter, could well be with Emile Zola's sensational *J'Accuse* revelation in the Dreyfus affair. It's not known which portions of the document Pehle read aloud to the president, but it is probably safe to say he started with its slam-bang opening sentence: "One of the greatest crimes in history, the slaughter of the Jewish people, is continuing unabated."

What was afoot here was an unprecedented governmental initiative. While it was not unheard-of for different departments of the federal government to clash and compete—and Secretary of State Cordell Hull more than once had complained about Secretary Morgenthau's penchant for acting "as if he were clothed with authority to project himself into the field of foreign affairs"[6]—this searing attack was like outright war.

The third paragraph of the report got right into it and proclaimed "that certain officials in our State Department, which is charged with carrying out this policy [saving the Jews of Europe] have been guilty not only of gross procrastination and willful failure to act, but even of willful attempts to prevent action from being taken to rescue Jews from Hitler."

Those certain officials were declared guilty of the following misdeeds, which were encompassed by a whole series of "not only, buts":

They have *not only* failed to use the *governmental machinery* at their disposal to rescue Jews from Hitler *but* have gone so far as to use this governmental machinery to prevent the rescues of these Jews.

They have *not only* failed to cooperate with private organizations ... to work out individual programs of their own, *but* have taken steps to prevent these programs from being put into effect.

They have *not only* failed to facilitate the obtaining of information concerning Hitler's plans to exterminate the Jews of Europe *but* in their official capacity have gone so far as to surreptitiously attempt to stop the obtaining of information concerning the murder of the Jewish population of Europe.

Plus, "They have tried to cover up their guilt by *concealment* and *misrepresentation.*"

The time wasted by the State Department was cited back at least to August 1942, when Gerhart Riegner of the World Jewish Congress in Switzerland first reported Hitler's proposed plan for the Final Solution, and then in November 1942, confirmed that Hitler was already carrying out his intentions, which led in December 1942 to a joint statement of the United States and European members of the United Nations denouncing the Nazis' diabolical atrocity.

"Since the time when this government knew that the Jews were being murdered," the Treasury report went on, "our State Department has failed to take any positive steps reasonably calculated to save any of these people." Whereupon, it referred to the Department's endlessly studying the problem and resorting to stratagems like the useless Bermuda Conference "to explore the whole refugee problem, making it appear that positive action could be expected when in fact nothing has been accomplished."

Assistant Secretary of State Breckinridge Long was first mentioned in the report in connection with the Bermuda Conference. Not mentioned was the fact that Long had made sure the meeting was held in such an isolated location.

But an extensive litany of complaints against the State Department followed, with special emphasis on condemning Breckinridge Long. Quotes from Long's main nemesis in Congress, the part-Jewish, part-German Catholic Emanuel Celler, were sprinkled throughout the transcript. One example was, "Frankly, Breckinridge Long, in my humble opinion, is least sympathetic to refugees in all the State Department. I attribute to him the tragic bottleneck in the granting of visas." And an accompanying beef was: "I brought this difficulty to the attention of the president. He asked Long to investigate at once. No, there has been no change in conditions. The gruesome bottleneck still exists."

Chapter and verse was included, on an inexcusably prolonged effort to help the World Jewish Congress save Romanian and French Jews in 1943, requiring intervention by the president himself, after nine months of delay.

The State Department's justifications for its recalcitrance were dissected and rebuked. Like the claim that any rescue operations must be for all refugees, not just Jews, "thus failing to distinguish between those refugees whose lives are in imminent danger and those whose lives are not in imminent danger." Or State's insistence that everything must be done through the Intergovernmental Committee on Refugees—a "committee [that] had taken no effective action to actually evacuate refugees from enemy territory." And Congressman Celler had been quick to point out that Argentina was one of the countries on the IGC executive board—a country where the Jewish press had been banned and "within whose borders Nazi propagandists and falangists now enjoy a Roman holiday." The other principal State Department excuse was based on its long-held paranoia that Nazi agents would be slipped in among any admitted Jewish refugees. The Treasury men suggested a remedy for this deliberately overblown fear. "The refugees upon arriving in this country could be placed in internment camps similar to those used for Japanese on the West Coast and released only after a satisfactory investigation. Furthermore, even if we took these refugees and treated them as prisoners of war it would be better than letting them die."

The accusers also hurled a charge at the State Department's "surreptitiously" attempting in 1942 to stop any further evidence that the Final Solution had begun from reaching the U.S. While Breckinridge Long is not specifically named in this instance, he is frequently criticized for his "misstatements" and twisting of facts.

Congressman Celler has the last word in the document and in no uncertain terms expresses his opinion about the assistant secretary of state: "If men of the temperament and philosophy of Long continue in control of immigration administration, we may as well take down that plaque from the Statue of Liberty and black out the 'lamp beside the golden door.'"[7]

Was President Roosevelt puffing smoke via his famous long-stemmed cigarette holder as he listened? Was he silently perturbed, hearing these attacks upon his old buddy, Breck Long? Did he recall the elaborate dinners at the Longs' expensive rented DC quarters in those World War I days, as these two wanna-be's and their wives—Frank and Eleanor, Breck and Christine—got together socially? Did FDR also dwell on the 1932 Democratic National Convention in Chicago, where Breck Long was one of his floor captains and helped him cinch their party's nomination? Or that in 1933 Breck had gotten him out of a political pickle by unhesitatingly agreeing to be the U.S. ambassador to Italy. Or that in 1936 his friend from St. Louis, barely recovered from a serious operation at the Mayo Clinic, had joined the re-election campaign on a whistle-stop train ride across the Middle West.

When all was said and done that Sunday, once John Pehle had finished, Roosevelt rather lamely tried to make excuses for Assistant Secretary of State Breckinridge Long. The claim was that Long had "soured" on refugees (read "Jewish refugees") after allowing into the U.S. a recommended list of them from Rabbi Stephen Wise and finding out afterwards that some were "bad people," an argument the president had apparently accepted without even asking how many were unacceptable and how they were "bad." Secretary Morgenthau countered that Attorney General Biddle had found only three cases of Jews who had turned out to have any ties to the Nazis.

Apparently, his one pro-Long sally was as much resistance as the president saw fit to exert. John Pehle, relating the story years later, reported: "The President asked questions and was very interested," and at "the end of the meeting, the President said: 'We will do it.'"[8]

What they would *do* was create the new agency so many people were clamoring for—the War Refugee Board, it came to be called—and its independence would later be assured by putting John Pehle in charge.

The entire meeting took 20 minutes. But this breakthrough in rescue policy, too little and too late though it was, did save lives—of an estimated 200,000 Jews and 20,000 non-Jews. By DC standards, it was fast action, dating back only to December 18, 1943, when the three "warriors" at Treasury presented a tough memo to Secretary Morgenthau, demanding that something be done to circumvent the State Department's hard-nosed obstruction tactics.

True, Roosevelt had brought a record number of Jews into his administration. However, for them, their status as Jews was a ticklish matter. Some even hid their Jewishness, like Oscar Cox, who has been credited with first proposing the idea of the War Refugee Board. Henry

Morgenthau Jr., whose cabinet post made him the highest ranking of his co-religionists, had always felt he had to walk a fine line. According to his daughter Joan, he "particularly felt he was being sabotaged by Breckinridge Long." But to impose upon his friendship with FDR and on a "Jewish matter," seemed too dicey to him, until he encountered that trio of determined Gentiles in his department, bent on action.

Once Morgenthau gave them his tentative approval, DuBois took on the task of writing a first draft and spent all of Christmas Day completing it. Still, there was cabinet protocol that had to be followed. Morgenthau first needed to see Secretary of State Cordell Hull. When his "boys" asked him what he would say to Mr. Hull, the Treasury Secretary half-seriously replied he would tell him, "After all, if you were a member of the cabinet today in Germany, you would be most likely in a prison camp and your wife would be God knows where, because Mrs. Hull is a Jewess, you know."

Underlined in this sarcasm was another instance of the anti-Jewish climate still prevalent in the U.S. Reportedly, Cordell Hull, often mentioned as a successor to Roosevelt, refused to run nationwide, fearful that his wife's Jewishness (on her father's side) would be used against him.

On December 20, 1943, Morgenthau did go to meet Hull. Forewarned, it seemed, the State Department was ready for him. Long was in the room, too, and reported a few steps they had taken that appeared to counter British attempts to stop all aid to Jewish refugees. In a private meeting afterward between Morgenthau and Long, the matter of the latter's anti-Semitism was frankly addressed. The Missourian stoutly denied any such attitude on his part.

Still, the thrust for a separate agency wasn't blunted, and as John Pehle has verified, on January 16, 1944, it received FDR's approval. Moreover, he told the Treasury officials to consult with Edward R. Stettinius Jr., the new under secretary of state, the Department's number-two man.

Stettinius had been named by FDR to replace Sumner Welles, whose abrupt if not mysterious resignation had taken place three months earlier. At any rate, when Morgenthau contacted Stettinius as the president had ordered, he found the new under secretary more than cooperative. Despite Long's attempts to butter him up, Stettinius let it be known he wasn't happy with Long's work and that an upcoming reorganization might strip him of most of his functions. The handsome silvery-haired Stettinius, a Republican, one-time head of U.S. Steel and then of General Motors, had previously run the Lend Lease program, where Oscar Cox was a leading lawyer. Whether Cox had influenced him to support the new War Refugee Board isn't known, but support it he most certainly did.

Morgenthau's strongly worded plea to him had been that "forthright immediate action" would be needed, if the American government "was not to be placed in the same position as Hitler and share the responsibility for exterminating all the Jews of Europe." Answering him, Stettinius said he was "not surprised about Breckinridge Long since Long had fallen just as badly and in an equally shocking way in the exchange of prisoners," and if he had his druthers, the Missourian's only duties would be congressional relations.

Yet like FDR, Stettinius sought to make excuses for Long and did not feel he had meant to hurt the Jews, but he had found him "no longer a young and perhaps never a vigorous executive, inefficient in everything he handled." When it was suggested that Adolf Berle, another assistant secretary of state, take over Long's duties in this area, Stettinius also said "there were grounds for believing Berle might be even worse than Long." He therefore declared he thought the Treasury Department's plan for a new agency "was wonderful."[9]

On January 22, 1944, President Roosevelt issued Executive Order 9417, which officially created the War Refugee Board.

At the State Department, there was barely contained anger that they had lost a bureaucratic battle to their arch rival, the Treasury. Secretary of State Cordell Hull himself, in his published postwar memoirs, initially stated drily that in 1944 the president had created the WRB and "the State Department fully cooperated in its institution and administration."[10] But his real feelings, barely kept in check, came out in the next paragraph:

Naturally the more extreme sympathizers in this country, especially among the Jews and some in high positions such as Secretary of the Treasury Morgenthau, found grievous fault with the State Department and especially with every official handling the refugee problem. It was but natural that, in their anguish over the projected extermination of their race in Europe, they should feel that even the strenuous efforts we were making were inadequate. Nevertheless, it can be safely said that the results accomplished by the State Department, up to the time of the creation of the War Refugee Board, at least equaled those of all other countries combined and that some hundreds of thousands of Jews are now alive who probably would have fallen victim to Hitler's insane enmity had not the Department begun so early and so comprehensively to deal with the refugee problem. President Roosevelt at no time complained to me that the Department had not done enough.[11]

Allegedly, one of the State Department insiders did not appear at all circumspect. James C. "Jimmy" Dunn, political advisor to Hull, was said to have been overheard exclaiming: "That Jew Morgenthau and his Jewish assistants like Du Bois [a Protestant] are trying to take over this place."[12]

What was Breckinridge Long's response? Never one to be straightforward about revealing his feelings, he put the best face he could on his defeat. The entry for January 24, 1944, of his Wartime Diary reads:

> The President has appointed a War Refugee Board consisting of the Secretaries of State, War and Treasury—they to appoint a Director. It is good news for me. This "Director," when chosen, will take over—this insures me staying out. What they can do that I have not done I cannot imagine.[13]

Further thoughts in the same paragraph expressed Long's *sui generis* belief that the move to the War Refugee Board was "good—for political reasons," referring to the four million Jews in the New York City region, "demanding special attention and treatment" and that the WRB's creation would "encourage them to think the persecuted may be saved." Quite smugly, Long continued: "But in my opinion the Board will not save any persecuted people I could not save under my recent and long suffering administration."[14] Washing his hands of the whole affair, he detailed hints that he wasn't going to cooperate with this matter and would tell Hull to involve Stettinius.

Otherwise, Breck Long acted as if nothing of any note had happened.

His next day's entry, however, started by dismissing the War Refugee Board. A meeting with Hull at the latter's hotel apartment (the secretary had been ill for two days) seemingly settled the matter. The Board would be an independent agency, with its own director, outside the Department and "the Department shall help whenever possible—but no longer be responsible."[15]

There is a temptation to pause here and take an objective view of Breckinridge Long at this juncture of his life. He was 63 years old. His career path, he was acutely aware, had brought him, in 1944, to the exact same position—assistant secretary of state—that he had held in 1916 when he was 35. His contemporary at the time, Assistant Secretary of the Navy Frank Roosevelt, had already been governor of the nation's then most populous state and U.S. president for nearly a dozen years. Did Breck not often feel he had never matched the luster of his Breckinridge progenitors? It was a family name that had resounded in American history. Had he not always insisted on being called by it, dropping his first two given names? Had he not daydreamed of adding his own name to the Breckinridge glory? Instead, didn't he now feel stymied, hemmed in by a country that no longer paid obeisance to its "better members" and had tainted itself with unworthy immigrants and would have done so even more, had it not been for his efforts to keep the riffraff out, efforts that not only had gone unappreciated but had even been reviled. One could well imagine that Breck was thinking a lot now about his Breckinridge ancestry and happier days in an older America.

Chapter Two

Breckinridges and Blairs

THE BRECKINRIDGES WERE IMMIGRANTS, TOO, but they came "across the water" fairly early on. No quotas existed in 1739, when the first of the line that led to Breckinridge Long—one Alexander Breckinridge, a native of Ulster in Northern Ireland—settled near Staunton, Virginia.

Had there been restrictions then, especially ethnic ones, the family might have encountered difficulties. They were Scots-Irish—Scottish Presbyterian dissenters from the Church of England, forced to leave their native hearths, seeking freedom to be themselves in Ireland, but having to uproot once again and choose America. Over here, they were considered (and called) "Irish" by the pure English and viewed as unfavorably as Irish Catholics were a century later.

Many of these Scots-Irish immigrants headed for William Penn's Pennsylvania, where the Quakers were rumored to be more tolerant. But a large number of them broke new trails, crossing the Appalachians, bringing their energy and feisty fighting spirit to western parts of Virginia, to Kentucky, to North Carolina, and to an area briefly known as West-sylvania, a conglomerate of pieces of Pennsylvania, Virginia, Kentucky, Ohio, and Maryland that in 1775 sought but failed to become a state. The names they contributed to American history still echo: Daniel Boone, Andrew Jackson, John C. Calhoun, Davy Crockett, Sam Houston, James G. Blaine, Woodrow Wilson, Ronald Reagan, Bill Clinton and, yes, John Cabell Breckinridge, vice president of the United States, candidate for president in 1860, and Breckinridge Long's great uncle on his mother's side.

The genealogy that followed from Alexander Breckinridge incorporated his wife Jane Preston, and descendants of theirs would include Prestons and Blairs, like Breck Long's wife Christine, who seemingly completed a full circle.

Through Alexander Breckinridge, we also get to his son Colonel Robert Breckinridge, who moved to Kentucky where he led a ranger outfit in the French and Indian War, became county sheriff and justice of the peace, and died in 1772, three years before Concord and Lexington. Alexander's second marriage, to another Preston, his cousin Letitia, produced the man known to posterity as the Honorable John Breckinridge, whose relatively short life was highly distinguished.

In fact when Breckinridge Long was seeking membership for his mother in the Daughters of the American Revolution, he cited this particular ancestor above all others as the basis of her claim.

The questionnaire had a space headed: "My ancestor's services in the assisting in the establishing of American Independence during the War of the Revolution were as follows," to which Long answered about great uncle John: "Was Attorney-General under President Jefferson, also a subaltern in the Virginia Militia and a member of the House of Burgesses in 1780." After independence, the Honorable John Breckinridge was likewise a U.S. Senator from Kentucky.

This application to grant DAR membership to Margaret Miller Breckinridge Long, although a bit skimpy on her ancestor's actual role in the Revolution, was approved on May 2, 1895.

The Miller connection showed up the generation after the Honorable John. His marriage to Mary Hopkins Cabell had produced the Reverend John Breckinridge, and he in turn wed Margaret Miller, daughter of the Reverend Samuel Miller, well-known Princeton professor and founder of the Princeton Theological Seminary. A Breckinridge connection to the famed Presbyterian college in New Jersey was further strengthened when the Reverend John's brother, Joseph Cabell Breckinridge, married the daughter of Princeton's president.

From the latter couple came the most famous of the Breckinridges, John Cabell Breckinridge. This Kentuckian, described as "handsome, witty, charming and charismatic," had a meteoric career, elected at age twenty-eight to a seat in the Kentucky Legislature, to a place in Congress at age thirty, and vice president of the United States (with James Buchanan) at age thirty-five, the youngest in the history of the country. He also experienced his first taste of military service during the Mexican War, becoming a major in the army, albeit seeing no real action. As a Southerner, he was consistently pro-slavery but never a fire-eating secessionist, and so his moderation allowed him, in 1860, to be the presidential standard-bearer for the Southern Democrats in the election of 1860. The Northern Democrats backed Stephen Douglas, and the split allowed the recently formed Republicans to elect Abraham Lincoln with 170 electoral votes. Breckinridge came in second with 72.

His next career, mainly a military one, followed his escape from Washington, DC, where he was a U.S. senator, to join the Confederacy, even though Kentucky had opted to stay in the Union. He declared he was "trading six years in the U.S. Senate for the musket of a soldier," and in November 1861 the Confederates named him a brigadier general. He fought at a number of important battles, including Shiloh, Chickamauga, and Cold Harbor, and was later in charge of a lesser-known campaign throughout the western parts of Virginia, winning the battle of New Market with the aid of cadets from the Virginia Military Institute (VMI). Shortly before the Confederacy surrendered, John Cabell Breckinridge was chosen by Jefferson Davis to be the South's last secretary of war. Post-Appomattox, fearing arrest, Breckinridge fled to Florida, then Cuba, then Europe, where he and his wife lived until a presidential pardon let him return in 1869 to Lexington, Kentucky, where he was prominent as a corporate lawyer, railroad president, and opponent of the Ku Klux Klan, until his death in 1875.

A biography of John Cabell Breckinridge, after describing his heritage, concluded: "In short, almost everywhere John turned, he had powerful examples of family achievement, models of leadership and useful supporting allies."[1]

How much better might such sentiments apply to Samuel Miller Breckinridge Long, born in 1881, who not only had Vice President John Cabell Breckinridge among his relatives, but a further number of post-Civil War distinguished ancestors to add to the mix.

Most especially there was his maternal grandfather, Samuel Miller Breckinridge, who had moved to St. Louis, become a member of the Missouri Legislature and then a judge of the Circuit Court. He was also extremely active in the Presbyterian Church, an elder of his local St. Louis parish, and on the entire denomination's National General Assembly. Ironically, he dropped dead while addressing this very same body at a convention in Detroit. He was married to the former Virginia Harrison Castleman, whose distant relations included Presidents Thomas Jefferson and William Henry Harrison. During the Civil War, Samuel Miller Breckinridge, a staunch Unionist and close friend of Abraham Lincoln, was able to have the president intercede for one of his wife's Southern relatives, John Breckinridge Castleman.

Breck Long knew his grandfather and on occasion spoke of him. He was also in touch with a noted cousin of his, Sophonisba Preston Breckinridge, the first woman to be admitted to the bar in Kentucky, a social worker at Hull House in Chicago, and a professor at the University of Chicago in public welfare. In 1933 President Roosevelt sent her as a delegate to the Pan American Conference in Montevideo, Uruguay, the first female ever to represent the United States at an international meeting.

Mindful of his distinguished family on his mother's side, Breck Long could look back, too, on a paternal past that, while not as celebrated, was similarly the stuff of genealogical pride. His relatives in that instance began with a James Webb, also of Scots-Irish parentage.[2]

Born in 1774, just prior to the outbreak of the Revolution, Webb forged a successful career as a physician and businessman in Hillsborough, North Carolina, a small city in the Piedmont section that was the original provincial capital of the state. He and his wife, the former Annie Alves Huske, were organizers of the local Presbyterian church and John Huske, her father, had been secretary to Governor Thomas Burke during the Revolution and captured by Tories but later freed in a prisoner exchange. The Long connection began with Osmond Fitz Long, who went into a business partnership with James Webb, after marrying the Webbs' daughter, Frances Helen. One of the Webb-Long side ventures was hiring out "slaves of widows or absentee or ailing owners." Osmond F. Long was also a medical doctor and, like his father-in-law, had gotten his undergraduate degree at the University of North Carolina and his physician's credentials from the University of Pennsylvania. The son of Osmond and Frances Helen, who became Breck Long's father, was William Strudwick Long, and his unusual middle name could be traced to his grandfather Webb's "ward and best known medical student," Edmond Charles Fox Strudwick, later a leader of the North Carolina Medical Society.

During the Civil War, Breck Long's father was a major in the Confederate 44th North Carolina Regiment of Volunteers and served as a clerk on detached duty at the notorious Libby Prison in Richmond. His reminiscences of his service to the Rebel cause included comments on the battles of Bristol Station and Cold Harbor, the Kilpatrick-Dahlgren raid against Richmond, escapes of Union officers from Libby, the conditions of exchanges of Union and Confederate prisoners, and camp life, morale and marches in General Robert E. Lee's Army of Northern Virginia. To complete Breck Long's exposure to the Southern side of the war, his father's sister, his Aunt Margaret Taylor Long, married Confederate General Rufus Barringer.

Such a welter of historical pedigrees, involving both sides of the War Between the States and between slaveholders and opponents of the "peculiar institution," became even more complex when Breck Long married Christine Graham, with her Blair and Preston ancestry.

One complication here is that American history knows *two* Francis Preston Blairs, father and son. The former, a newspaper owner in Washington, DC, had no direct connection with Missouri. His highly influential *Washington Globe* was closely tied to President Andrew Jackson and the Democratic Party, and its companion, the *Congressional Globe*, was a forerunner of the *Congressional Record*. Another gift to our posterity was his home in the capital, Blair House, still used today for the federal government's guest quarters. From 1856 on, the older Blair's anti-slavery views led him to support the newly formed Republican Party, and in 1860 he worked hard for Lincoln's election. But in the Reconstruction period, his opposition to the Radical Republicans' hard-nosed attitudes toward the South led him back into the Democratic Party fold.

Like father, like son. The Missouri-based Francis Preston Blair Jr. followed exactly the same political pattern of Democrat, then Free Soil Republican, and finally Democrat again, running for vice president with Horatio Seymour in 1868 and losing to Ulysses S. Grant. James G. Blaine, in his massive two-volume *Twenty Years in Congress*, had this to say about Christine Blair Graham Long's grandfather, who had entered Congress as a senator from Missouri in 1871.

> General Blair's political career had been somewhat checkered and changeful. Originally a Democrat of the Van Buren type, he had helped to organize the Republican Party after the repeal of the Missouri Compromise . . . A Republican until Andrew Johnson left, he joined the Democrats and became so vituperatively hostile that the Senate in 1866 successfully rejected his nomination for Collector of Internal Revenue in the St. Louis District and for Minister to Austria.

"He was a "good soldier," Blaine went on, "a Major General who received a commendation from Grant . . . His defeat for the Vice Presidency had, if possible, increased his antagonism to the Republican Party and he came to the Senate as much embittered" against them as he had been against the Democrats ten years previously. Blaine concluded that Blair was "a generous minded man of strong parts" whose career had been hurt badly by "the unsteadiness of his political course."[3]

It was Francis Preston Blair Jr.'s military prowess, perhaps more than his political skills, which led to his being immortalized by that statue in St. Louis's Forest Park (another statue of him was contributed by Missouri to the National Hall of Statuary at the Capitol building in DC). His fast action at the start of the Rebellion kept the "Show-Me State"—originally a slave state—in the Union. The Missouri governor in 1860, Claiborne F. Jackson, was pro-Confederate, and when President Lincoln made his call on the states for troops, he deemed it "illegal, unconstitutional, revolutionary, inhuman, diabolical and cannot be complied with." Jackson's own Missouri troops that he controlled were massed by him at Camp Jackson near St. Louis, planning to attack the Federal arsenal in the city. But Blair had raised one thousand volunteers from a pro-Union organization called the Wide-Awakes, many of them anti-slavery German immigrants, and they moved the arsenal's weaponry across the Mississippi to Illinois and then surrounded the state guards at Camp Jackson and forced them to surrender.

The famed journalist Horace Greeley in his book on the Civil War hailed the importance of Blair's initiative. "Had not these machinations been countervailed, Missouri would have fallen . . . helplessly and passively into the hands of the Confederates . . . But for St. Louis on one side and Kansas on the other, Missouri could scarcely have been saved."[4]

Blair's reward was to be commissioned a brigadier general in August 1862, with a promotion to major general the following November. As commander of the 1st Brigade, Blair had infantry under him from Illinois, Missouri and Ohio, also artillery and cavalry, and he saw lots of fighting, heading up a division at Vicksburg and Chattanooga, and was one of William Tecumseh Sherman's corps commanders in Georgia and North Carolina.

An interesting sidelight connection between the Blair and Breckinridge families occurred early in the Civil War, when Confederate troops under the command of General John Cabell Breckinridge were on their way to capture Washington, DC. Arriving at Silver Springs, Maryland, they took possession of a home abandoned by the Blairs, and General Breckinridge made it his headquarters. In describing the event, Breckinridge Long, who had obtained an 1861 letter signed by Francis Blair Sr., wrote:

> Breckinridge discovered that Blair had left his good liquor, some barrels of whiskey. It was brought forth and passed around the Confederate staff in such quantities that the attack on Washington scheduled for 5AM the following morning was postponed till nearer 10AM. In the meantime, the Washington forces were

augmented, the attack failed and General Breckinridge was forced to retreat.

Long included a passage from the letter in Francis Blair Sr.'s own words:

I am under great obligation to Breckinridge and all his comrades for the sentiment that prevailed in my favor and saved my house and some of its furniture, but I am sorry it did not extend to my neighbors and the poorer sort . . . Although they spared my house, they took everything out of it that a soldier could use . . . Some fellows dancing in my clothes and one, in Betty's riding habiliments; many drunk with the whiskey they had enjoyed.[5]

The Blair-Breckinridge relationship was an obvious background for Breck Long to consider in marrying Frank Blair Jr.'s granddaughter—a counterpoint to his own father's service as a Confederate officer—and besides, the younger Blair had been a Princeton graduate, like Long, and both Blairs had ended their political careers as Democrats, which Long had already become well before marrying Christine.

According to a local history of St. Louis published in 1909, three years before their marriage,[6] Breckinridge Long is described as "a stalwart advocate of the Democracy and in 1908 was [the] candidate of his Party for the State legislature." The biographer, at this early stage of Breck's career, had high hopes for him, although there is no indication whether or not he won in his attempt to represent St. Louis in Jefferson City (apparently he did not). The author notes that Mr. Long is practicing law "at the St. Louis bar with a large clientage" and "comes of [a] family noted for strong intellects," adding that "the strong intellectual force and laudable ambition of Mr. Long are the basis upon which his many friends rest their predictions as to a successful political career for him." The author's conclusion: "He is a splendid representative of a progressive type of young manhood, and nature and education have vied in making him an entertaining and cultured gentleman."[7]

So Breck Long obviously had a lot going for him once the new twentieth century was underway. In 1904 he had gotten his undergraduate degree at Princeton and in 1906 completed his law studies at St. Louis's prestigious Washington University and passed the Missouri bar. A trip around the world followed, before he settled back home to practice law, opening an office in the downtown Commonwealth Trust Company.

In 1908 the conventional tenor of his life was briefly ruffled by the abrupt, impulsive marriage of his only sibling, his sister Margaret, to one of his Princeton classmates, Harold Gould "Chat" Chatfield. Even *The New York Times*, on February 10, 1908, carried the story of how Chatfield, a New York socialite, arrived suddenly in St. Louis, proposed an immediate marriage, and the couple called her mother, the widowed Margaret Breckinridge Long, her brother Breckinridge Long and several intimate friends and "urged them to hurry to the 2nd Presbyterian Church." A year later, in another slight deviation from his nose-to-the-grindstone law work, Breckinridge Long succeeded in obtaining a Master of Arts Degree from his Princeton alma mater.

Already there were hints of the predicted Breckinridge Long ambition to be more than merely a successful provincial attorney. The one thing this up-and-coming young Ivy Leaguer may have felt he still lacked was having sufficient money at his disposal, and that situation was soon remedied in 1912 by his snagging an heiress.

Long no doubt was a good catch. Although someone once referred to him as "tiny and raw-boned," his younger pictures show a good-looking fellow, clean-cut in a Scots-Irish fashion, along the lean lines of an Andrew Jackson, with a mien that can only be described as—*long-faced*. Well-educated, with manners finely honed enough to serve as a host to royalty and other dignitaries during his State Department career, he certainly had appeal for the opposite sex. In his high school days in St. Louis, he ran on the track team—skinny and lithe. By the time he married Christine Graham, he was thirty-one and she was twenty-four.

After perusing Breckinridge Long's voluminous writings, one comes to the conclusion that he is sedulously circumspect about his life's companion or just plain neglectful, for he rarely mentions her. In general, he expresses contentment in his marriage yet infrequently has moments of exasperation, acknowledging in one diary entry how she went without him to "some dance at the country club" and did not come home until 3:30 a.m. On another occasion, they quarreled over expenses—she wanted "a whale of a house" and he didn't think they should spend so much. "We had tears at lunch and much displeasure."

Lest Christine be thought something of a flibbertigibbet of a co-ed, just a few years out of college, Long has included various letters among his papers from her years at Smith. Most of them have to do with a gift of $25,000 she gave to build an addition to the art gallery. The president of Smith, L. Clark Beelye, addressing "Miss Christine Graham," personally thanked her, assured her the trustees had agreed to use her gift as directed, would present the plans for her approval and "P.S., Your wish in regard to publicity will be respected." A subsequent missive, in June 1910, thanked Christine for a "supplementary gift of $2,500," and while understanding that she wanted to remain anonymous when still a student at the school, would "she object to revealing her name later?"

Whether she said yes or not isn't revealed by any of the documents. One bit of correspondence kept for posterity does raise an eyebrow, however. It was sent to Christine in her freshman year, dated October 3, 1906, from her mother in St. Louis to Miss C. A. Graham in Northampton, Massachusetts. "My darling daughter—we had a comfortable trip home though the car was full of people, principally Jews, I think."8

What should anybody consider about this remark? Proof of anti-Semitism? Or simply a Pecksniffian commentary from a wealthy Midwest dowager with social pretensions (she was a vice-regent of the Mt. Vernon Association), traveling back from having dropped her daughter off at a very exclusive college. Avowedly, we can be sure that Mrs. Christine Biddle Blair Graham approved of her daughter's choice of Samuel Miller Breckinridge Long for a husband. On June 1, 1912, the couple was married at Christ Church Cathedral in St. Louis, with the reception afterward at 5145 Lindell Boulevard, in the very same grand house they were eventually to occupy and dazzle the entire city's upper crust by adorning it with their own private art gallery.

Chapter Three

From Missouri Politics
to the
National Scene

A 1950s ARTICLE IN THE *Dictionary of American Biography* on Breckinridge Long more realistically describes him in St. Louis prior to his marriage, engaged in a "small criminal and civil practice" and that he "had considerable difficulty in obtaining clients and collecting fees."[1]

Obviously, the alliance with the Graham family changed everything. Despite the fact that Benjamin Brown Graham had died in 1904, his widow had remained a power among the social elite of St. Louis. As the granddaughter of Francis Preston Blair Jr., she commanded the respect due this great hero of the Civil War, in addition to her lady-bountiful role in her native city. Like her daughter, she endowed buildings, most memorably the Benjamin Brown Graham Chapel on the Danforth Campus of Washington University. Dedicated in 1909, the chapel is patterned on King's Chapel at Cambridge, England. One of its outstanding features is said to be a stained-glass window that—given the Mrs. Graham's quote in reference to Jews—ironically depicts the dedication of King Solomon's Temple in Jerusalem.

The late Mr. Graham was an Ohioan who came to St. Louis as a fifteen-year-old, joined the Missouri pro-Union Militia and built the Graham Paper Company into a major worldwide distributor of paper products. As long as he lived, he was highly influential on the St. Louis scene—a director of the Merchant's National Bank and St. Louis Union Trust, the president of the St. Louis Mercantile Library, active at Christ Church Cathedral, and a charter member of the city's University Club, claimed to be the oldest exclusive club of its type in the country.

Consequently, a son-in-law of the deceased Benjamin Brown Graham was a figure in St. Louis and had family influence at work for him. The same *Dictionary of American Biography* article states: "In 1913, through his wife's political connections, U.S. Senator William Stone and Representative Champ Clark, both Missourians, urged Long's appointment as third assistant secretary of state. But Secretary of State William Jennings Bryan objected and the appointment was not forthcoming."[2]

In November 1912, Woodrow Wilson had been elected president. It seems entirely likely that Breck Long played some role in his national campaign, if only in St. Louis. There is evidence Wilson knew Breckinridge Long as a student in one of his Princeton classes, especially the future president's constitutional law course. Some years later, Long used his study of colonial governments under Wilson to publish a book called *The Genesis of the Constitution of the United States*. Incidentally, for his master's degree in 1909, Long's thesis bore a title he might have wanted to retract half a century afterward, which was: *The Impossibility of India's Revolt From England*. However, uttering wrong pronouncements on foreign policy matters with strong assertiveness and being unabashed about them seems to have been a habit with him. Still, the work on India did at least give Long some credentials in making his pitch for a State Department post.

Let us now enter the labyrinth of Missouri politics in the second decade of the twentieth century. That these politics strayed into national politics in this era was due in large part to Champ Clark (actual name James Beauchamp Clark), Speaker of the U.S. House who in 1912 contested for the Democratic presidential nomination with Woodrow Wilson. If there is a haziness about Breckinridge Long's role in this primary election, it may be he did what most intelligent politicians do when caught in a political crossfire—he lay low. His natural allegiance should have been instinctively to Wilson, his teacher and the president of his university—it is said that Wilson's organization at the 1912 Baltimore Democratic Convention was composed "in the main of young college grads of Princeton" and other Ivy League schools[3]—and yet Champ Clark was Missouri's favorite son and, indeed, a favorite to capture his party's nomination. If Breck Long hoped to have any career in Missouri public life, he couldn't desert Champ Clark.

Most people have forgotten the bruising fight between Clark and Wilson and how it was settled on the 46th ballot, basically because of William Jennings Bryan's intervention. On the 14th ballot, Bryan convinced his own Nebraska delegation to switch its vote from 13 Clark, 3 Wilson to 12 Wilson, 4 Clark. Champ Clark saw this move as having "robbed" him of the nomination. Right after he lost the final vote, Clark declared he had "never scratched a Democratic ticket or bolted a Democratic nominee" in his life and "I will support Governor Wilson with whatever power I possess." But the Speaker could not stifle his anger against the Nebraskan. "I lost the nomination solely through the vile malicious slanders of Colonel William Jennings Bryan."[4] Later he added: "Bryan's animus against me at Baltimore grew out of two facts: First, he could not pull me around by the nose in my conduct as speaker. Second, his ambition to be nominated himself."[5]

For Clark, a year afterward, to be willing to go to bat for Breckinridge Long could well have been due to the lawyer's ancestry. In his memoirs, Clark, originally from Kentucky, called John Cabell Breckinridge "the handsomest man, the most majestic human being, I ever clapped eyes on. I saw him frequently while I was attending Transylvania University at Lexington and I was in the vast concourse who listened to his speech on his return from exile." In giving aid to Long's ambition for a job in the State Department, Clark possibly considered that Bryan, rewarded by Wilson with the plum office of secretary of state, would want to make a conciliatory gesture. Nothing of the kind. Bryan gave a quick thumbs-down in 1913 to the Princetonian from St. Louis.

The following year, as if to enhance his credibility for public service, Long entered a Democratic primary race for the Missouri state Senate. Unfortunately, it did not go well. A news clipping from August 2, 1914, probably from the *St. Louis Republic*, a paper owned by former mayor and governor, David R. Francis, a leading Democrat, carried this headline:

LONG IS INCENSED AT VOTERS' LEAGUE
SAYS IT MADE A "LAMB" OF HIM BY NOT INDORSING HIM FOR STATE SENATE

HE IS OUT TO FIGHT

This outraged candidate for state Senate in the 32nd District was in a three-person race, and he condemned the League's nod to one of his opponents, Chilton Atkinson, the other being the favorite, David Nelson.

"Long is one of the most highly respected members of the local bar," the reporter wrote, "and a member of the commission appointed by Governor Elliot Major to recommend changes in legislation as to court procedures." Then, the writer detailed Long's disappointment with the Municipal Voters League when they "failed to place him in the same class with Atkinson." Long is quoted as saying, "I called up the League and was informed that the reason I was not indorsed was that they wanted to defeat Dave Nelson for the nomination. I do not see why I shouldn't have been picked for the purpose of defeating Nelson." The article went on to state that the failure to endorse Long "came as a big surprise to the *Democrats* of the District and throughout the city generally."

Having the leisure, since his marriage, of not having to worry overly about money, Breckinridge Long could afford to buttress his political ambition by doing pro bono good works for worthy causes. It was only three months after his wedding that he received a letter from the Executive Committee of the Civic League of St. Louis telling him how pleased they were at his "acceptance of a place on the new Short Ballot Committee of the League."

Short Ballot, by the way, was seemingly a hot-button item in 1912— a nationwide movement whose leader was Woodrow Wilson. His two opponents in the 1912 election, current President William Howard Taft and former President Theodore Roosevelt, were also visible supporters of the initiative. Wilson had issued a ringing statement of endorsement, saying: "I believe the Short Ballot is the key to the whole problem of popular government in this country," and even after he was in the White House, he remained at the head of the movement. Its idea was to mandate that "all administrative and clerical positions should be filled by appointment," rather than by election, thus producing a smaller list of names with which the voters would have to cope.

Of more immediate significance was Long's appointment to the Missouri Code Commission in May 1913. Its task was "to consider revision and simplification of the civil and criminal procedure of the State of Missouri." Long had a history of making himself useful in such activities, always volunteering to take on much of the nitty-gritty work, and thus it is no surprise to find him chosen as the secretary of the commission. Its final report was presented on December 3, 1914. To no one's surprise, they found widespread dissatisfaction with the status quo, that people wanted more simplified, less expensive operations, and higher professional standards. For Breckinridge Long, it was a maiden taste of government in action.

Also, there was his service in the St. Louis Art League, a natural for a man whose wife seemed to be such a devotee of the arts. Christine was a member, in fact an officer on the board of governors, and in 1914, her husband was made a member of the Executive Committee. The following term, 1915–1916, Breckinridge was elected president of the League, an imposing private organization, which in 1916 had more than 1,100 members and 100 on its governing board. That summer, the Executive Committee turned its attention to environmental matters, urging the mayor to stop the city park commissioner from building a road through Forest Park to Lindell Boulevard. Noted was the fact that nineteen "large and beautiful trees" would need to be destroyed and other roadways were in "a poor and deteriorating condition," and any city construction funds should be used to repair them, not to construct an unneeded thoroughfare.

It is curious to observe, in view of the charges of anti-Semitism later frequently made against Breckinridge Long, that the chairman of the Executive Committee of the St. Louis Art League was Dr. Max A. Goldstein, obviously Jewish, but also obviously highly respected. Actually, when Long stepped up to become president in 1915, Dr. Goldstein was his vice-president.

In November 1915, one year before the presidential election of 1916, Long entered without any inhibitions into the campaign to re-elect Woodrow Wilson. He had recently begun the first of his many diaries, and its initial entry has him attending a "series of conferences in St. Louis to start a Democratic Club." The party apparatus in the city was seen as "so weak that its Republican results might carry the whole State." Among the participants in these efforts, he cites Rolla Wells, a former two-time mayor of St. Louis, Harry B. Hawes, who next year would be elected to the Missouri House of Representatives and subsequently to Congress and the U.S. Senate, and—surprisingly in the Democratic column—George Herbert "Bert" Walker, the maternal grandfather of the first President Bush and great-grandfather of the second.

So was born the "Wilson Club." Rolla Wells was offered the presidency but turned it down, and thus the always-available Breck Long had to assume the top responsibility. They rented a clubhouse, had a big housewarming and brought together *all factions* of the local Democrats, including followers of ex-Governor Joseph Folk, ex-Governor David Francis, Harry Hawes, Rolla Wells, etc. "Within two days," Long wrote, "the Club had a membership of 120 of the most prominent men, financially and politically, in the city."[6] Within a year, he was to report, the number of members had climbed to three thousand.

Pushed by the local Businessmen's League, one of their first tasks was to try to snare the Democratic National Convention for St. Louis. There was a Democratic National Committee meeting scheduled for DC in December 1915, where a decision on the location would be made.

Off to Washington went Breck Long and Harry Hawes, arriving well ahead of time, so they could enlist help from the state's top Democratic elected congressional officials, like Speaker Clark, U.S. Senator Stone, and Missouri's other U.S. senator, James Reed.

Added to the lobbying effort was Rufus Hollister, later an official at the Democratic National Committee, and Charles Higgins, the Senate Sergeant at Arms, and together they planned a dinner at the glitzy Willard Hotel for all of the Missouri big shots in the capital. Included was Edward Goltra of St. Louis, an iron and steel manufacturer, who served as Missouri's Democratic National Committeeman. Eventually, the Willard became the site of the group's headquarters, and to everyone's surprise little St. Louis beat out much bigger competitors like Chicago and Dallas.[7]

Early in January 1916, William F. McCombs, Chairman of the Democratic National Committee, arrived in St. Louis to make preliminary convention arrangements, and Breckinridge Long was his host. The Longs put on a dinner for him in their home. One item under discussion was a proposed visit to St. Louis by the president, in response to an invitation from the Businessmen's League for him to give a breakfast speech. Going over McCombs' head, Long fought for a much more public event—a Wilson speech that eventually *did get to take place* and drew sixteen thousand people. The ambitious Princeton grad could write that he sat at Wilson's table during the breakfast, and "I had a few minutes chat with him at the train as he left." The idea of the third assistant secretary of state had been revived by the fact that William Jennings Bryan had resigned in 1915 after a fight with Wilson. Needless to say, any such dream was dependent upon Wilson's re-election.

Long was soon back in Washington, this time as the legal representative of the Busch-Sulzer Brothers Diesel Engine Company and the Lake Torpedo Boat Company. He did manage to see President Wilson again but "could only wave," walking by him in the senate wing with Senator Stone and Champ Clark.

Back in St. Louis, the Wilson Club got busy preparing for the convention, which was to be held at the Coliseum, June 14 to 16. Long wrote in *Diary 1*: "My standing with Mr. McCombs was not of the best." A request by McCombs for two thousand tickets, he added, was "coolly received."

There was no suspense in St. Louis in 1916, no cliffhanger between two strong primary candidates as in 1912. Wilson was re-nominated by acclamation. So was his vice president, Thomas R. Marshall, a former governor of Indiana.

Except the campaign ahead of them was anything but a slam dunk. The Republican candidate, picked a week earlier, was Supreme Court Justice Charles Evans Hughes, a formidable foe and one who would be well financed.

With a real worry about funds in mind, the Honorable Rolla Wells, then treasurer of the Democratic National Committee, saw to it that *deep pockets* Breckinridge Long was introduced to the Chairman of the DNC's Finance Committee. This was Henry Morgenthau Sr., father of the future Treasury secretary. The two men met at St. Louis's Jefferson Hotel, and Morgenthau asked the wealthy Missourian to join the Finance Committee and, furthermore, could he meet with him in New York City the following morning?

In those days, long-distance travel was mostly by train. It was a jovial crowd that boarded at St. Louis, Senators Stone and Reed and their colleague John Sharpe Williams of Mississippi, along with Mr. and Mrs. Breckinridge Long, and a certain amount of horseplay on the overnight ride east centered around "12 small bottles of whiskey" given Senator Stone (this was before Prohibition) and the prank of removing them from under Senator Williams' berth, where they'd been hidden, and slipping them (Breck Long did this) into Williams' pocket, "a continuous joke the whole way from St. Louis." Also included in this diary segment of Long's was the intelligence that Jim Reed had a quart bottle of whiskey he and Stone kept sampling.

At the New York end, Long met Henry Morgenthau Sr. in his office, and the two of them examined a campaign headquarters location on the second floor of the building. Right afterward, Long took off for a three-week vacation on Nantucket at Christine's family's summer home, and then, back in New York City, he inspected the up-and-running Wilson operation, before returning to St. Louis and involving himself in the August 1 Missouri Democratic primary.

Describing the events of this period, Breck Long seems careful to eschew discussing those actions of his that really opened the door to his eventual appointment to the State Department. It remained for one of Woodrow Wilson's biographers—Arthur S. Link—to divulge this information and its obvious conclusion in his monumental study of Wilson's career, *The Road to the White House*.[8] In Volume 5 of his tome, talking about the 1916 race, he relates the money problems the Democrats suffered, notably after the passage and signing by Wilson of the Adamson Act that brought in an eight-hour workday and alienated many business leaders who began sending donations to Hughes. Link quotes one of the major Democratic workers, Robert Woolley, head of publicity for the party, telling of Breck Long's coming to the rescue of the new DNC chief, Vance McCormick, an All-American football star at Yale, who had replaced Long's bête noire, McCombs. The day after the Adamson Act was signed, the Missourian walked into McCormick's office on 32nd Street in New York City, handed him a check for $5,000, and told the Democratic leader he would also loan the party up to $100,000. There were no individual spending limits in those days. As it turned out, McCormick did borrow $30,000. It was Woolley's contention that Long's largesse kept the campaign office open. Now, that kind of effort could land you a spot in the State Department, once the Democrats were victorious. In his diary, Long only speaks of having lunch in Ohio with Mr. McCormick, after being sent to Columbus by Morgenthau to raise money.

But he has left no doubt that another of his ambitions was to succeed Edward Goltra as Missouri's DNC member. He originally planned to run against the incumbent, who was a close friend of President Wilson's. But a man by the name of Rumsey intervened. Although Long stepped aside for him, after Goltra was re-elected, Long loudly complained: "If I had been the candidate instead of Rumsey, Goltra would have hardly received 50 votes in the State."[9] Later, we shall see that this event would have a significant effect on Breckinridge Long's 1920 attempt to become chairman of the Democratic National Committee.

Another complaint by him concerned ex-Governor David Francis, a close friend of Ed Goltra's, who used his newspaper, the *Republic*, in a way that antagonized Long. Therefore, he once paid a man to have one offending edition bought up and destroyed so that only eleven copies out of eighteen hundred were circulated. In the future, Breckinridge Long would try to buy the *Republic* from Francis.

Breck Long seemed especially aggressive in his politicking in the 1916 election. In September, when the presidential results were known from Maine (which voted ahead of the nation), "the returns were most discouraging." Among Long's actions in Missouri, the most controversial was setting up a fake St. Louis Society of Criminology to search records for criminals who might be supporting Republicans. A list of them was used to challenge voters at the polls. The mayor of the city and the chief of police both attacked this practice, but Long stoutly defended himself and carried St. Louis for the state and federal tickets. The Republican city administrator tried to have him indicted, but he proved he had done nothing indictable.

Woodrow Wilson was re-elected, albeit narrowly. On January 10, 1917, Breckinridge, returning to St. Louis from a trip to Jefferson City, received word from Secretary of State Robert Lansing, who had succeeded William Jennings Bryan, that he was being offered the position of third assistant secretary of state. After receiving Christine's blessing, he wired Lansing his acceptance.

On January 12, Long wrote: "My nomination as Third Assistant Secretary of State sent to the Senate by President. A number of telegrams of congratulations have arrived."[10]

Whereupon off he went to Florida with Christine, who had to recuperate from a bout with pneumonia, bringing their infant daughter, also named Christine, nicknamed "Teenie"; he described his wife "in a wonderful humor" and entranced by the quarters they had taken at the Poinciana Hotel in Palm Beach.

On January 26, 1917, Long received a summons from the secretary of state to report to Washington immediately to start his job.

On January 27, he left Palm Beach at 7:50 p.m. and traveled all the next day. On January 29, he reported to the ornate State, War and Navy building near the White House and declared he had "a delightful office, open fire, negro messenger, and male clerk."[11] His new career had begun.

Chapter Four

Under Wilson

THE YEAR 1917 WAS A crucial period for the Wilson administration. Before it ended, the United States would be at war, while until then a good part of the Wilsonian foreign policy had been to broker a peace between the opposing forces in Europe. Some authors have claimed the originator of the famous 1916 Wilson campaign slogan, "He kept us out of war," had been none other than Breckinridge Long, and many political pundits have credited that voiced sentiment with having propelled Wilson to victory over Charles Evans Hughes.

Yet on the very next day after Breck Long reported for work, the German government announced it would resume its policy of unrestricted submarine warfare, thus unleashing new tensions with the still-neutral United States.

That same January 30, 1917, the new kid on the block from St. Louis paid a visit to the president's private secretary, Joseph Tumulty, and requested an appointment to see Mr. Wilson. It was granted for 12:30 p.m., and Long had a chance to thank the chief executive for his confidence and found him very cordial and gracious. Long wrote: "The whole time we were talking . . . his face lighted up with an expression of real pleasure at seeing me."[1]

Even before going to the State Department building, Breck had stopped by the Capitol, seeking to find Senator Stone to thank him for his support but Stone was in Missouri, and to see Senator Reed who wasn't in either, but Speaker Champ Clark was there with his son Bennett (later to be a U.S. senator), and so was Breck's friend, Charles Higgins, the senate sergeant-at-arms. Finally, at the State Department, he was received by the secretary of state himself, Robert Lansing, and met two other top Department officials, William Phillips and Frank L. Polk, with whom he would have various interactions over the years to come.

On February 1, his diary records: "Read dispatches of today up to 11:30 delivery. At 1 PM, lunched at Secretary Lansing's table at the Metropolitan Club." Here, in a venerable building on the corner of H and 17 Streets, was the exclusive inner sanctum of Washington, DC's professional world, and Breck Long soon became a member and eventually one of its board of governors.

Next, on February 2, he was having breakfast with Democratic National Committee Chair Vance McCormick, and on February 5 with Henry Morgenthau Sr., discussing how to fix the party's financial deficit.

All the while, he was being exposed to some of the most serious issues facing the nation. "German situation looks ominous," he reported on February 3, and on February 5 he went to the Capitol with Senator Stone in connection with an immigration bill that President Wilson had vetoed the previous December. Overwhelmingly, the Senate overrode the president's objections, and the Immigration Act of 1917, which banned illiterate immigrants over sixteen and certain classes of handicapped people, became law. Little did Breck Long realize, as he listened to the debate, how his own future would be tied to this perennially contentious issue. Long merely commented that he spent the next day reading Senator Jim Reed's speech on the subject.

What, though, in 1917, was his precise job as third assistant secretary of state supposed to be? One definition has been given in a book published anonymously in 1921, entitled *The Mirrors of Washington*, and it states: "The Third Assistant Secretary of State is the official Social Secretary of the Government. When royalty or other distinguished persons come to this country as the guests of the nation, the Third Assistant Secretary is the Master of Ceremonies . . . and occupies a minor place in the hierarchy."[2] This was written in an essay about Secretary Lansing and how he had once hoped to be a third assistant secretary, but instead had had to take the job of legal counselor to Secretary Bryan, and was rushed into filling the Nebraskan's shoes when he suddenly resigned in 1915 after his fight with Wilson.

In any event, in Breckinridge Long's immediate exposure to the ceremonial aspect of his work, he wasn't just a "greeter." Rather, on February 10, 1917, he was assigned to escort the German ambassador to the U.S., Count Johann Heinrich von Bernstorff, *out of* the country. The German government had recalled its envoy, and Long was to accompany him to New York City and "see him and his party safely aboard ship."

William Phillips, Long's superior at the time, has left a record of the incident.

Long and Warren Robbins have been instructed to be at the station at 10 o'clock tonight in top hat to receive Count Bernstorff on his arrival . . . Long and Robbins will accompany the party on the special which leaves at 12:10 AM and will escort them to the steamer tomorrow morning. Long carries a farewell letter from the Secretary to Bernstorff which he is to deliver at the last moment in order to avoid the possibility of Bernstorff's publishing it.

This was on February 13, 1917. On February 14, Phillips wrote: "Count Bernstorff's party got off last night and sailed today at 2 o'clock. Thank God!"

Then, on February 15: "Long returned this morning from seeing the Von B party off. He reports the greatest show of police ever. Every bridge between Wash and NY was strongly guarded by police and from the train to the boat the police were as thick as ants. Everything passed off without a hitch."[3]

His first mission satisfactorily accomplished, Breck Long's next job was to sit down with Frank Polk and others and begin to purge from the State Department rolls all consular officials with obviously German surnames. This was still a month before the U.S. declared war.

Politically, he was still trying to help solve the fiscal dilemma of the Democratic National Committee. During March, he met with a number of wealthy donors, many of them Jewish, like Bernard Baruch, Mr. and Mrs. Henry Morgenthau Sr., Julius Rosenwald of Chicago (an owner of Sears, Roebuck and Company), Mrs. Solomon of Chicago, Mr. and Mrs. Eisenman of Cleveland, and "Joe" Pulitzer, publisher of the *St. Louis Post-Dispatch*, whom he must have known from home. The end result of all this effort was that on March 16, Vance McCormick asked Breck to underwrite the DNC for $10,000 for one year, and Long agreed and signed a contract to do so.

In his personal life, he was concerned with the art gallery he and Christine were installing at 5145 Lindell Boulevard. By the end of January, it still hadn't been finished, and he noted in his diary that he "passed on tapestry for gallery at home and on designs for medallions on loggia." Although he could not have realized it then, his Missouri mansion was to be brought into his ceremonial duties soon after the U.S. entered World War I.

By the middle of March, he appeared to be wrapping up the task of weeding out potential enemy aliens from the Department. "I have caused about 15 officers to go," he wrote on March 16, "Consuls, Consul agents and clerks—because of German nationality or sympathy. Board today ruled only native Americans be designated for exams and that I use discretion in selecting those with foreign names. Our service will be in much better condition if I can carry out my ideas in Americanizing it from top to bottom."[4]

There was no countervailing effort by him to examine the fairness of what he was doing, nor—as with his World War II efforts vis-à-vis German refugees from the Nazis—to put himself in the place of those being fired or denied entry. At best, he did allow that this new field of work made him "fretful and irritable."

Long's involvement with another major event of 1917—the Russian Revolution that overthrew the Czar and ended with a Communist regime in place—was due to the fact that ex-St. Louis mayor and Missouri Governor David Francis had been made U.S. ambassador to Russia. Notwithstanding Breck's annoyance at the editorial policy of the newspaper Francis owned, he considered David Francis an old family friend. "No word from Francis at all," Long recorded his concern on March 17. "AP cables get there, but no word from Francis." Four days later: "We have requested Francis to recognize the new Russian government, as per his request and advice."

As it turned out, Francis had written from Petrograd to Brett Long on March 12, congratulating him on his appointment as third secretary and "to express the hope that our official relations may be as pleasant as have been our social relations since you were able to talk. I knew your Mother and Father before they were married," adding he was friends with Long's father until the latter's death and hoped he was still friends with Long's mother. He also cited a cable he had sent to Frank Polk at the State Department, saying he had recognized the new Russian government and that the U.S. was the first country to do so.[5]

In his communication to Polk, the ambassador made sure to send his regards to Secretary Lansing, to Bill Phillips and "also to Long, whom I have known from his birth and who has always been my political friend."[6]

The U.S. declaration of war on Germany and its allies, equally momentous, which occurred on April 6, 1917, received only a short notice in Long's diary. On April 4, he went to listen to the debate in Congress on the War Resolution, heard Senator Stone deliver "a strong speech" and was "moved to tears." Right afterward, he took Henry Morgenthau Sr., Mrs. Vanderbilt, a Madame Ekergran of Sweden, and Christine to lunch at the Shoreham Hotel. Two days later, his curt entry was: "War at 3:15 AM. I wonder how many realize what it means."[7]

Personally, for Long, all it meant immediately was a marked increase in his ceremonious duties of escorting foreigners.

Military and political personnel missions from Allied governments were soon flocking to the United States, and it was Breckinridge Long's task to smooth their path and make their visits as pleasant and fruitful as possible.

Consequently, we find him in the wilds of northeastern Maine, in the tiny town of Vanceboro on the Canadian border, about to cross into New Brunswick to the railroad terminus of McAdam, where he would greet and take charge of a British Mission led by Foreign Minister Lord Arthur Balfour. Then, in the last week of April, came the French, and eventually there would be Italian, Japanese, Russian, Rumanian, Belgian and even Brazilian and Serbian contingents among the friendly belligerents who arrived. In the case of the French, Long had a special assignment—one he might have suggested, himself. He was bringing the group headed by Maréchal Joseph Joffre, the top commander of the French military, and René Viviani, ex-premier and current minister of justice, to St. Louis, a city named for a French king and having had a strongly Gallic presence prior to the Louisiana Purchase.

Among the letters in the David R. Francis Collection at the Missouri Historical Society in St. Louis is one that Ambassador Francis's son had mailed his father on April 30, 1917, in which he mentions the awaited arrival of Maréchal Joffre and Minister Viviani, that they will stop at Breck Long's house, and that he has been invited to have breakfast with them. He also tells how much he is complimented because of the ambassador's "prompt action in Petrograd" and how everyone thinks he is "the right man in the right place."

In a letter on May 15, 1917, which Long himself sent to Francis, whom he addressed as "My dear Governor," he too wrote of the Joffre-Viviani stay in St. Louis, stating he'd held a "small reception" for the visitors at his home, that the art gallery had been opened for the first time, and they all had traveled throughout Missouri as well, "and I saw a great many of your friends."

In another of the Long-to-Francis letters, Breck reported that President Wilson (a close friend of Francis's) was looking well, that Christine was at Nantucket and "if you want anything in a hurry, mark it 'for Long' and I will do my best." Back came a request from Francis to help a Mr. Joseph Kerrigan who'd been doing relief work in Siberia and would be coming to DC. "He is a good Democrat, which I cannot say of all the men who have served with me in Russia." Kerrigan wanted a commission in the army. And added was a P.S.: "Can't you find time to write me a personal letter about the inside of the State Department?" Francis, it seemed, was furious about rumors there that he had been drinking too much and was also upset about whispers that he was pro-German.

In response, Long said he had asked help for Kerrigan from Secretary of War Newton Baker, and tried to calm the ex-governor about any rumors against him, because no one who counted for anything at State had said a word.

The Italian Mission arrived on May 22. Others were not far behind. Yet Long managed to involve himself in various other activities, too. Over at Navy, for example, he and Assistant Secretary Franklin Delano Roosevelt interacted on problems of communications to U.S. ships in the Pacific. Thus was formed a lasting friendship between the two young bureaucrats.

One event Breckinridge Long found time to witness was the ceremony of the sale of the Danish West Indies to the United States. A check for $25 million was given by Secretary of the Treasury William Gibbs McAdoo to Secretary of State Lansing to buy what were to become the U.S Virgin Islands.

The rest of 1917 was apparently very busy for Long on all fronts.

The foreign missions kept arriving and departing and requiring his attention. His aging and ailing mother moved to Philadelphia, and in spare moments he spent time visiting her. He mentions contacts again with prominent Jewish Americans, lunch with Justice Louis Brandeis, a meeting with Felix Frankfurter, a social evening with Henry Morgenthau Sr., and a visit he and Christine made to the Belmonts in Newport, R.I. August Belmont, the patriarch of the family, was a naturalized German Jew who represented the Rothschild banks in the U.S. and was for a period the head of the Democratic Party. His son Perry, a former congressman whom the Longs were seeing, was born of a non-Jewish woman, the daughter of Commodore Matthew Perry, and raised an Episcopalian.

A specific happening in November 1917, recorded by Long, was the death of John Watson Foster, who was the father-in-law of Breck's boss, Secretary Lansing, and the grandfather of another secretary of state, John Foster Dulles, and who was secretary of state himself for several years at the end of the Benjamin Harrison administration. Foster's funeral in Washington was a State affair and Long boastfully pointed out in his memoirs that he had escorted President and Mrs. Wilson to and from their seats in the church.

His final comments for 1917 touch upon this sense of importance he was gaining for himself in his thirty-sixth year, although leavening his remarks with a touch of humility.

> During the year I have dealt with some of the large problems of my country and have helped master them, have been part and parcel of the greatest period in the world's history, have come in contact, intimate contact, with the world's greatest statesmen and thinkers and have held my own. I am proud, not conceited, but tired.[8]

Chapter Five

1918-1919

THE FOLLOWING YEAR—1918—BEGAN with a personal jolt for Breckinridge Long. On New Year's Day, he received a message from Philadelphia that his mother had suffered "another stroke." He reached her bedside at half-past three in the morning and found her very ill. A worried call was placed to his sister Margaret Chatfield in Boston. But the next day Mrs. Long seemed better, and there were periods of ups and downs until January 6, when Breck decided to return to Washington. On January 9, he was testifying before the House Committee on Foreign Affairs and soon jotting in his diary that Teddy Roosevelt had arrived in DC to cause trouble for President Wilson.

As earlier noted, Breckinridge Long liked to indulge himself in prognostication—especially of a political nature. Here in the first month of 1918, he was telling his wife he had a "presentiment that peace would soon come," adding, "How I know not. I feel it strongly."[1] One can argue he was eleven months shy of the November Armistice date, but at least he had the year right.

That same January, he made a stab at political organizing on a national scale to benefit the Wilson administration. He named some of the people he wanted for his "War Council"—Vance McCormick, DNC secretary Rufus Hollister, Senator Willard Saulsbury Jr. of Delaware, Daniel Roper, chairman of Wilson's 1916 campaign and currently IRS commissioner and George Creel, head of U.S. propaganda in World War I[2]—but at the initial meeting in the Hotel Shoreham dining room, only Roper and McCormick showed up.

Maybe this early in 1918 a bee was already in Breck's bonnet about running for federal office. No matter that he had twice failed to be elected on the state level. He was in a different league now and felt he had acquitted himself well.

It might also have entered his mind that he was a bit of an anomaly in the State Department. As a political appointee, he could see he was not on a career track, nor did he necessarily want to be. Most certainly, Breck had learned about the bifurcation in the State Department's employment structure—between the diplomatic corps and the consular service, and the caste system it imposed—diplomats at the top, consuls inferior. Not until 1924 was something done about this split through a piece of congressional legislation called the Rogers Act, which reorganized everything. Credit for this "leveling of the playing field" at State and the creation of a unified Foreign Service has always been given to a determined veteran State Department bureaucrat named Wilbur J. Carr, who during Breck Long's first tour was the director of the consular branch.

From Long's diary, one cannot tell exactly when he initially began *thinking* about a run for the U.S. Senate. His War Council on March 13 at a dinner in his home discussed the proposed Senate candidacy of Joseph Davies, the recently retired head of Wilson's Federal Trade Commission. Involved were Messrs. McCormick, Roper, Hollister, and a newcomer, Attorney-General-to-be A. Mitchell Palmer. Less than a month later, U.S. Senator William J. Stone died unexpectedly, leaving a vacancy in Missouri itself. Long says he took part in an effort to have Champ Clark appointed by the state's Democratic governor, Frederick Gardner, but Clark decided he preferred to stay on as Speaker of the House. The interim seat went to a man with the unforgettable name of Xenophon Wilfley.

In the course of such deliberations and maneuvers, Champ Clark allegedly told the young Missourian he should consider contesting for the position at an upcoming special election in November. "Champ Clark—re Senatorship—encourages me to activity,"[3] Long wrote on May 9, 1918.

It was apparent that Xenophon Wilfley had just been a place-holder. But as much as Long might have been tempted to run, he was wise enough not to rush into a Democratic primary. The nomination eventually did go to a former governor, Joseph W. Folk, a strong candidate. October found Breck Long smugly declaring: "I am amused myself in writing a letter to Judge Spencer, the *Republican* nominee for Senator in Missouri, responding to a letter he wrote me asking for my support. I told him I could not do it."[4] However, in that November 1918 contest, Governor Folk was not able to win for the Democrats.

On the other hand, former appeals court Judge Selden P. Spencer's defeat of ex-Chief Executive Joe Folk offered, in a sense, a real opportunity for Long. There would be another election two years hence when Senator Stone's term officially ended, and he could set his sights on being the Democratic choice to face Spencer. There would be plenty of time to plan.

By now, Breck and Christine had moved into very elegant rented quarters within DC—the "Pink Palace" at 2600 16 Street NW—built in 1910–11 by Franklin MacVeagh, President William Howard Taft's treasury secretary. It was a place where they could hold elegant dinners, as they did at Christmas for 50 to 75 exiles from St. Louis, living in the capital city. During the summertime, the Longs left the Potomac heat for York Harbor in Maine, renting one of its mansion-like seaside "cottages." Breck was alternately feeling weighed down by overwork and then refreshed by his mini-vacations.

For example, at the end of March 1918, after a month-long bout with utter fatigue, he waxed rhapsodic about "a good rest" at the Virginia farm of a subordinate of his, during which he went horseback riding every day and studied the Richmond campaign of the Civil War (in which his father had taken part). "Also read Bancroft's History of the United States . . . wrote 20 pages of reminiscences about the French Mission . . . enjoying beautiful sunsets . . . fields growing green and nature at its most encouraging." Finally, his Presbyterian conscience bade him add: "Now I am back, refreshed, heartened, ready for more work and eager for accomplishment. Lots to do about Japan and Japan in China and Siberia."[5]

Throughout this year, he had a number of contacts with his friend at the Navy Department, Frank Roosevelt. In one case, he was requesting a warship to transport the body of the Chilean ambassador, who had died in DC, back to his homeland. In another, he was asking to have an admiral assigned to the party greeting a member of British royalty, Prince Connaught, when the nobleman arrived in New York City. In addition, he had some meatier international issues he was working on, mostly in the Far East. Handling a major bank loan for China, he found himself having to leave York Harbor at the end of June for New York City and a bankers' conference about a fund for the Chinese. While in the Maine resort, he and Christine twice drove south to coastal Magnolia, Massachusetts, to visit Colonel Edward House, President Wilson's closest advisor.

Eager to be involved in policy-making, Long had come up with an idea that belatedly—a quarter of a century later—brought him recognition for his clairvoyance. This was his proposal for the ultimate disposition of the Caroline and Mariana Islands of Micronesia and other nearby Pacific archipelagoes, which were to be taken from the defeated Germans. Japan, an Allied nation, was loudly staking its claim. Breck Long just as vehemently argued the U.S. should gain possession, letting the Germans remain in charge, so they could later sell these strategic outposts to the U.S. At the State Department, no higher-up was interested, so the League of Nations awarded them to Japan, which broke its promise not to erect fortifications, and as a result thousands of American lives were lost in World War II battles at places like Truk and Palau and Peleliu.[6]

On the domestic front, Breckinridge Long was listened to a little more seriously, no doubt because of his gifts of money to the Democratic Party. But here he wasn't as far-seeing. He predicted the off-year November elections would return a Democratic Senate and House. The reason it didn't happen has been attributed to Wilson's abandonment of his nonpartisan war-president's stance and his active campaigning for the Democrats.

The results in fact, for the party of Woodrow Wilson and Breckinridge Long, were disastrous. In the House the Democrats lost twenty-five seats, and in both bodies couldn't hold on to their majorities. The five Senate seats that changed hands included the one taken by Judge Spencer in Missouri.

Election Day was a week before the Armistice, and on December 4 the president set sail for France. Breckinridge Long was not among the State Department personnel chosen for the U.S. delegation to the Paris Peace Conference, although he hinted in his diary that he had been scheduled for Paris, but Frank Polk, filling in for Secretary Lansing, had cancelled his mission.

While all eyes in America were on the president and the tumultuous welcome he received overseas, Democratic bigwigs in Washington were mulling over the election results and building their strategy for the presidential election of 1920. Breck Long, while participating, also was eyeing his own future. Assistant Secretary of the Treasury Tom Love, a political friend of his, was now urging him to go for the U.S. Senate and to start early. Breck's response was, "I agree, but doubt the advisability of announcing now. It would be too long a race."

Planning early was something else, though. On December 20, he lunched with Rufus Hollister, and they talked about the need for a good Democratic newspaper in Missouri. "I will buy one in St. Joe," Long stated in his diary, "Consider purchase of one in Kansas City and will ask Francis if he will sell the *Republic*."[7] As for a Senate candidacy, he again insisted it was too early to announce and even hedged whether he'd "definitely decide" to do it. He saw primary competition from a number of heavyweights: Folk, Gardner, Hawes—all from St. Louis, and Frank Walsh from Kansas City.

Still, the itch was truly there. On December 23, he noted a speech by Senator Henry Cabot Lodge attacking the League of Nations, and Long experienced a need to speak out. Except he was, as he put it, "gagged by the State Department," forbidden to wade into politics while on the government payroll.

Toward the end of the year, his thoughts briefly turned to his family. "Christmas—much excitement for Teenie and a very pleasant day at home." Also, a pang of guilt about not going to see his ailing mother in Philadelphia. "But it is best that I do not see her. She is so excitable that it affects her badly. Doesn't realize what is going on."[8]

As the year ended, he for once spoke openly about his wife, quite sentimentally; his "little wife," as he referred to Christine. "She, too, has done her part and the praises should be sung—and someday I will do it—the wifely, the lovely, the constant devotion to me during my days and nights and months of labor, her solicitude, her care, her constant attention, her devotion—all manifestations of a great love."[9]

The beginning weeks of 1919 had been set aside for Breck to test the political waters in Missouri. He had been scheduled to leave shortly after New Year's, but on January 4 the basement of their rented palatial home was flooded right while they were entertaining the vice president of the United States, Thomas R. Marshall, and his wife. Until he could get the cellar pumped out, Breck had to stay in DC. Previously, a talk with Champ Clark had revealed how bad conditions were for a Democrat to run in Missouri. The would-be candidate went to seek advice, too, from Senator James A. Reed, but found the now senior Democratic senator was out of town.

Later these two men would encounter each other on a train ride to St. Louis. Both were to speak at a National Convention of Retail Shoe Dealers. En route, Long got an earful from Reed, whose nickname was Fighting Jim and whose reputation was that of a fiery, colorful speaker with outspoken opinions. "Reed discussed President Wilson in bitter and sarcastic terms—on every occasion," Long wrote. "He has a strong personal antipathy to him . . . He is jealous of the President . . . Maybe because someone called the President the smartest man in the world . . . Besides his jealousy, there is bitter hatred."[10]

Before the shoe dealers at the Statler Hotel in St. Louis, Reed spoke first. The subject was supposed to be foreign trade. Instead, Reed turned his speech into a harangue against the League of Nations. When Long's turn came, he vigorously defended the League. Knowing he wasn't supposed to do so as a State Department official, he wired Frank Polk and "practically" offered his resignation. Polk wired back that he approved of Long's intervention.

In St. Louis, Long found plenty of encouragement for his possible candidacy. "I am being mentioned for and spoken to about running for Senator on all sides," he confided to his diary.[11] Nevertheless, he also recorded that the Democratic situation in Missouri was indeed "bad." Three reasons were given for the party's downfall: that the Democratic Congress had fixed the price of wheat but not of cotton; that the president's appeal for a Democratic Congress had rallied the Republicans; and so had the attacks by Senator Lodge and Teddy Roosevelt on Wilson for not demanding "unconditional surrender." Also hurting were Prohibition and "Holy Joe" Folk's reputation as a strongly moralistic enforcer of blue laws.

Making the political rounds outside St. Louis, Breck went to Kansas City, which was famous for its Democratic bosses and their "machines," most notably Tom Pendergast's, but no less powerful was that of the lesser-known Joseph B. Shannon. Pendergast, who brought Harry Truman into public life, called his followers "the goats," and Shannon's men were "the rabbits." Since Pendergast was away, Long had to be satisfied with a talk with Joe Shannon. Going on to the capital at Jefferson City, he met Governor Gardner and "many others." The state senators wanted a speech from him, and he obliged, yet felt afterward he hadn't done a good job. Coincidentally, on the way back to DC he ran into Boss Shannon on the train, and they rode together to Washington.

On January 23, 1919, the Peace Conference formally opened in Paris. Plaintively, Breck Long declared in his diary, "If the South Sea Islands are taken up and I am not sent for, I probably shall not be sent for at all. I am not expecting it."[12] Nor was he incorrect. Wilson and Lansing never brought him over for any reason.

Another issue making headlines at the time was the Russian Civil War that followed the Bolshevik overthrow of the Kerensky Provisional Government in the fall of 1917. Ambassador to Russia David R. Francis had remained in Petrograd, although technically there was no government to which he could be accredited. Because of this, Francis was charged by the Republicans with incompetence.

Be that as it may, on February 25, 1919, Francis returned to the U.S. in the company of President Wilson, paid a visit to Breckinridge

Long, who commented, "He looks very well considering what he has been through." And on March 1, he consented to be Long's houseguest. Actually, the ex-St. Louis mayor and Missouri governor was recuperating from an operation that had left him with a painful wound caused by the removal of his prostate gland and a more-than-half-inch bladder stone. "I thought I could get in more quiet and rest there" (at Long's home), he informed a friend in St. Louis in a letter.

Through David Francis's correspondence, we get a look from outside at the Longs, as they were perceived in those early months of 1919. Francis writes:

> Breck Long and his wife, Christine, stand remarkably well in Washington society and especially in official circles. He is very responsive, an untiring political worker and is by all odds the best politician in the State Department if not in the entire Government. Christine has captured everybody she has met, strange as it may seem. She has improved very much in looks and has learned the forms so that she can entertain with taste and judgment in this fine residence which is in fact a palace.[13]

And in another letter penned the same day, "It seems that both of them have developed wonderfully since I saw them last."[14]

Chapter Six

Running for U.S. Senate

T HE "LOVE FEST," SO TO speak, between David Francis and Breckinridge
Long was not to endure throughout the rest of 1919. Their quarrel
arose over the latter's desire to buy the *St. Louis Republic*, in order to
boost his chances if he ran for the U.S. Senate in 1920. Rather, *when* he
ran; Long had become increasingly frustrated by what he termed "the
stifling policy of the [State] Department versus political expression."
After his speech to the shoe dealers, he had felt himself pressured to
be a leader in Missouri on the League of Nations issue, particularly as
a counterweight to Jim Reed's apostasy. "They seem to look to me for
leadership in Missouri and I am willing to try even though I recognize
and appreciate the force, ability and strength of Reed. He is an able, a
very able, orator and a fighter."

About ten days later, "Fighting Jim" Reed made himself outrageously
obnoxious attacking the League before the Missouri Legislature. So
insulting was he to President Wilson and Colonel House that sixteen
Democrats got up and walked out, to the cheers of Republicans. Later,
fifty of the party's sixty-seven members signed a resolution condemning
Reed and calling on him to resign. The irate Democratic solons then put
out another resolution, inviting Breckinridge Long to come and address
them in favor of the League.

On May 12, Governor Francis, who had gone to the spa at White
Sulphur Springs, West Virginia, to recuperate, stayed overnight at the
Longs' on a visit to the capital. By now Breck was ready to sound out
the publisher about selling his newspaper. "He will sell," Long reported.
"Depends on price." Breck told Francis he could raise half a million and
spend an extra $100,000 of his own money and make the *Republic* "a
great paying investment and a very influential paper."

Ten days later, one of David Francis' sons wrote his father, "Have you
heard from Breck Long?" He was to communicate his offer to Francis

Brothers and Company by May 21. When Long's answer did come in on May 23, it reiterated his original bid—half a million borrowed, plus his own $100,000. The verdict: "Breck Long's proposition, of course, is out of the question," followed by a cautionary, "I do not see any possibility of Breck's making the property a success as, if he says, he intends to remain in politics." Melville E. Stone, a nationally known newspaperman and an advisor to the Francis family, voiced the same argument in a slightly different syntax, "that if Long could forget politics, he would be the very man to control the *Republic*."[1]

But that wouldn't happen. The Francis family soon had a better deal. It took some time for David Francis to reach Breck Long who was at York Harbor and tell him he planned to sell his newspaper to a Sam Lazarus for $100,000 more than he had offered it to Long. Stunned, Breck said he would go back to DC and see if he could raise more money. Stone had told Francis he should get at least $700,000 and there was also talk of selling the paper to Hearst.

In the end, the *St. Louis Republic* was sold to another Missouri organ, the *Globe-Democrat* (despite its name, a Republican paper). Long commented bitterly to his cohort Rufus Hollister, "Francis' action may have a material bearing on my ambition to go to the Senate next year—by contributing to the election of a Republican." He then mailed out 1,500 letters to Democrats in Missouri, touching on his proposed candidacy. "These letters ought to reach the addressees just as they are in the midst of feelings of revulsion about Francis and his sale of the paper . . . This ought to turn their minds to me instead."[2]

Before we leave David Francis completely, one other letter to him from Long should be mentioned because it touches on the frequent query about Breckinridge Long's reputed anti-Semitism. It was an invitation Long forwarded to Francis from a Rabbi in Baltimore, wanting the ex-ambassador to Russia to speak to his congregation. The Rabbi was Morris S. Lazaron, and he and Breckinridge Long considered themselves *good friends*.

The correspondence between them gleaned from the Rabbi's papers at the American Jewish Archives in Cincinnati only goes back as far as 1934, but obviously from this 1919 request to David Francis, their acquaintance can be dated much earlier. They may have met in connection with the League of Nations Association, of which Rabbi Lazaron was a member.

Cynically, one might say that Rabbi Lazaron was Breck Long's type of Jew—American born and raised (in Savannah, Georgia), Reform in his intra-Jewish religious affiliation, ecumenical in his relationships with Catholic and Protestant clergy, and above all strongly assimilationist and rabidly anti-Zionist. "Few individuals were judged more traitorous by American Zionists than Rabbi Morris S. Lazaron," is a quote taken from a biography of the noted American Protestant preacher, Harry Emerson Fosdick.[3] Rabbi Lazaron in 1942 helped found the American Council for Judaism, a fanatically anti-Zionist group known for working against the State of Israel, and he gained some notoriety at the time by declaring "unfortunate" the visit of Dr. Chaim Weizmann to the U.S. Meanwhile, over the years a stream of letters was going out from Breck to "My dear Rabbi," usually closing, "With every good wish."

Two more clues in his 1919 diaries do not answer definitively Breckinridge Long's attitude toward Jews as such, but they raise intriguing questions.

The first appears on June 10, 1919. It starts off with Long's expressing his annoyance at the U.S. Senate for passing a resolution in favor of a free Ireland, which was then under British rule. In his best high-hat State Department manner, he declares Ireland's status "none of their business." But he goes on and excoriates even more a second meddlesome Senate resolution that he labels "a tearful expression about anti-Jewish pogroms in Poland, etc., even after advice that the reports were exaggerated and in many instances unfounded."

What we have here is a one-sided view of a public spat in the press on events in the newly independent, reformulated nation of Poland and its likewise new neighboring countries of Lithuania and the Ukraine. All were wracked by civil strife resulting from the breakup of the Czarist Russian Empire. Once more, it seemed, during the fighting, pogroms had erupted against the Jewish populations. But the U.S. minister to Poland, Hugh Gibson, had backed the position of the Polish government in maintaining there were only a few isolated anti-Jewish incidents and no pogroms at all. From Breck Long's remarks quoted above, it is evident he unquestioningly upheld the contentions of his colleague and friend, Hugh Gibson.

A welter of conflicting *New York Times* headlines tells the entire story. *The New York Times*, June 8, 1919:

GIBSON DENIES POLISH POGROMS
Our Minister to Poland Says He Knows of None Outside of Pinsk.
Investigated Vilna Affair, Found It Was Not a Jewish Massacre.
Some Jews Hostile to the Government.

And right underneath, this contrary intelligence:

SAY POLISH TROOPS SLEW 1,500 IN VILNA
ALLEGATIONS OF CRUELTY SHOWN TO JEWS STILL BEING MADE TO THE
PEACE CONFERENCE.

The New York Times, June 11, 1919:

TO AWAIT DETAIL IN POGROM INQUIRY
HOUSE COMMITTEE PUTS OFF REPORT UNTIL MINISTER GIBSON MAKES
FULL REPORT. PRELIMINARY ADVICES FROM WARSAW SAY AGITATION IS
BASED ON UNWARRANTED REPORTS.

The New York Times, June 17, 1919:

ASSAILS GIBSON REPORT ON POGROMS
LOUIS MARSHALL SAYS THE MINISTER IS WHITEWASHING POLISH
ATROCITIES. CITES EVIDENCE OF KILLINGS AND ASSERTS THAT GIBSON HAS
DISREGARDED ADMISSIONS BY THE POLES THEMSELVES.

There is no mention of Louis Marshall in Breckinridge Long's writings. This pugnacious, strong-willed New York German-Jewish lawyer, who had the nerve to challenge Minister Hugh Gibson's veracity, could fit the same bill as the pushy "radical Jews" whose aggressiveness would enrage the Missourian a quarter of a century later. In 1919 Breck Long was only a bystander in the controversy about what had or had not happened to Jews in parts of Eastern Europe. But his predilection obviously bought into the idea, heavily promoted by the Polish government with Gibson's aid, of Jewish "overblowing" if not outright deceit about injuries inflicted upon their people. It was a charge often made in the past by Czarist perpetrators of pogroms. Shades of the Holocaust-denial to come.

As a defense counsel, Louis Marshall had a reputation for fierceness. To Gibson's publicized insistence on how the isolated atrocities that did occur could not constitute a *pogrom* because they were not government sponsored (as in Russia), Marshall roared back ferociously, "Anyone familiar with Polish affairs would consider Gibson's report *astounding*. He has apparently spoken out of the fullness of his ignorance." Getting warmed up, Marshall then condemned Gibson for basing his opinion "on the merest hearsay, parrot-like repetition of what has been told him in court circles, within whose sacred precincts Jews are not permitted to enter."[4]

Marshall issued this rebuttal from Paris, where he had been attending the Peace Conference as president of a "Combined Jewish Committee" of observers. A founder of the American Jewish Committee in 1906 organized to fight pogroms in Czarist Russia, he also had helped create the American Jewish Joint Distribution Committee upon the outbreak of World War I, a group dedicated to assisting their co-religionists caught in the war zones. In taking on Hugh Gibson, Marshall cited the names and fates of actual individual victims: "Israel Bensky was shot to death in his home . . . Rose Stein was killed because she protested the killing of her husband . . . M. Pilnick was killed because he refused to surrender a sum of money demanded of him,"[5] and all this information was presented to President Wilson in Paris.

Hugh Gibson stoutly returned the New Yorker's fire and at once raised hackles by admitting that, yes, the killing of thirty-seven Jewish men by Polish troops in Pinsk had happened, but their behavior "was such as to invite trouble" and likened these Jews to gunmen in New York City (i.e., Jewish gangsters) "who caused the police so much trouble."[6] Following his biased declaration, the U.S. minister to Poland spoke about Polish-American World War I veterans who had joined General Jozef Haller's Polish army, and offered the chilling argument that

> [Haller] said they had never before seen the Orthodox Jew with his long beard and cloak, his greasy ringlets and none too clean appearance. When they heard the tales that the Polish peasants and townspeople had to tell about the profiteering and other offenses of the Jews their sense of justice was aroused and they set out to show "how the matter would be handled in America.[7]

Confronted in Paris with this dichotomy, President Wilson reacted swiftly by calling upon his old friend and supporter Henry Morgenthau Sr. to lead an inquiry, and the report was delivered in the middle of January 1920. It really did nothing to settle the controversy. Although fixing blame for the "excesses" (it never used the word "pogrom") on Polish troops, it did find "extenuating circumstances." The number of Jewish victims it acknowledged was limited to 280, and the group called for a new commission to be appointed by the (as yet uncreated) League of Nations.

As a final word, an article, "Hugh Gibson and Diplomacy," asserts that this career envoy—

held a common stereotyped opinion of Jews—that they were frequently sly and conniving, rather than straightforward and that he, like many other White Anglo-Saxon Protestant Americans aired certain prejudices of which he was not even fully aware, so much were they a part of him.[8]

Could not the same be said of Breckinridge Long? His indignation over the fact that a State Department stalwart like Hugh Gibson could be challenged was an automatic reflex, no doubt. This notion once planted that Jews were exaggerating their sufferings will appear again, and Long's apparent belief in it would play a tragic part throughout the years when the Holocaust was happening. At the tail end of December in 1919, Breck Long wrote to his friend Hugh Gibson at the American Legation in Warsaw. New Year's greetings were included. So was insider gossip about the Department and how things were so busy they'd never had time to get a photo of the secretary and his three assistants. At the end was a request from one buddy to another: "By the way, if you have an opportunity to cut a few Polish stamps off your mail I wish you would send me some of them for a young friend of mine who is collecting."[9]

The year 1919 was not yet over when Breck Long's diary contained another entry related to anti-Semitism, one that was unexpected and shocking, yet still not really revelatory of his own true feelings on the issue.

In late October 1919, another job he had was to escort King Albert I and Queen Elizabeth of Belgium throughout their visit to the United States.

This was a *very big deal.* Although partly of German heritage and married to a Bavarian princess, Albert had won worldwide cheers for refusing to allow German troops to cross neutral Belgian soil to attack France and leading his own Belgian army personally against the Kaiser's invading forces for the next four years. No king was better loved by his people, revered as their liberator from the Teutonic yoke, and as a man of the people and ardent reformer. This trip to America was his second; he had also come in 1898, when he and his lovely queen were greeted everywhere in the U.S. with great warmth.

The arrangements made with Breckinridge Long in this instance were a bit unusual. In DC the Longs were to turn over their palatial rented house to the royal couple, and they would stay with a Blair relative of Christine's. Breck's October 29 diary entry was: "Christine and I had a unique experience—to be guests for luncheon in our own house. The King gave a lunch [for 75 people] his last day."[10] Also unusually, Long had been assigned to accompany the king and queen on shipboard when they sailed back to Europe.

It was during this voyage that King Albert—and Queen Elizabeth, to an extent—said some things so unlike their benign images that Breck had to record them.

> Extended discussion with King of Belgium. Feared constitutional monarchy wouldn't last. Attacks on monarchy from press. Said press controlled by Jews. Reuters and Havas were Jewish, that all attempts to start a competitive Christian newspaper distribution association had failed. Then, he proceeded to analyze the control of fundamentals—news, money, credit, supplies—by the Jews and the possibilities of world control. He spoke of the Talmud and its teachings, particularly that to save money and to lend it and to control by controlling the funds, etc. He had not heard of the Jewish Protocols and was much interested in my account of their general nature. He had not an intimate knowledge of Russia and doubted the Jews had been as influential and powerful there as they really have. He mentioned the fact that the radical press, always clamoring against society, wealth and control, never mentioned in an antagonistic way the Rothschilds or the other Jews of prominence and power. He also connected the Zionist influence with the general trend of extension of Jewish influence.[11]

For anyone wishing to examine Breckinridge Long's bona fides as a genuine anti-Semite, there is quite a bit to parse here. The business about the "Jewish Protocols," for example. Breck knew about them, so presumably he had read these infamous *Protocols of the Elders of Zion*, a Czarist forgery stolen from the plot of an obscure French novel, and yet in 1919 they were basically unknown in the United States until at least a year later when Henry Ford's rabidly anti-Semitic publication, the *Dearborn Independent*, began publishing that scurrilous piece of propaganda. That they came up in the conversation must have been at Breck's instigation, since the royal couple apparently was ignorant of them.

Another sentence of Long's to wonder about is when he opines the king is not well enough informed to know how powerful the Jews in Russia really were—although you can probably add, *among the Bolsheviks.* It may be noted Long didn't try to argue with his majesty—that's understandable—but on the diary pages there was not even a tut-tut.

When their ship briefly docked at the Azores, Breck Long received word his mother had died and a radiogram from President and Mrs. Wilson conveying their condolences.

Europe-bound again from the Portuguese islands, Breck had dinner with King Albert and Queen Elizabeth. Once more, we have a characterization of Jews that he repeats in print.

> Dinner on board—discussing with King and Queen events in Russia—the part played by the Jews in Bolshevism, then designs for control of the world. The King regretted the reported defeat [of White armies] and the Queen spoke several times of Jewish ambitions and connected the Zionist movement with it. She asked about Justice Brandeis, of the propriety of his connection with Zionism and attributed it to his idealism.[12]

It may be wondered if Long's mind flashed back to the past spring and an evening having dinner at Frank and Eleanor Roosevelt's home with Justice and Mrs. Brandeis.

Now it was November. Their ship docked in Brest, France, on the 11th, the one-year anniversary of the Armistice. After a quick trip to see the battlefields and have dinner with Frank Polk and his wife in Paris, the third assistant secretary of state was on his way back to the U.S.

How much longer would he remain in his present post? The ceremonial job was wearing thin. When the president-elect of Brazil came to visit the U.S., Long was tickled by a Pathé newsreel showing him greeting the dignitary's arrival, which preceded a feature film drama about the fall of Richmond in the Civil War featuring his famous kinsman John Cabell Breckinridge. "It was funny to be on the same stage with my ancestors," he mused. Less funny were the antics of Senhor Epitácio Pessoa and his entourage. The relieved comment in Long's diary was, finally "they have gone! Bag, baggage, 80 trunks, 107 pieces of hand luggage, maids, valets, dogs, wives, husbands and Pessoa."[13]

On the day before Christmas, Breck's crony Rufus Hollister bought the *Daily Capital News*, the main morning newspaper in Jefferson City. Long was financing the purchase and in describing it added an optimistic postscript: "I feel my prospective candidacy for the Senate is becoming very rosy."[14]

Chapter Seven

Losing for U.S. Senate

A HIGH POINT OF THE stay of King Albert and Queen Elizabeth in Washington, DC occurred when their host Breckinridge Long escorted them to the White House to see President Woodrow Wilson. Ordinarily, this sort of state visit would have been replete with ceremonies and formalities. But in October 1919, Wilson was recuperating from a partial stroke he'd suffered in Colorado when campaigning for his League of Nations idea, and the president received the royal couple while in bed. They were the first visitors he'd allowed since his collapse. Breck Long was appalled by Wilson's appearance.

Discussions in Democratic circles about the presidential race of 1920 had included consideration of a third-term try by Wilson. This was possibly what Long was hoping for in connection with his own race for U.S. Senate. But one look at the gaunt figure in the White House bedroom told him it was never to be (even if Wilson himself kept thinking he might still yet run). Brett Long realized he would have to take on his Republican opponent without any added help from the national ticket—that is, if he won his primary.

The Missouri Democrats would make their selection in August. As it turned out, Breck was to have not one but five Democratic opponents, which was a good thing for him. The most formidable was ex-Federal Judge Henry S. Priest, whom Senator Jim Reed had hand picked to oppose Long, because Priest was anti-League of Nations, an outspoken "wet" on Prohibition and also backed by the Kansas City Pendergast machine. Next came Charles M. Hay, a St. Louis lawyer and Prohibition leader, the driest of "dries," but pro-League of Nations. The three other very minor candidates were a minister (also pro-League and pro-Prohibition), the owner of the *Sedalia Democrat* (for the League and changes in the Volstead Act), and a total unknown. Breck's position was solidly in favor of the League of Nations, naturally, but ambivalent regarding Prohibition.

On January 4, 1920, the first public announcement of Breck Long's intent to run for U.S. Senate was made. From then on, he was to endure the vicissitudes of worry and spurts of euphoria that any contender for office experiences. Right from the start, there was a rumor that Champ Clark might enter the race and obviously would be a formidable opponent. This news was brought to DC by a group of Missouri Democrats in town to convince the Democratic National Committee once again to pick their state for the site of its upcoming national convention. The critical meeting on this choice was held at the Shoreham Hotel January 8, 1920, and Breckinridge Long was present, although not a member of the committee, showing his aptitude for clever political maneuvering by persuading his friend Homer Cummings, the DNC chair, to let him use the proxy of an absent Puerto Rican member. Kansas City might have had a shot, he later claimed, if they had improved their offer. The nod instead went to San Francisco, the very first time the party had gone west of the Rockies.

The threat from Champ Clark soon began to fade. About a week after the DNC action, Long boastfully declared: "Clark was about to get into the race, but Hollister wrote him a letter which will scare him off. Probably will not run."[1] When official word came in mid February of Clark's demurral, Breck sounded positively cocksure of himself. "Good news," he declared, "though I'll beat him if he does run."[2]

However, he still had to sweat out the potential entry of other Missouri Democrat heavyweights, like Governor Gardner, ex-Governor Francis, and ex-Governor Folk.

Then, too, the rumor mill went on churning. In February a story had emerged that Wilson would appoint Breckinridge Long ambassador to Switzerland. As Breck told it, he declined and offered his resignation from the State Department, which the president refused to accept. A hidden meaning here involved the evident rift that had developed between Wilson and Secretary of State Lansing, who had been sandbagged by the alleged offer to Long. Actually, Wilson fired Lansing on February 15, 1920 (that is, forced him to resign), the real motive being that the latter had criticized the League of Nations.

In the following weeks, it seems, Breck Long may have been living in a fantasy world. He still carried on at his assistant secretary job, notwithstanding that he was already an announced candidate for the U.S. Senate. On March 5, 1920, in a *New York Times* article about him, the headline was: LONG TO REMAIN AT POST. The reason he gave to the press was that in view of the resignation of Secretary of State Robert Lansing, the appointment of Under Secretary William Phillips as ambassador to the Netherlands, and the pending retirement of Acting Secretary Frank Polk, he, Long, "should remain at his post." In fact, if he did leave, it would not be until after the Missouri primary election in August.

Implicit, conceivably, in this little cutesy game of political timing was Breck Long's unspoken assumption that with Bill Phillips gone, he might be moved up to under secretary of state. For that plum, no doubt, he would gladly abandon his intention to run for senator. Nevertheless, on March 18, 1920, he was still following the news from Missouri. "Clark out. Francis out. Folk probably out. Hay says No. [He would later say yes.] Gardner still to be heard from."[3]

What a difference a day makes. On March 19, 1920, the worst nightmare of the Wilsonians became reality. In the U.S. Senate, the Republicans delivered a crushing defeat to the treaty of peace which the Central Powers had worked out so tirelessly at Versailles and, even more devastating, refused to allow the U.S. to join the League of Nations. For the ruin of his own dreams, Wilson was loudly blamed—at least by the Republicans and opposition Democrats. If only he'd been more flexible; if only he'd caved in to Henry Cabot Lodge, been less stiff-necked and so on . . . But, no, Wilson had made it plain that the terms he'd negotiated in Paris were nonnegotiable in Washington, DC.

At the State Department, the new secretary was an ex-Republican, Bainbridge Colby, who had left the GOP in 1912 to join Teddy Roosevelt's Progressives and afterward was a strong supporter of Wilson's. The day following Colby's confirmation, Long noted that a project he'd worked on, a "consortium" loan for the Chinese, had been consummated, and he crowed grandiloquently, "It is the most important accomplishment of my life so far." Yet it was soon clear to him he wasn't going to be the next under secretary.

So his eyes not surprisingly turned back to Missouri. For two weeks he campaigned, drawing five hundred supporters at a St. Louis testimonial and culminating his efforts at the Democratic State Convention in Joplin. There, an extraordinary event took place. The anger against Jim Reed for his continual anti-Wilson remarks literally exploded, and against all tradition the senior senator was denied delegate status at the Democratic National Convention in San Francisco.

The first effect on Breck Long's ambitions of this stinging insult to Reed was—quite plainly—the entry of Reed's candidate Judge Priest into the Senate primary race against Breck Long. On June 4, 1920, Long filed his nomination petitions and seemingly had no opposition until, at the last moment, Reed's man entered, followed by Charles Hay and the three lesser candidates. Although this was two months before the vote scheduled for August 3, Breck decided it would be better if he left the State Department right away. So on June 7, he met with Colby and Polk, resigned, and according to *The New York Times* suffering a high fever from tonsillitis, took to his bed, and followed doctor's orders not to see anyone.[4]

Breckinridge Long was now a bit of a celebrity, attracting attention from national newspapers like *The New York Times*, which soon ran another story about him not related to the Missouri U.S. Senate race. This was a bizarre incident about a professor from the University of Minnesota named Stanley L. Rypins who claimed that during World War I while working in Military Intelligence, he had opened the mail of Third Assistant Secretary of State Breckinridge Long. Immediate denials from the Army and State Department helped stir this tempest in a teapot that ended with the professor saying it wasn't Long but a third assistant secretary of war he wouldn't name.[5]

As Breck's Missouri campaign unfolded, far more serious canards were hurled at him, especially by Senator Jim Reed. He called Breckinridge Long "a dandy" and "a pink tea candidate" and even said he should be in jail, although not saying for what. When criticized by the press for these personal attacks, Reed archly replied he didn't really mean it and that Breckinridge was "as nice a little gentleman as ever carried a Duke's grip from his steamer to his hotel." Against such sharp-edged sarcasm, Breck Long could only lamely manage to fire back by calling Reed "an alleged Democrat."

Jim Reed, it should be added, was the darling of the most WASP-tongued of all American journalists of that era, H. L. Mencken. Both were contributors to the *American Mercury* magazine. Some years later, in a heartfelt tribute to Fighting Jim, Mencken emphasized, "The important thing is that he fights. Were there greater gladiators in the Senate in the Golden Age? I presume to doubt it." His weapon, the columnist added, was his rapier-like wit. "He knows how to make it go through stone and steel." Like Reed, Mencken had no use for Woodrow Wilson, and he called Wilson's idealism "that shabby scam by Calvinism out of McGuffey's Fourth Reader."[6]

By beating Reed's candidate, Long merely accelerated the hostility between the two Democrats.

For once, on August 3, 1920, Long's prediction of voting results was accurate. "Primary Election today. Early returns tonight indicate an easy victory for me." The August 4th *New York Times* had Long ahead and, a day later, beating second-place Judge Priest. With all votes tallied, Long had crushed the Reed proxy by about twelve thousand votes. On the Republican side, the incumbent Selden Spencer had beaten his challenger, Colonel Dwight F. Davis, by a like amount.

Meanwhile events at the Democratic National Convention in San Francisco had added a new—and potentially harmful—dimension to Breck Long's quest. No third term for Woodrow Wilson materialized, and the party had deadlocked on top names like Wilson's son-in-law Treasury Secretary William Gibbs McAdoo, William Jennings Bryan, and Attorney General A. Mitchell Palmer, until settling for a dark horse on the 44th ballot, Ohio Governor James M. Cox. Even though Cox was a League of Nations man, Breck Long could not have been pleased to see the national ticket headed by a man of less than star power. The one consolation was that his friend Frank Roosevelt had been chosen for vice president. One might expect Long to be thinking that he and FDR were on parallel tracks to the big time in American politics.

But reality was quick to sink in. Candidate Long and his sidekick law partner Frank Thompson traveled to Ohio to meet candidate Cox at his home near Dayton. And whom should they find there but Fighting Jim Reed, on an errand to convince Cox to drop his support for the League of Nations. There was a scene. Breck Long confronted Reed and demanded support for his U.S. Senate race in Missouri. Reed "blew up" and refused. Tit for tat, Long declined to have his picture taken with the senator. Sometime later, when Cox was alone with him, Breck learned that Reed had threatened to have a Senate committee investigate Long's campaign expenditures unless—his price was that Cox change his position on the League. Cox told Reed no, and Breck remarked in his diary, "No wonder Reed was mad yesterday."[7] Jim Reed never did support any Democrat in Missouri in 1920, except the Honorable John M. Atkinson for governor.

A document from that campaign, urging support for both Long and Atkinson, sheds an interesting sidelight on Missouri elections during this period. The handbill in question was addressed: To THE COLORED VOTERS OF MISSOURI, by the Afro-American League, headquartered in Kansas City. It exhorted:

> STAND BY THE LEAGUE OF NATIONS.
> VOTE TO CONTINUE GOOD TIMES AND HIGH WAGES.

Then in a full page, it pushed for Hon. Breckenridge [*sic*] Long,

HE IS THE MAN FOR UNITED STATES SENATOR.

and Hon. John M. Atkinson,

LET'S HELP ELECT HIM GOVERNOR.

In Long's favor:

> He stands for a square deal for our people and we must vote
> for him and place him in a position where he can and will do
> the most good. It was the Breckenridge Long Democrats, led by
> Senator Mike Kinney, who defeated the segregation ordinances
> for St. Louis and be it remembered that the Republican precincts
> and wards gave the Jim Crow ordinances the biggest majorities,
> while Democratic precincts went against it and we urge every
> thinking colored voter to vote for Mr. Long.

Judge Atkinson's appeal was based in part on the information that
"he belongs to the highest type of white people, the class who believes
in treating us and all men fairly."

Another campaign leaflet contains an extensive exposition of
Breckinridge Long's platform and qualifications. It is a document that
begins by looking back at Long's government service—"two [years] of
active warfare and one of efforts to restore peace"—in which he praises
the record of the Wilson administration in overcoming "the greatest
military autocracy the world has ever known and putting the Stars and
Stripes on the ramparts of the Rhine," followed by an attack on the
Senate for having rejected the peace treaty and jeopardizing the payment
of American claims of property damage to the tune of $800 million, and
he also attacks a "subtle and well-organized attempt to hold the President
responsible for the failure [of the treaty]." He touches upon hot-button
issues like Prohibition, going so far as to state: "I am unalterably opposed
to the re-opening of the saloon" (playing to the dries) but simultaneously
(playing to the wets) saying he thought certain features of the Volstead
Act were unconstitutional, and he would await the decision of the U.S.
Supreme Court before taking any action.

Considering that his connection to the Consular Service in World
War II proved so controversial, it is interesting to note how much time

he spent praising his role in it during World War I. After stating that this State Department function paid for itself and in 1919 deposited $1.5 million in the U.S. Treasury, he twitted a Republican presidential hopeful, General Leonard Wood, for not even knowing there was an American Consular Service, never mind that it was "the foremost in the world." Throughout his campaign, Breck Long continued to blow his own horn about his work with the Consular Service, that he had been "President of the Consular Board," directing all assignments, as well as being in charge of the Bureau of Citizenship, the country's passport office, and on the Diplomatic Board that conducted the Foreign Service entrance exams.

Larding his resumé were other examples of his work in the Far East, China, Russia, Eastern Europe, and the Pacific Islands. Specifically mentioned was his helping to arrange the withdrawal of American troops from Siberia in 1919 and placing the Chinese financial system on a sound basis. Nor did he shrink from boasting of his ceremonial duties—namedropping some of the celebrities he'd entertained, like Lord Balfour of England, the Joffre and Viviani mission from France, the king of the Belgians, Dr. Masaryk, the president of Czechoslovakia, numerous Latin American dignitaries and various other international groups.

Possibly considering that Missourians might not be too bowled over by all this foreign stuff, it was added that Breckinridge Long was "a clean campaigner, possesses a wonderful personality and he has clearly shown that he has a thorough knowledge of the national problems which confront the country today." More important, no doubt, was that the candidate had married the granddaughter of Senator Frank P. Blair and was directly descended from the well-known Breckinridge family of Kentucky; his mother was Miss Margaret Breckinridge, a daughter of Judge Samuel Breckinridge of Kentucky and his father Major William Long of North Carolina, who was wounded in the Confederate Army.

Pride of heritage, his place in society, the high level of his service in Washington—all these elements had to buoy Breck Long, when he measured his *curriculum vitae* against that of his opponent. He had once described Selden Spencer as "a cheap vaudeville actor on a world stage."[8]

Indeed, as the campaign heated up, the Republican candidate did resort to a few political tricks. One was a charge he hurled—in mid October— at President Wilson, claiming he was prepared to send American troops back across the Atlantic if troubles broke out in Europe. Spencer alleged Wilson had made this promise to Premier Bratianu of Romania, a story vigorously denied by the White House and by the stenographer present at the meeting of the two men. Also, as Jim Reed had threatened, Long was hauled before a Senate committee to answer for his campaign expenses—the only one of seventy candidates to be so treated—and before a committee on which Selden Spencer sat.

Such gamesmanship, though, was hardly instrumental in the final outcome of the Spencer-Long race. It turned out that the election of 1920 was one of those electoral tidal waves—like 1932 or 1964 or 2008—that sweep over the American political scene, carrying all before them. At the top of both tickets were essentially two nonentities from Ohio—Cox and Harding—but the GOP standard-bearer was running on a platform perfectly fitted to the public mood—a return to *normalcy* after the sacrifices of the war years.

Breck Long never saw the Republican surge coming. Shortly after the polls closed on November 2, he was bold enough to jot in his diary, "Returns available up to midnight indicate my election," despite the fact that he'd already recognized it was "Harding by a large vote."

November 3 brought more sobering news: "Returns are worse and worse. The State has gone Republican . . . My defeat is not yet conceded. I am running in the lead of my ticket and may be elected in spite of the Republican victory."

No such luck. On November 4: "It is all over. Our defeat is certain and overwhelming. I am at the head of my ticket but even so am defeated by a large vote." Selden Spencer, "the cheap vaudeville actor," beat Breckinridge Long by 130,000 votes.

The only squeal of pain Long allowed himself to put in his diary was: "So—has been at least temporarily eclipsed, the goal of my ambitions."

Breck's postmortem blamed Cox and that he'd abandoned the League of Nations as an issue. Simultaneously, the GOP had spent "an enormous sum of money—$600,000 in Missouri, alone, while the Missouri Democrats had expended a mere $50,000 and owed $32,000. Anti-Wilson voters prevailed, Germans who resented him, cotton and wheat farmers unhappy, the economy souring."

Upon reflection days later, Breck was able to put a better face on what had happened. He had enjoyed the experience immensely, he declared. "Two hard fights in six months. I was nominated—but defeated in the general election—but I am not yet 40 years old and youthful enough to be optimistic."[9]

Chapter Eight

One More Try

A FULL YEAR AFTER BRECK Long penned his optimistic view of the future following the 1920 defeat of his political ambitions, he posted in his final diary entry of 1921 a more sobering estimate of where he was.

> Before I go, I will bring to a close—a record of a rather unfruitful year. I have not done well during 1921—health demanded rest, started in disappointment, unemployed for many months . . . I am practicing International law and have some business. But that is all . . . I have lost prestige, power, influence and money.

On the bright side, however, were some compensations.

> But I am happy and that is a lot. My dear wife and I are most congenial . . . Our dear child grows strong and develops . . . New year coming in which to return to progress further—to work and to achieve.[1]

His day-by-day recording of events in 1921 was commensurately skimpy. He did not even write anything until February 12, when he noted his and Christine's return from Miami, Florida, to DC. They had taken their *first long trip together* (their honeymoon in 1912 had been interrupted by his need to attend the Democratic National Convention in Baltimore). Part of their present trip had been on a chartered houseboat off the east coast of Florida, with cruises to the Keys and Cuba, then docking at the Miami Yacht Club and staying at the Flamingo Hotel in Miami Beach. There were a few political musings about the incoming Harding administration, how Bill Phillips and Joe Grew would probably be kept on because they were Republicans, and later the fact noted that the new president had made Charles Evan Hughes his secretary of state.

By the last week of February, Long had decided his immediate future. He would practice law in both DC and St. Louis, and he and Christine would give up their pink palatial rental at MacVeagh House and buy a more modest place in the capital—a move they consummated by April. Meanwhile, he and his sister Margaret had divided their mother's estate. He mentioned that his share included a large silver ladle, which had been in the Long family since 1800, and a china cup and saucer belonging to his great-grandfather Long.

Further remarks in 1921 were reserved for specific criticisms of the Harding administration's appointments to the State Department, plus a special personal rant over what he called "political plagiarism." The Harding folks at State were giving the president credit for the Chinese banking "Consortium" that he, Breckinridge Long, had so painstakingly put together and had so proudly crowed about.[2] Next, on April 12, 1921, Breck recorded his profound disgust with the Harding administration in its dealing with defeated Germany. "America today officially notified the world at large she was temporarily divested of honor," he started off, furious that Harding had told Congress he would sign a separate peace treaty with Germany, "a complete divorce from the League of Nations and taking the League out of the Treaty."

Most likely unbeknownst to Breckinridge Long was that across the Atlantic in Munich, Germany, an Austrian transplant and wounded war veteran named Adolf Hitler had gained the leadership of a small political group called the National Socialist German Workers Party, one of the many voices already raised in Germany condemning the Versailles Treaty.

Closer to home in 1921 and also left out of his diary—perhaps deliberately—was an intra-Democratic Party fight in which Breckinridge Long was intimately involved. As expressed in his swan song after being trounced by Selden Spencer, he had no intention of giving up his political ambitions. His next step in that direction, though, will appear quixotic. It was nothing less than an attempt to be elected chair of the Democratic National Committee. Adding piquancy to this move was that the man he planned to challenge for the job was Cordell Hull, his future boss a dozen years hence.

Hull, a Tennessee congressman, had been defeated in the 1920 Republican landslide. Whatever hubris led Breck Long to believe he could take on this veteran of fourteen years in Congress (and Hull was to serve ten more after being returned in 1922) never did get explained. Perhaps Breck thought he might have an edge since the DNC meeting was being held in St. Louis. But Hull's biographer Harold B. Hinton tells how Long's impertinence was easily squelched.

> Hull had to be the favorite. His closest contender was Breckinridge Long, who suffered under the handicap of not being a member of the committee. Eligibility for him even to run required that he persuade Edward F. Goltra of St. Louis, the Missouri committeeman, to resign so that he could be elected to the vacancy and nominated for the chairmanship. Goltra cleared up the whole situation by refusing to resign and Hull became the unopposed compromise choice.[3]

While it is doubtful that Long would have succeeded in any event, at least here he could blame Ed Goltra. Besides, it was hardly a good time to be heading up the Democrats. The final communiqué from the Missouri meeting, as Hull's biographer put it, actually even *piggy-backed* on a GOP initiative, praising the disarmament "Washington Conference on the Limitation of Naval Armament," convened by President Warren Harding upon the advice of Secretary of State Charles Evans Hughes.[4]

Within Missouri, meanwhile, the fratricidal rancor between Wilsonians and anti-Leaguers continued apace. Less than six months later, Breckinridge Long was being urged to run for the U.S. Senate again—this time against incumbent Jim Reed in a primary race.

One of his most persistent champions was none other than Charles Martin Hay, the Prohibitionist leader, who had run against him unsuccessfully in the previous Senate primary. Hay's first letter to Long on the subject was dated October 8, 1921, and sent from Hay's law office in St. Louis to Long's law office in DC. It began by stating that "an organized effort is already underway to re-nominate and reelect Reed," which in Hay's opinion would be "abhorrent" to all high-minded Democrats. "Do you not think something should be done and done soon since no movement to organize against Reed appears to be in sight?"

Three days afterward, Long wrote back to "my dear Charlie," apologizing for the delay because he'd just returned from Nantucket, where he'd been keeping "assiduously away from politics for some months."

Yet it was obvious he'd been giving this matter lots of thought. Coyly, cautiously, he'd admitted he'd been "in communication with persons in several parts of the State on general political topics" but felt there was no need "to do anything very soon" because "there is a natural inclination to oppose Mr. Reed for re-nomination." This movement would eventually jell, he insisted, and by the way, they could continue the discussion in three or four weeks, when he planned to be in St. Louis.

Presumably their talk had been held by the end of November 1921, when Hay wrote to a political friend in St. Joseph, Missouri, named C. E. Betts, to tell him that Breckinridge Long was a possible candidate to take on Senator Reed, but so was a Judge Williamson of Kansas City. "I could easily support either one of them," Hay confided. But the next month, on December 27, 1921, he informed Betts that it looked like Long would make the race and Judge Williamson most probably *wouldn't*. Optimistically, Hay added, "Of course, if Long runs, we should get behind him and do what we can to put him over. I think he will easily beat Reed."

His positive rationale for such confidence was soon outlined by Hay in a letter to the highly influential Virginia U.S. Senator Carter Glass, and it was based on statistics from the 1920 primary race. Underlining that he had only entered it on the last day of filing, he had still garnered 45,000 votes, second to Long, who had 65,000, while Reed's man, Judge Priest, trailed with only 40,000. Thus, the combined pro-League, pro-Wilson, tally had been 110,000 as opposed to the pro-Reed, anti-League forces' total of 40,000. This was Hay's pitch to a fellow Wilsonian, beseeching him to halt a movement among U.S. Senate Democrats rumored to support Reed's re-election.

Plainly indefatigable, Hay kept exhorting his likeminded friends to rally behind Breckinridge Long. Trying to dissuade a Judge Ewing Cockrell of Warrensburg, Missouri, from running, he argued that "Long has a strong organization, is amply able to make a vigorous campaign and will get a substantial vote." To G. W. Bibb of Montgomery City, who had pressed Hay to offer himself, he firmly replied, "My intention is to support Mr. Long . . . Long made a good race before and I think will be acceptable to a majority of the Democrats this time." And at the very end of his letter to Senator Glass, Hay is close to apoplectic in his denunciation of Fighting Jim Reed, declaiming: "It ill behooves any man who was a friend of the last administration to try to embarrass the administration's genuine friends in this state who have suffered so much humiliation already at the hands of this man."[5]

Therefore, it will come as no surprise that Woodrow Wilson, himself, sick as he was, should participate actively in this bitter Show-Me-State primary. Not only was there a sharp-elbows public debate between the two contenders about whether or not the incumbent Democrat senator had *slandered* the former president but also Wilson on at least three occasions sent letters to be published in the Missouri press, excoriating Reed and evincing his support for Breckinridge Long. Incidentally, the offending remark of Reed's was reported by Long to be a reference to Wilson as "that long-eared animal that goes braying about the country." But Reed denied, in effect, having called the president *an ass.*

Then Wilson made public his own striking characterization of Reed. As befitted an erudite ex-academic, he used a term seemingly archaic but perfectly apropos to Reed's conduct vis-à-vis the League of Nations. A Wilson missive that appeared in *The New York Times*, as well as the Missouri papers, ended with: "Certainly Missouri cannot afford to be represented by such a *marplot.*"

The meaning of *marplot*, according to Webster, is: "One who by his officious interference mars or defeats a plan."[6] Reed exactly fit the definition in this case. Otherwise, Woodrow Wilson used less intellectual language for his denunciations of the senator from Kansas City. In a communication to the *St. Louis Globe-Democrat*, he declared Reed is "incapable of sustained allegiance to any person or any cause . . . has forfeited any claim to my confidence . . . I will never consent to any further association with him."[7] Or, writing ex-Missouri Governor Loy V. Stephens: "I shall hope and confidently expect to see him repudiated by the Democrats at the primaries."

This spectacle of the ailing former president of the United States rising from his sickbed to intervene in a state election was at first thought to give his candidate a real boost.

TIDE IN MISSOURI SETS AGAINST REED
WILSON NOTE HURT REED

was an April headline in *The New York Times*. The body of the story editorialized that an expected backlash against Wilson's butting in hadn't materialized, that Reed was "seriously injured" by Wilson's attacks "and that Mr. Long's chances have been improved correspondingly."[8]

Helping, too, was Wilson's son-in-law, William Gibbs McAdoo, the ex-secretary of the Treasury, who repudiated a statement by Reed that, he, McAdoo, had said the League of Nations was now a dead issue. Not so, the Californian riposted in a telegram to Breck Long that was immediately made public. McAdoo also took a shot at the GOP in general for having "lied," claiming they would find an alternative to the League when they had no intention of doing so.

There did turn out to be *some* negative reaction to Wilson's involvement. Hay reported to Long that "a very astute politician up in Callaway County" had written him with the following message: "If you know of any way to get Wilson to let up on letter writing get busy as this will react sure as you are born." There were those, too, who felt the president should have stopped with a single letter and that his flurry of activity showed he wasn't as sick as he was made out to be.

Today we would call Jim Reed "a piece of work," that is, a formidable and unpredictable personality, with a gift for acerbic, witty language. In his own day, he'd been called "This Rabelais-reading Jeffersonian," and "This steely-eyed, iron jaw play boy of the Senate, this Voltaire-tongue bastinado of the uplifters," who "could fill the Senate galleries whenever he spoke."[9] Also, he was daring and peremptory. On one occasion, his second wife Nell Quinlan Donnelly, a very successful dress designer and manufacturer in Kansas City, was kidnapped and held for ransom. Fighting Jim summoned the most notorious local criminal kingpin, Johnny Lazzia, and told him he wanted her back immediately unharmed and unpaid for, and within hours this was done.

Mostly forgotten in our day, Reed's memory—to an extent—has been kept alive on the Internet by an arch-conservative group of the Ron Paul Libertarian persuasion. They admiringly posted on their website the full text of an attack made by Reed in 1914 on the Migratory Bird Act. He thought it dastardly that this law for protection of egrets, then being hunted to extinction for their feathers, had been in his shocked words "enacted in response to a manufactured sentiment created by an organized lobby." Federal government protection of this sort was clearly unconstitutional, he loudly proclaimed.

The race between Reed and Long no doubt received the national attention it did because of Woodrow Wilson's role in it. One pundit wrote that without Wilson's support, Long would not have had the slightest chance of winning. Yet it was a tight race. On August 2, 1922, the early returns from the larger Missouri cities brought the following headline to the front page of *The New York Times.*

REED SEEMS VICTOR AT MISSOURI POLLS
BUT VOTE IS CLOSE

The outcome still remained cloudy, however, and the story stayed on the pages of *The New York Times* for at least a week. On August 3, it even drew an editorial. Both men were characterized: Reed, a transplant from Iowa to Missouri, as having "a quick mind, a biting tongue, a genius for humorous-vituperative epigram and epithet," and "the art of making warm friends and prominent enemies," while Breckinridge Long was deemed "an accomplished and cultured young man" but "who had had five disastrous candidacies for office" and "no considerable popularity."[10] The editorial writer also touched upon what later was to emerge as the most important factor in Long's defeat—noting that the Missouri Primary Law allowed Republicans to take part in a Democratic primary. Later on, it was estimated (by Long) that 40,000 to 50,000 of the GOP had taken Democratic ballots in order to support Jim Reed and reward him for his stands, particularly against the League of Nations.

Reed had carried the two biggest Missouri cities by 43,000 votes, doing much better than expected in Breck Long's hometown of St. Louis as well as triumphing in his own bailiwick of Kansas City. Long's plurality in the rural areas was only 40,000.

On August 4, 1922, *The New York Times* headline was:

NOMINATION OF REED NOW SEEMS CERTAIN
BUT LONG KEEPS HOPE

One last straw for Breck to grasp at was that the Missouri National Guard vote of several thousand had not yet been counted. Labor unrest in the state had caused the governor to call out the reservists to protect factories, and the guardsmen had had to vote by absentee. The vast majority hailed from rural areas, and Long saw them as his voters.

By August 5, a mere 58 precincts were left to be counted, and Reed was ahead by 5,972. Already, Long was raising the issue of Republican voters and arguing that Democrats alone should have been allowed in their party's primary.

Then, with defeat certain, the issue shifted. Would Breck Long himself or one of his followers run as an Independent, thus drawing off large numbers of Democratic votes in the general election and electing Reed's Republican challenger? That person turned out to be a man named R. R. Brewster, the winner over five other candidates in the GOP primary.

Such a strategy was the focus of a meeting Long had with state Democratic leaders, whose consensus was against a *sorehead* move. One Long supporter, Frank H. Farris, a nominee for state Senate, summed up their feelings: "We'll hold no post mortem. We have lost."

Still, Long refrained from issuing a concession statement. Instead, he publicly proclaimed: "The Democrats in the State are fighting mad.

I have received over 1,000 telegrams since it became apparent I was not nominated and they are seething out there."[11] He even said he was contemplating asking for a recount. The next day a former Missouri congressman, W. D. Van Diver from the college town of Columbia, publicly said Long should run as an Independent, claiming that 100,000 Democrats would stay home unless a "real Democrat" was on the ticket. Nevertheless, Breck Long finally let it be known he would accept his defeat, wouldn't ask for a recount and would even disassociate himself from any efforts of the anti-Reed forces to run a third candidate."

Charles Hay did supply a sort of "post mortem"—beyond the obvious, if unfair, intrusion of Republicans into a Democratic family spat. To a friend in Ohio, Dr. E. J. Moore, he wrote on August 21, 1922: "There is but one explanation . . . for Long's defeat and that is the weakness of Long, personally, on the stump, set over against Reed's transcendent ability as a campaigner."

A perfect illustration from the campaign coverage bears him out. Reed's language, it is clearly seen, always had the power to stir a crowd. For example, he came right out and called the League of Nations "a corpse around the neck of the party," and followed this up with a brilliant bit of simile that the common folks could understand, smile at and nod at.

> Some of you men have at some time owned a horse that you thought had speed. But did any of you ever have your horse beaten by 7 million miles [he was referring to earlier remarks of his about Harding's 7 million plurality in 1920] and then re-enter him again at the first opportunity with the same rider and put your money on him. Now, that's exactly what 'Brecky' wants to do.

Eleven years later, the *St. Louis Globe Democrat* called the 1922 contest "a campaign that made history in Missouri politics."[12]

Incidentally, in the 1922 *general election*, Jim Reed handily defeated his Republican opponent, R. R. Brewster, calling him "a tool of Walter S. Dickey," the "Old Guard" GOP leader whom he had beaten in 1916. Always a showman, Reed took a circus tent with him on the hustings and had women appear with him on the same platform when he blasted the Prohibitionist Anti-Saloon League. His margin over Brewster was 44,258 votes.[13]

Chapter Nine

Nativists and Anti-Semites

TOWARDS THE END OF 1922, Breckinridge Long was writing in his diary: "Ever since the primary election, I have been endeavoring to determine what my course should be."[1] The main prospect still seemed to be the law, but where his heart really lay (in politics), was best expressed by him in unspecified terms: "I have tried to do my part—and been denied official authority but I shall continue. Others can't. So I will," and he phrased his stated goal as a mushy pledge to "work for the attainment of proper and helpful objectives."[2]

Continual rehashing of his situation went on for the rest of the year. He complained constantly about the unfair if unfortunately not illegal organized influx of Republicans that had helped defeat him. He fretted over the failure of the anti-Reed Missouri press to back him openly. Even Rufus Hollister's Democratic newspaper in Jefferson City, which he had bankrolled, had adhered to its longtime policy of staying neutral in a party primary. Finally, he needed to decide where he and his family should live—Washington, DC or Missouri.

The answer may have seemed simple. "Christine likes Washington. She dislikes St. Louis." The gateway city on the Mississippi held bad memories for her: the deaths of her parents, her grandfather Francis Blair's defeat for U.S. Senate, her husband's two defeats." Yet Breck also had to admit, "On the other hand, I like politics."[3] That is, being in Missouri political life.

Nonetheless, in November, he wryly had to acknowledge, "I have returned to Washington," adding, "Christine and Teenie had returned a few days ahead of me, arriving from New York where C. has been engaged in the annual pastime of depleting the dressmakers and hat makers of their most expensive wares."

Long's future really was a blank slate at this point. Events were happening elsewhere that would intersect with his own life in ways utterly unimaginable during those first years of the 1920s. The closest occurred in that very same Missouri Democratic primary of 1922, when Harry S. Truman of Independence won the nomination for Eastern Judge of Jackson County. It is to be wondered if Breck Long had heard of him and, if so, discounted him as just another hack employed by Tom Pendergast's machine, which had helped their pal Jim Reed beat him. In 1922, Breck Long could never have dreamed what lay ahead, neither for Truman nor, for that matter, his friend Frank Roosevelt.

It was only a year after the 1920 election—in August 1921—that Frank Roosevelt had contracted polio. By 1922, he was being fitted for the heavy metal braces he would have to wear the rest of his life in order to stand upright. FDR's prognosis of having a continued public career was aptly summed up by one of his biographers. "Clearly, any person who survived a severe case of paralytic polio in the 1920's faced a depressing and uncertain future."[4]

Definitely not in Breck's thoughts, except as names in the newspapers, were two foreign figures who came into notice during those early 1920 years. In Italy, Benito Mussolini, a man Long would come into direct contact with a decade later, began on October 27, 1922, a *March On Rome* that brought this one-time Socialist turned Fascist leader into power. In Germany there was Adolf Hitler, who in 1923 would win worldwide notoriety for a failed *Putsch* in Munich. As he wrote about settling down in Washington, DC, Breck Long seemed blissfully innocent.

> My life here can be both pleasant and interesting. We have the entrée to the diplomatic circles, though most of the chiefs of mission are changed since my official connection with the Government . . . We know Cabinet officers and my acquaintance among Senators and members of the House and with Army and Navy officers is about the same as when I was here.[5]

However, starting up an office again might not be so easy. Mrs. Cunningham, his former secretary, had had a nervous breakdown and attempted suicide, but he still wished he had her back. "I have no secretary, no clerk, no stenographer and I can't get one easily because I am not easily satisfied." Nevertheless, he was soon writing, "I am trying out a young woman who has been with Thomas Nelson Page as a confidential secretary."

Parenthetically, this Thomas Nelson Page was a Virginian friend of Woodrow Wilson's, a diplomat—actually, a forerunner of Long's as ambassador to Italy—and a novelist of some national repute, usually writing about the South but spending his summers in Maine, in York Harbor, where in 1922 Breckinridge Long and family passed five weeks during July and August. Page's home was in the fancy Norwood Farms area of the resort, and Long rented quarters nearby, so the two men undoubtedly had to have known each other.

In his 1922 diary, Long devoted a full section to his family's vacation activities. It was a lazy aftermath to a hectic spurt of activity and, most likely, in Breck's mind, a mere interlude. He wrote:

> I sleep late, breakfast in the sun parlor, read the papers, write a few letters or a few pages in the preceding account of the campaign. The child plays around. Christine puts endless stitches in a sofa cover . . . We go driving 60–80 miles . . . sometime just to buy glass—up the coast, down the coast . . . My wife goes to curio shops . . . She enjoys it. I endure it . . . I sit in the car most of the time while she is in shops or houses . . . Christine is very knowledgeable about antiques . . . Off to the foothills of the White Mountains for an auction . . . I stay home and take Teenie out to Nubble Light and search for sea urchins in recesses of the rocks at low tide . . . As far north as Bath, as far south as Ipswich—to Manchester, New Hampshire, Portland several times—often go to shops in Portsmouth.[6]

When their summer idyll was over, the Longs returned to DC. Soon, Breck was rushing back into national politics.

Colonel Edward House, the Texas Democrat who had been President Wilson's right-hand man and chief guru until the two men had a falling out, stayed with the Longs for a few days. An intimate discussion about the future of the Democratic Party followed a dinner party at Breck's abode—he and House, joined by Cordell Hull in his capacity as chairman of the Democratic National Committee and U.S. Senator Carter Glass of Virginia. In Long's private workroom, this powerful quartet "discussed the 'State of the Union'" and the Democratic Party's chances in 1924. Their conclusion, duly reported by Long, was: "Al Smith, we thought, could not be elected, but would get a lot of eastern support. McAdoo would not do well in the east, but would in the west."[7]

There was no discussion of Missouri's recently re-elected Senator Jim Reed. But Breck saw him "ipso facto a candidate for President."

Despite the fact that in the end he had faithfully voted for Democrat Reed in 1922, he was drawing the line if Fighting Jim sought the party's presidential nomination in 1924. Breck expressly declared in his diary: "I shall fight him looking to the State Convention in the spring of 1924—18 months from now. I shall oppose him then . . . there will be no Republicans there."

Democratic hopes for 1924 grew stronger as 1923 saw the incumbent Warren Harding in ever more hot water. Scandals of significant proportions occurred in the Veterans Administration, the Departments of Interior and Justice and other agencies of the federal government, not to mention Teapot Dome, the outrageous attempt to turn U.S. Navy property over to Harding cronies for their private profit. Although the Democratic nomination would now be fiercely contested, it was considered worth something, and a complete reversal of the disaster of 1920 was contemplated.

That was before Harding had the bad grace to die suddenly in August 1923, with the result that Vice President Calvin Coolidge, a much different individual, and squeaky clean, supplanted him.

Previously, when party insiders like Breckinridge Long had carried on their speculations, their choices were narrowed to four main possibilities: Al Smith, William Gibbs McAdoo, Samuel Moffett Ralston, U.S. senator and former governor of Indiana and—although it seems strange to us now—carmaker extraordinaire, Henry Ford Sr.

Per usual, Breck Long doped things out dogmatically: McAdoo was ahead but not by enough; Smith would have New York, New Jersey, New England; Ralston would take Indiana, Kentucky, Iowa, Illinois, etc.; while Ford would carry Michigan, Mississippi, and unnamed *others*. "I do not care for any of them except McAdoo," Long declared, but still worried that the Californian would face bitter opposition in the east. During the same period, Long was actively politicking in Missouri, successfully seeking to make his ally Frank Farris chair of the State Committee and working to control the state's delegation to the 1924 Democratic National Convention.

With the mention of Henry Ford as a national politician, a not-so-new but especially jarring note entered the American political scene in the 1920s. Rabid anti-Semitism wasn't confined to places like Germany, Poland and Russia. It was alive and well in the public discourse of the United States—and no one worked harder to make it respectable than Henry Ford. In the long run, the seeds of hatred that he planted in the fertile ground of the 1920s bore fruit in the 1930s and polluted the civic atmosphere even well into World War II. In retrospect, one can see why Colonel House in his discussion of potential Democratic presidential candidates with Breck Long had labeled the automaker "a dangerous experiment." How dangerous was illustrated by a *New York Times* headline in December 1922:

BERLIN HEARS FORD IS BACKING HITLER
BAVARIAN ANTI-SEMITIC CHIEF HAS AMERICAN'S PORTRAIT AND BOOK IN HIS OFFICE.

The question has also been asked, Did Ford's money also find its way to the Nazis' Brown House headquarters? This is one of a number of unanswered questions about Ford's attacks on the Jews and, despite later attempts at backtracking, why he seemingly remained pro-Germany, even while the U.S. was fighting the Nazis. Some writers have pointed to the influence of his closest aide-de-camp, Ernest Gustav Liebold, American-born in Detroit, although suspected by U.S. Military Intelligence in World War I of spying for the Kaiser. Liebold is also suspected of having inspired Ford's weird 1915 "peace mission"—dubbed "Ford's Folly"—when he sailed to Europe in a vain attempt to halt the hostilities begun in August 1914. The Ford book given to Hitler, entitled *The International Jew. The World's Problem*, was a compilation of articles from his *Dearborn Independent*, which he inaugurated in 1919, accompanied by a blast in the *New York World*, claiming Jewish financiers were behind all of the world's wars.

Allegedly, Ford's newspaper was the first to bring the notorious Russian forgery, *The Protocols of the Elders of Zion*, to public attention in the United States. This murderous fairy tale, responsible for uncounted Jewish deaths, is still around, even after the Holocaust, with its preposterous caricature of a rabbinic conspiracy to control the world. Breck Long, we learned from his self-reported talks with the king and queen of Belgium, knew of it and most likely had read it.

After a number of years, Henry Ford abruptly ended the *Dearborn Independent's* hate campaign. One explanation was that Jews were no longer buying his automobiles, and he had lost too much business. He seemed genuinely puzzled that Jews might be upset by what he was having written. His neighbor, a Rabbi Franklin, offered a case in point. Why on earth, he wondered aloud, had the rabbi become unfriendly? And as soon as Ford was sued for libel, he ended up printing a blanket retraction of all these anti-Semitic ravings and allowed the *mea culpa* language to be dictated by Louis Marshall, the plaintiff's attorney. Coincidentally, Ford's own lawyer in the case was Senator James A. Reed.

Possibly the most damaging part of the *Dearborn Independent's* Jew-baiting screed, once the publication had really revved up, was its insistence—subsequently incorporated into Holocaust Denial—that if Jews protested at being murdered, they were faking. Louis Marshall, it will be remembered, refuted such a claim when it was made by Breck Long's colleague, Minister Hugh Gibson in Poland in 1919, precipitating the third assistant secretary's huffy haste to back up his crony. Meanwhile, the Ford newspaper was spewing out such poison as,

> This propaganda of pogroms—"thousands upon thousands of Jews killed"—amounts to nothing except as it illustrates the gullibility of the press. No one believes this propaganda and governments regularly disprove it.[8]

The rise of anti-Semitism in the United States has been documented by many authors. A seminal year cited for its modern beginnings in the New World is 1881, when the assassination of Czar Alexander II led to a fulsome repression in Imperial Russia and an exodus from there of Hebrews on a scale unheard of since Biblical references to the Pharaohs. Soon the aftermath of that fatal bombing would not seem so far off to America, nor be taken so lightly. The "pogroms," which the anti-Semite deniers insisted were nonexistent or exaggerated, fostered a movement of millions of persecuted Jews seeking safety, especially in the U.S.

For example, my own paternal grandfather. At age sixteen in 1886, he fled from Bielorussia to escape conscription into the Czarist Army— one of the draconian measures enacted by Alexander II's reactionary successor—a literal death sentence for any young Jewish male, who had to serve for twenty-five years and rarely ever survived. Waves of Eastern European Jewry kept coming across the Atlantic, causing ever-increasing irritation among non-Jewish populations.

But it wasn't only Jews who were resented. On the European side, Poles and other Slavs were deemed undesirable, likewise non-Scandinavian Baltic types such as Lithuanians and Latvians, plus Italians from the southern areas of the Boot, who were as impoverished as most of the Jews. Asians? In 1882 Congress passed the Chinese Exclusion Act—no Orientals allowed. Lynch mobs had dealt with them in San Francisco and the Pacific Northwest. To save face, the Japanese signed a "gentleman's agreement" not to send their countrymen to work in America if the

Americans did not include them on the exclusion list. Africa, with slavery abolished, wasn't a contributor any longer. Funny enough, given today's big to-do about Hispanics, Latin Americans were allowed free entry.

Among those resisting this concerted drive to rescind America's Statue of Liberty appeal to "Give me your tired, your poor, your huddled masses yearning to breathe free, etc." were strong Jewish voices. None were more effective than Mary Antin, brought to Boston as a child from Russia, speaking only Yiddish, who became a literary sensation in 1912, when Houghton Mifflin published her autobiography, *The Promised Land*, and it turned out to be a bestseller.

But in most respects, Mary Antin was swimming against an irresistible tide. The Chinese Exclusion Act had been followed by the Immigration Act of 1903, which added other categories of people to be excluded, and then came the call in 1911 by a U.S. Senate body, the Dillingham Commission, to require all incoming aliens to pass a literacy test. This was a particular sore spot for Mary Antin, for she had been illiterate when she came to the U.S., due to the fact that Jewish girls weren't allowed to go to school in her section of Russia.

In 1916 the anti-immigration movement was given an intellectual boost through the publication of *The Passing of the Great Race* by a Park Avenue socialite named Madison Grant. It was the prime example of a *pseudo-science* known as "eugenics," then rising in favor in the western world. The *Great Race* was the *White Race* (minus certain Caucasian groups such as the Jews, who were deliberately mislabeled a separate race), and Grant's thesis was the threat of its destruction by "mongrelization" with lesser ethnic groups. Such was the power of this idea in the early 1920s that a well-funded eugenics think tank was created at Cold Springs Harbor on Long Island, New York, from which white supremacist dogma was spread around the world, reaching among others Adolf Hitler, who wrote Madison Grant that his book was "my Bible."

A prime financer of this operation was Mrs. E. H. Harriman, wife of the railroad tycoon, and the director was Harry H. Laughlin, originally from Missouri, a Princetonian and a devotee of thoroughbred racehorses. One wonders if these three attributes—also applicable to Breckinridge Long—meant that the two men knew of each other, although Laughlin is never mentioned in Long's diaries.

By 1924 the principal promoter of the eugenicists' line of thinking in the U.S. Congress was the Washington State Republican Representative Albert Johnson, a "chunky, hard-faced"[9] small-town newspaper editor from the lumbering center of Gray's Harbor. Reputedly, Johnson had led a mob attacking Japanese workers in 1907, and also a mob attacking foreign-born millworkers on strike. He has been denoted an anti-Semite, too, and it is no surprise that in 1923 Albert Johnson was elected president of the American Eugenics Association. More importantly, as a congressman he rose to be the head of the House Immigration Committee, and his goal was to pass a comprehensive immigration law that would freeze out those ethnic populations he deemed inferior, and preserve the ascendancy of the so-called Nordics (Anglo-Saxons, Germans, Scandinavians, etc.) from northern Europe.

The Johnson-Reed Bill of 1924, establishing quotas for the first time in America, was the result, and its effects are being felt to this day. The Senator Reed who lent his name to the legislation in the upper body was not Missouri's Jim Reed, however, but David A. Reed from Pennsylvania.

There was State Department involvement here as well, primarily through the participation of Wilbur J. Carr, whom Breckinridge Long would get to know well during his tours of duty. In the annals of the State Department, this career bureaucrat, who was a fixture from 1892 until 1939, is considered something of a hero. His tireless efforts to break down the barriers between the consular and diplomatic services have led to the creation of the Wilbur J. Carr award for those who show equal devotion to the Foreign Service. Less well advertised have been his efforts on behalf of immigration restrictions.

That references to anti-Semitism were rife at the State Department are underscored by Wilbur J. Carr's words in a letter he wrote to Congressman Albert Johnson. "The great mass of aliens passing through Rotterdam are Russian Poles or Polish Jews of the usual ghetto type. They are filthy, un-American and often dangerous in their habits." His claim was: These "abnormally twisted" and "unassimilable Jews" were swamping the U.S.[10]

Backstopping such inflammatory language was the articulate journalist from Maine, Kenneth Roberts, destined for fame as America's foremost writer of historical fiction. He served as an unpaid advisor to Congressman Johnson's committee, after penning a series of biting articles for the *Saturday Evening Post*, which had sent him to Europe to interview potential immigrants. Out of this activity also came a book by Roberts entitled *Why Europe Leaves Home*. Quotes of an anti-Semitic nature did not come from the author himself; rather, he let others speak their minds and recorded them. One American consul beefed that

nine-tenths of all the emigrants which pass through here on their way to America, are from Poland, and nine-tenths of them from Poland are Hebrews. They have no political principles or convictions, are entirely without patriotism and usually are evasive, dishonest and incapable of appreciating any responsibility toward any government.[11]

A footnote Roberts included in his book repeats Madison Grant's dictum that because

the Polish Jew, whose dwarf stature, peculiar mentality and ruthless concentration on self-interest are being engrafted upon the stock of the nation, the man of the old stock is being crowded out of many country districts by these foreigners, just as he is today being driven off the streets of New York City by the swarms of Polish Jews.[12]

Roberts's sympathy fastened on the poor State Department officials who had to deal with these matters.

I'd seen consular officers shed tears of fury at the unending streams of slum-stunted throngs pouring through their consulates to become added burdens on America . . . I had to keep on saying the things that our consular officials were unable to say aloud and describe conditions until an awakened America came to the support of senators and representatives and gave them the courage to take action.[13]

Against this flood tide of prejudice, the voices of the Mary Antins and the Louis Marshalls were effectively drowned out. Additionally, all this was happening in the America of the early and middle 1920s *when times were good*. The worldwide Depression that followed in the 1930s already had a prior built-in scapegoat—"International Jewry." And with the backdrop of such a maelstrom, Breckinridge Long—in his second tour of duty at State—played his part.

Meanwhile, the die had already been cast by the Johnson-Reed legislation and its later revisions. Discriminatory quotas were set, seemingly in stone. Italy, which under a 1921 law was allowed 42,000 immigrants a year, found itself reduced to 4,000. Poland went from 31,000 to 6,000. Greece dropped to 100 from 3,000. The open-door policy of the U.S. was now a dead letter. World War II and its horrendous refugee problem were just around the corner.

Chapter Ten

Treading Water

WHEN DID BRECKINRIDGE LONG START to accumulate racehorses?
His infatuation with the ultimate trappings of a gentleman
squire, which would consume much of Breck's time and attention in his
retirement, was touched upon in various diary snippets as early as 1923.
We find him on Nantucket that summer, and he writes he was riding his
"saddle mare" every day. But even earlier, he had speculated in print that
his friend Dr. Cary Grayson, who had been Woodrow Wilson's physician,
bred "nice" horses. Therefore, he would take his mare to Grayson's stable
to have her inseminated and would watch the resulting colt carefully. "If
it has any possibilities, I will race it," he declared.

Earlier, there was a trip to the Kentucky Derby. His host in Louisville
was John Clancy, apparently a Princeton classmate, and "I found a warm
welcome and a considerable quantity of Bourbon whiskey."[1] He and
Clancy proceeded to consume "more liquor than was necessary, went
to the races, lost a little, met Desha Breckinridge [Breck's cousin], played
poker all night in the Seelbach Hotel . . . I lost more money than I like
to think about . . . Had to sell some stocks to pay for the fun." But
he won back some money betting on Desha's horse, which was named
after their common ancestor, Robert Jefferson Breckinridge. Another
aspect of English country aristocracy, American style, concerned Breck's
penchant for bird shooting. He stayed on Nantucket long enough in
1923 to go duck hunting. His favorite haunt was an area called the Day
School between the islands of Nantucket and Tuckernuck, a sandy shoal
only two feet above the ocean, where he waded in hip boots, set decoys
with the help of a local guide, and then fired away. "I am a very fair shot,"
he boasted, and always bagged "plenty of duck."

We are also informed that daughter Teenie learned to ride that
summer, that wife Christine liked neither horses nor sailing . . . and that
the Long family left Nantucket on Sunday, October 28.

Their destination was Washington, DC, and the joys of rural life were once more ceding their place to politics in Breckinridge Long's order of priorities. He was not giving up on anything, neither his own advancement in public life nor the Democratic Party's response in now having to cope with Calvin Coolidge as their opponent instead of the late Warren Harding. Long already had arranged an appointment with Democratic National Committee chair Cordell Hull, written a long letter to Colonel Edward House, would see Dr. Cary Grayson (RE: politics, not horses) and he was angling also to meet with Senator Carter Glass.

The upshot of his return to the political wars was that he pledged his wholehearted support to the presidential candidacy of William Gibbs McAdoo. This decision kept him embedded within the Wilsonian camp (although the president and his son-in-law McAdoo did not much like each other).

On February 3, 1924, Breck recorded Wilson's demise, along with a few gossipy sidelights of pettiness that came out of the funeral arrangements: Colonel House not invited; Joseph Tumulty, the faithful press secretary, not invited; Bernard Baruch taking pleasure at Colonel House's discomfiture. Under the date of February 6, the funeral was described: "Rain turned to snowflakes and wind blew hard . . . took an hour and a half to seat everyone . . . the services were rather brief, formal after the manner of the Episcopal church, dignified."[2]

Even in death, Woodrow Wilson was still an inspiration for Breck Long in his next political sally, which was to do all he could to injure Jim Reed, who had announced a run for the Democrats' presidential nomination. On March 3, 1924, the *Cleveland Plain Dealer* carried this headline:

REVEALS BLAST AT REED BY WILSON
Long Shows Letter From Late President Denouncing Missouri Senator

The release was aimed at the Missouri Democratic State Convention, set for April, where Long sought to win a majority of delegates for McAdoo, or at least deny Reed enough delegates from his home state to cause him acute embarrassment. The letter was one Wilson had sent to Long in March 1922 but never made public. Its introduction two years later was to counter a move initiated by Reed's forces to claim the late president hadn't been so anti-Reed. Long was saying, Here's what Mr. Wilson really thought of Fighting Jim. The most punishing quotes were:

"I consider Reed my implacable opponent in everything that is honorable and enlightened . . . I never have dealt with a man who more thoroughly and completely earned my distrust."[3]

Missouri was allowed 36 votes at the Democrats' National Convention. Most did go to McAdoo and helped dim any prospects Jim Reed might have had, by supplying that most fatal of whispers: *Why, he can't even carry his own people!* A Missouri newspaper spoke of "hopelessly outnumbered adherents of Senator Reed"—who included "Boss" Tom Pendergast. And Breckinridge Long's triumph might have been thought complete, since he was able to swing all but one of the delegates to McAdoo, and she herself was anti-Reed.

"Boss Long"? Well, not quite. Had he left well enough alone, Breckinridge Long would have chalked up an impressive victory and solidified a high position in Missouri Democratic politics. But his ambition to be elected to something, anything, continued to haunt him, and his earlier unrequited desire for a place on the Democratic National Committee led him to run and try to unseat his old antagonist Edward Goltra.

Call it revenge. Tom Pendergast entered the fray by getting a third person into the DNC race and giving him the full support of the Kansas City-Jackson County machine. Moreover, he chose his man very shrewdly, picking William T. Kemper, a well-respected Kansas City banker. When the balloting for national committeeman began, the first and inconclusive results were: Kemper, 507 and one-third; Long, 451 and one-third; and Goltra, 179 and one-third. And there was only a second ballot. The one-thirds were dropped, and Kemper was declared the winner, 673 to 451, after Goltra threw him all of his support. To Breck Long's chagrin, this new setback to his ambitions was featured in the Missouri media.

REED FORCES DEFEAT LONG IN ELECTION OF KEMPER

The 1924 Democratic National Convention itself was held in Madison Square Garden and stretched out from June 24 to July 9. One reason for this seemingly interminable length was the party's two-thirds rule whereby no one could win without gaining two-thirds of the delegates' votes. Breckinridge Long's man—William Gibbs McAdoo—generally stayed in first place in the more than 100 ballots that were cast. His archrival, Al Smith, kept pace with him, though. A distant third was John W. Davis, whose corporate address was New York but who ran as a West Virginian. On the 103rd ballot, McAdoo and Smith gave up their battle and settled upon Davis as a compromise choice they could both support. By his own account, Breck Long played a major role during those sweltering days in Manhattan. He afterwards declared, "It was a wonderful experience but not one to be repeated. I had been asked to organize all the McAdoo forces for the Convention work and to assume the floor management of the forces, and with some reluctance I entered upon the work."[4] He started off by dividing the U.S. into sections of states and assigning a man to each of these divisions. There was also a Board of Strategy that he chaired, and it would meet regularly in room 401 of the Vanderbilt Hotel. Of his fellow workers he said,

> By their kindly acceptance of my dictatorship and by their respective abilities, we all cooperated to execute the most remarkable fight in the history of American politics and all under the generalship of McAdoo. We waged a political battle for 102 ballots, to see Davis nominated on the 103rd.[5]

Long did claim that at one point when his man had 505 votes, he'd tried to broker a deal with Al Smith, but the "Happy Warrior" was too drunk to negotiate. There followed some uncomplimentary words about "the Irish" and their disruptive presence in the Democratic Party. A sarcastic nickname for this particular convention that has survived is The Klanbake, signifying that the most serious divide in that Democratic Party gathering was what to do about a revitalized Ku Klux Klan. An anti-Klan plank was proposed for the party platform and seemed specifically devoted to boosting the candidacy of Al Smith, an Irish Roman Catholic. So should McAdoo come out against it, trying to capture pro-Klan delegates? Long advised him to stay neutral, which McAdoo did, and in the end, the rebuke to the Klan failed by a single vote.

Did Breck Long ever reveal his inner feelings about the racist, anti-Catholic, anti-Jewish, anti-immigrant sentiment rising in the country? Did he sympathize with this fiery nativism? If he had a preference, he didn't reveal it, except for what might be seen as political expediency. For example, once John W. Davis's national campaign got underway, Long upbraided him (at least in his diary) for

> his untimely, unnecessary denunciation of the Ku Klux Klan [that] has lost him strength in States where it was needed and has added nothing in States he could not possibly carry.[6]

As for immigration, Breck Long was not unmindful of the action in Congress that year. But he was careful in alluding to the Johnson-Reed Bill, which he called the "Japanese Exclusion Act," and merely stated that the Senate had before it "the troublesome quota provisions of its immigration bill but expects passage of the measure by the end of the week . . . then must reconcile with the House." Seemingly, Long had first disapproved of the measure, citing its discrimination against Italians and Czechs who had fought alongside the Allies during World War I, yet ended his comments with,

> but we can't permit the red and brown races to come in large numbers without destroying our racial integrity.

On the surface, the above statement seems to pinpoint Breckinridge Long as squarely in tune with a preponderance of Americans of his era who feared an alien tide. It's interesting, though, about his choice of races to depict pejoratively—*red* and *brown*. Not the *black* race, not the *yellow* race, but *red*—which signifies specifically Native Americans, who are already here—and *brown*, usually meaning at first blush Filipino or Malaysian or Indonesian.

That Long was following the progress of the Johnson-Reed Bill is indisputable. He revealed in his diary that he had spoken to senators who'd assured him they had the votes to override a Coolidge veto, if one occurred. Also, he'd learned that despite Teddy Roosevelt's gentleman's agreement with the Japanese, their countrymen would now be juridically excluded from the U.S.

When the vote was taken in the senate, the new immigration law passed by a landslide count of 71 to 4. There was no veto from President Coolidge. In happily signing the measure at a Rose Garden ceremony, the president's only caveat was a fleeting murmur of disappointment over the naming of Japanese to be excluded. None had been coming, anyway. Or perhaps he could foresee the mischief this "insult" would cause in future Japanese-American relations.

Otherwise, Breck Long remained silent on the impact of the law— pro or con—although the ambience at the State Department, had he been there then, would probably have put him on the side of Wilbur J. Carr and the unhappy consuls described by Kenneth Roberts. Had he read those *Saturday Evening Post* articles?—he doesn't say. Had he read *Why Europe Leaves Home*? Silence again. If it bothered him that former comrades-in-arms like the Czechs and Italians (and add Serbs,

Rumanians, Montenegrins, and Poles) were having their entries to the U.S. reduced, it was nothing to get excited about. As for the Eastern European Jewish masses—well, his high-placed *our crowd* German Jewish friends didn't think too much of them, either.

But maybe Breck simply shrugged, never imagining that the Johnson-Reed law would someday touch him, and he simply focused on pleasanter things, like his horses and a nifty ship model he had just acquired for his collection—"the *Royal Gem*, fully rigged, running rigging, standing rigging, clean lines, etc., etc., sails and all . . . she is by far the finest model I have ever seen," and less pleasant but always fascinating, there was the political present. Since McAdoo had lost, Breck offered his services to Democratic nominee Davis, and subsequently he made some pointed comments about his experiences. He went to St. Louis in the fall and soon felt the Davis campaign was "hopeless," although he thought the local Dems might win the governorship. "From the first, it seemed Davis is beaten," he wrote. "He has seemed himself to be surrounded by incompetents." At the state headquarters, Long found "no organization, no plan—only hope." Earlier, from Nantucket, he'd telegraphed Davis, offering support. "No answer." He'd offered advice. "No answer." Meeting Davis in New York, he'd offered advice again. "No acceptance."

The result was not unexpected—but the size of the GOP victory was startling. Nationwide, the Democrats were utterly routed. Coolidge won the popular vote by 25 percent, actually carried New York City, and the electoral vote ratio for him was 3 to 1. In Missouri, the Republican juggernaut carried everything before it. Even Harry Truman lost his judgeship. Although gaining 60,000 more votes than Davis, Arthur W. Nelson, the Democrat for governor, was still defeated. Here, Breck Long's comment was symptomatic of his tendency to overrate himself. He began musing that if Nelson had been elected and Jim Reed died, "I probably would have been appointed to the Senate [vacancy]." His predilection for wishful thinking reflected a false rumor that "those who have seen Reed say he is very ill and cannot long survive."[7]

Fighting Jim, on the other hand, proved to be very much alive—and active. Reed stayed in the Senate until 1929 and pursued an energetic campaign for the Democratic presidential nomination in 1928. Breck Long, once he had been disabused of his arch-rival's impending demise, saw this move coming. Back in 1926, Long was to write: "This time Reed might seriously be a candidate for the Presidency and I will have to fight him again. I should think his last experience in Missouri when I beat him so badly would have satisfied him for a while."[8]

Precipitating this thought, it could be surmised, was an incident that prompted the following mention in his diary.

> February 14, Valentine's Day. Went to Small's Flower Store to buy some roses and violets for Christine for Valentine's Day—and met Jim Reed buying flowers! It was the second time I have seen him since '22. The first time in the ante chamber of the senate and he refused to speak and passed me by—shortly after the election of '22. Today, he was polite. He spoke, advanced toward me and extended his hand, which I accepted. We exchanged a few innocuous words . . . He looks well—much better than I have been led to believe.

Then, lo and behold, thirteen days later, Breck and Christine attended a dinner party hosted by a Chinese diplomat identified solely as Sze. Who should be there but Reed and his wife, and the Longs were seated with only "one lady" between them and the Reeds.

> We bowed our recognition. Mrs. Reed bowed and I bowed, could not suppress a smile. Christine looked Jim plumb in the eye, but gave no sign of recognition . . . After dinner, the gentlemen retired . . . Reed excused himself twice during the time and left the room for short intervals. All the rest of the company seemed to shun him . . . As the guests were departing, Mrs. Reed passed immediately by me, smiled, said "Good night, Mr. Long," started to extend her hand, then withdrew it. I smiled, said "Good night, Mrs. Reed," extended my hand partway but exactly as she had extended hers and withdrawn it, and kept it that way as she passed. It was a very amusing experience . . . Funny I should have met him St. Valentine's Day and again so soon after years of no contact.[9]

Although Jim Reed had helped successfully torpedo U.S. membership in the League of Nations, there was strong support in the Senate for the U.S. to join the World Court. The opposition of Reed, who teamed up with Republican William E. Borah of Idaho, as Breck Long put it, "in a crusade to nullify our entry into the World Court," went down to a crushing defeat as the senators voted 76 yo 17 in favor of the move. In the final analysis, however, the anti-Wilsonians exerted enough pressure to water down American participation, but a spot was still held open for an American judge to sit in what is now the International Court of Justice in the Peace Palace in the Hague, built by Andrew Carnegie.

In 1926 a further retrospective of the Wilson era occurred with the publication of Colonel Edward House's diaries. Not pleased with them, Breck Long wrote scornfully in his own diary that "Colonel House is being universally condemned for his 'Papers.'" That same year, too, Long had his first book published—by the MacMillan Company—and no such controversy surrounded *The Origins of the Constitution of the United States*, a re-working of a college thesis he had done. Like any author, Breck was pleased to see his work in print, and he traveled to Boston on an ostensible book tour, speaking to the Massachusetts Senate and also to the local Sons of the Revolution at their annual dinner, regaling them, he self-mockingly stated, "on the exciting subject: the contribution of Colonial New England to the principles of the Federal Constitution." He stayed at nearby Dedham with his sister Margaret and her husband Henry "Chat" Chatfield, and it was there that the initial copy of his opus had reached, him and he inscribed it to his nephew "little Henry."

Now a bona fide intellectual, Breck was likewise a practicing attorney, consulting with the General Manufacturing Company of Brooklyn, which owned properties in Mexico and needed his legal help. Nonprofit work was similarly on display when he took a volunteer position as Chairman of the Jeffersonian Centennial Foundation Committee. All the while, he was setting himself up to be the owner of thoroughbred racehorses, breeding his mare and declaring, "I would like to see my colors on the track for the first time."[10]

Dilettante! Dabbler! Words that convey a shallow inconstancy of purpose and fragmented direction come easily to mind. Yet Bret Long would have argued that he had solid accomplishments to his credit. At his Princeton Class's twentieth reunion, he was bold enough to include himself among the "three most prominent men" in the group. The others were Arthur B. Reeve, a movie maker and detective-story writer, and Pax (Paxton) Hibben, "a diplomat but a Socialist, almost a Bolshevik, [who had won fame feeding starving children during the Russian Civil War] and a bad egg." Unsurprisingly, their get-together had been a wild, drunken affair, despite Prohibition, with forty barrels of *real beer*, twenty kegs of applejack and fifty gallons of gin. Breck and Hibben had had words over the latter's attack on the U.S. government, and Arthur Reeve, he tattled, got "sloppily, ungentlemanly drunk" one night. Later of great satisfaction to Breckinridge Long, '03, was that he alone of his classmates would someday obtain the exalted rank of member of the Princeton Board of Trustees.

Speaking of Bolsheviks, Breck wrote at this time of having lunch in DC with Alexander Kerensky, the last non-Communist leader of Russia after the Czar's dethronement. Joining them was a man named Bakhinstief, once Kerensky's envoy to Washington. Long's diary includes an unusual conversation with this person. It is another of the rare entries where Jews are mentioned and possible anti-Semitism subtly expressed through quotes by others. On the Russian's part, bias definitely existed. He told Long that the Bolsheviks were purging their top Jews, like Trotsky and Zinoviev. Bakhinstief's emphasis, as recorded by Long, was that the peasants in Russia had associated Trotsky with the Jews, and they were resentful and deeply anti-Semitic and someday would show their animosity in an outburst of pogroms. "A result of the divorce of the Jews from control," Long was told, "would be the Bolsheviks having less engagement in international propaganda and confining attention to Russia's own soil."[11] No comment was forthcoming from the diarist.

Breck's financial condition during these years when he held no paying job is also hard to discern. A hint at least of his thinking about scrimping was when he decided to forego a dinner in New York City sponsored by the Woodrow Wilson Foundation, because he felt he "could not afford the expense."

The poor house, however, never did loom. Just the opposite. The vision of a glorious mansion located outside DC soon beckoned to Breckinridge and Christine Long. It was in horse country, had beautiful grounds (70 acres) and a pedigreed name, like the British country estates wealthy WASPs so much admired. This elegant pad in Laurel, Maryland, was called Montpelier.

The Georgian redbrick edifice had been built in 1781 by Major Thomas Snowden on a plantation then covering 9,000 acres. During its ownership by the Snowden family, which lasted until 1890, it had entertained a number of famous visitors, including Abigail Adams, George Washington en route back and forth to the Constitutional Convention in Philadelphia in 1787, and Martha Washington, traveling to her husband's inauguration in 1789. Breck Long first mentioned the place on January 20, 1927. "Have been waiting all day expectantly to hear of my offer to buy Montpelier," he wrote, and explained that the offer was made to the court "now in charge of its involved affairs."[12]

A week later, he was reporting: "No word yet of Montpelier" and at the same time, no word either about a stallion named Catalan he had proposed to buy—costing $25,000—and going "halves" on it, "if they will take my note for my half." Certainly at this stage money did not seem to be his problem. Indeed, he was soon gloating over a coup he had scored by betting on Princess Rose, who finished second in a race at Miami—a $100 bet that netted him $1,785, and "if she had won, I would have had to buy a bank . . . Had never won so much on a race . . . the market has been good to me the last month, too." Also, he told horse trader Reid Riley to purchase him a two-year-old colt and find a horse for Teenie, as well.

On March 5, he took his wife to Montpelier. "It is lovely but needs some restoration and some repair. Some vandal has broken in and stolen the huge brass lock from the front door—the original old brass of about 1740. The box bushes are wonderful . . . crocuses were in bloom on the south side."[13]

It was not until 1928 that the property was secured and on February 15 Breck would state: "Went to Montpelier today for the first time in the role of proprietor." Ten days later, his daughter Teenie, now a student at the exclusive Foxcroft School in Middleburg, Virginia, accompanied her father and her Aunt Margaret and Uncle "Chat" to see the family's new home, one it would occupy for the next thirty-three years.

Since 1928 was a presidential election year, Breck Long found himself once more drawn into the vortex of Democratic politics, and Montpelier had to wait until November to be groomed the way the Longs wanted it and Samuel Miller Breckinridge Long could start fully to assume his "Lord of the Manor" style of life.

Chapter Eleven

From Al Smith to FDR

A FTER HIS ABORTIVE TRY IN 1924 for the Missouri seat on the Democratic National Committee, Breckinridge Long never again competed for a contested position to which he had to be elected. Forever afterward, he simply continued his role of "volunteer," whether in politics, where he participated in campaigns behind the scenes, or in leadership positions in what today we would call NGOs—nongovernmental, nonprofit, private organizations.

A major one that consumed much of his attention from 1925 to 1929 bore the jaw-breaking title of the National Jefferson Centennial Committee of the Thomas Jefferson Memorial Foundation, where he served as chairman.

The purpose of the group was to raise money for the restoration of Monticello, Jefferson's home in Charlottesville, which had been bought by the Thomas Jefferson Memorial Foundation in 1923. Thus the complicated masthead of Breck Long's stationery; on top was the National Jefferson Centennial Committee, Breckinridge Long, chairman, and below a listing of Honorary vice-chairs, among whom the best known names were Will H. Hays, postmaster general under Harding but most famous as Hollywood's film censor, William Gibbs McAdoo, and William Green, president of the American Federation of Labor. Further below this grouping was The Thomas Jefferson Memorial Foundation Inc., presided over by Stuart G. Gibboney, who seems to have been its founder, and it had a committee of state governors plus its own board of governors, which included a host of illustrious Americans, such as Calvin Coolidge, Theodore Roosevelt, Dr. Nicholas Murray Butler, the president of Columbia University, ex-Secretary of State Bainbridge Colby, and banker Felix Warburg. Breckinridge Long also was listed on this distinguished roster.

Underlying the actual purchase of the Jefferson property in 1923 was a long-running drama that, believe it or not, exhibited overtones of anti-Semitism. Since 1836, the Virginia plantation site had been owned by a family named Levy—bought in that year by U.S. Naval Lieutenant Uriah Levy, the first Jewish commissioned officer to serve full term in the navy, and the property was handed down by him to his son, Congressman Jefferson Monroe Levy of New York. In detailing how the eventual purchase took place, there were definite instances of anti-Semitic charges and statements made, particularly against Congressman Levy for at first not wanting to sell, for charging admission and, when at last putting Monticello on the market, asking too much money for it. In the end, in the 1923 transaction, Jefferson Levy settled for $500,000, which he claimed was half the sum he'd sunk into the buildings and grounds, and it was said he openly wept when he signed over the deed. Previously, it should be noted, his father had tried to sell the Jefferson estate to Congress and been rebuffed three times. His will actually stipulated that if Congress still failed to set up the farm school for U.S. Navy orphans he'd envisaged, he would leave everything to three Portuguese Jewish congregations in New York, Philadelphia, and Richmond.

As a result, Breck Long took very seriously his role of needing to raise private money for Monticello, since Congress continued refusing to accept any responsibility for preserving such a precious relic of our history.

The connection with Thomas Jefferson was properly natural for a Breckinridge and a St. Louisan. The city had always considered itself a gateway to the territory gained by the United States through Jefferson's Louisiana Purchase. Later, in the 1930s and 40s, even into the 50s, Long would become invested in another Jeffersonian project, this time with federal National Park assistance, leading to the famous St. Louis Gateway Arch along the Mississippi River.

In the 1920s, Long's Jeffersonian work was strictly concerned with Monticello. Looking for a vice-chair, he wrote on October 25, 1925, to an important person in Iowa with whom he had worked in Democratic national politics—Edwin T. Meredith of Des Moines, owner of the publishing company that put out the ever-popular *Better Homes and Gardens* magazine. Ed Meredith had been President Wilson's secretary of agriculture and also a strong supporter, along with Breck, of William Gibbs McAdoo in 1924.

The group had three main purposes,[1] Breck informed Meredith:

- To "spread a better understanding" of Jefferson's ideals of democracy as embodied in the Declaration of Independence
- To raise enough money to free Monticello of debt and make it into a "patriotic shrine," and
- To prepare for a national celebration on July 4, 1926, the 100th anniversary of Jefferson's death and the 150th anniversary of the signing of the Declaration of Independence

"With your state-wide knowledge and capacity for organization," Long went on, "it would be the matter of but a few hours for you to choose certain key men to serve as Chairmen in various locations," and that "it will be very little work to keep in contact with them when occasions arise."[2]

The answer was not exactly what Breck had wished. The Iowa publisher said he'd be glad to serve as *one of the vice-chairmen* of the National Committee or *chair the Iowa effort* or find someone else who would. Thereafter a steady stream of communications went from Breckinridge Long at the national headquarters in New York City to Des Moines with reports of what actions were being taken countrywide. Among them were a collection taken up in all of the New York City schools, with a request that the schools in Iowa do the same thing, a "Transcontinental Birthday Party," explained in a enclosed folder, that would solicit funds nationwide on April 13 and a "Birthday Party Tour to Seven European Countries" to which any organization raising $5,000 for Monticello would be entitled to send a representative, whose trip would be entirely free. Hoping Iowa would join in all these efforts, the chairman ended with the news that "yesterday we received an anonymous twenty cents from Alaska."[3]

Left unstated in this correspondence was whether or not the two men were, in 1926, still working on a political project they had discussed in 1924. This was to abolish the two-thirds rule required for presidential nominations at Democratic National Conventions. In an earlier letter to Meredith, Long had argued that the operation of the rule "gives to the cities of New York and Chicago, each of which dominates its State and certain political parasites in their respective neighborhoods, the power to amass one third of the Convention and to set at naught the will of a majority. It is really not a two-thirds rule, but a one-third rule." Long's last words to Meredith on this score were : "I hope you will do everything that is necessary to get Iowa properly instructed before 1928."[4]

Unfortunately, Ed Meredith died on June 17, 1928, nine days before the Democratic Convention opened in Sam Houston Hall in Houston, Texas. Ed Meredith had actually been proposed as a favorite son from Iowa. In contention, on the other hand, as the balloting started—no doubt to Breckinridge Long's dismay—was Senator Jim Reed, Missouri's favorite son, which must have added to Long's decision to drop his previous objections to Al Smith, the leading contender. The two-thirds rule had not been abandoned but on the first roll call, Smith had 724 and two-thirds votes, only 10 short of the needed amount. Ohio then gave Smith its votes and other states followed suit, and consequently the New York governor clinched the nomination right at the outset. To Long's delight, Jim Reed ended up with an exceedingly distant 52 votes, in fourth place, behind Smith, Cordell Hull, and U.S. Senator Walter George of Georgia.

Texas oilman Jesse Jones had used his money to influence the Democratic National Committee to hold its meeting in the South for the first time since just before the Civil War. He'd fibbed about the Houston weather in the summer, not revealing how brutally hot it would be, which also may have helped account for only one ballot. Yet unmistakably Al Smith had the votes, once his sole real competitive rival, William Gibbs McAdoo, decided not to run. Another feature of this convention was Franklin Delano Roosevelt's appearance, giving the nominating speech for his fellow New Yorker. Propped up by the metal braces on his legs, FDR, as he had done at the 1924 convention, spoke of Smith as "the Happy Warrior," a line borrowed from a Wordsworth poem, which had enjoyed great popularity. FDR's presentation drew rave reviews. The *New York World* wrote of "A figure tall and proud even in suffering; a face of classic profile; pale with years of struggle against paralysis . . . most obviously a gentleman and a scholar." Al Smith, listening on the radio in Albany, told him afterward that it "brought tears in the Mansion when you spoke it."[5] The convention ended with a positive feeling that despite Smith's vulnerabilities as a Catholic, an outspoken opponent of Prohibition, and a New Yorker with a heavy city accent, the Democrats had a fighting chance to reverse their string of defeats since 1920.

Breckinridge Long, who'd participated in the convention, had no hesitation in switching his wholehearted allegiance to Al Smith—i.e., supporting a Catholic for president and urging Americans to be *tolerant*. He wrote on June 30, 1928: "The Convention adjourned *sine die* yesterday afternoon. Smith and Robinson [Senator Joseph Robinson of Arkansas] are the nominees . . . I served on the Resolutions Committee and enjoyed the work . . . Spoke in support of the Foreign Relations plank

and the Law Enforcement plank."[6] Also, he went before the National
Committee and the Presidential Committee, arguing for his Missouri
delegation to be seated, rather than a rival one [presumably pledged to
Jim Reed]. While in Houston, he stayed with T. W. House, a nephew
of Colonel Edward House, and he didn't go right back east following
the end of the convention. On July 4, he found himself in El Paso,
where the temperature was 114 degrees in the shade. There, he gained
his first inkling of what the Democrats would face during the Smith
campaign—a fiery cross was burned by the Ku Klux Klan on a nearby
mountainside.

In the meantime, he'd been combining his political trip with a
business matter that took him into Mexico. It was a law case—a divorce,
in fact—and his client, sued by his second wife for the dissolution of
the marriage, was a fascinating character. An English citizen and Scottish
laird, Sir Charles Ross was one of the largest landowners in the British
Isles and had become famous for his development of Ross's rifle, which
he'd invented during the Boer War and that had been mass-produced
for the Canadian Army in World War I. This second wife, who had
been pursuing her case since 1927, was an American, the former Patti
Ellison of Louisville, Kentucky, and Long had been Sir Charles's lawyer
starting then, but the matter wasn't finally settled until 1930. The huge
Ross estate in Scotland was called "Easter Ross," and at one point the
eccentric Baronet, trying to escape U.K. taxes, declared his ancestral land
to be a territory of the United States, causing the British government to
declare him a *rebel* and *outlaw* for a time. Once severed from number-two
wife, Sir Charles promptly acquired a third mate, also an American.

Finally, back in action politically, Breck Long went to Poughkeepsie,
New York, where he attended a Smith campaign meeting at the local
Democratic headquarters. Since Hyde Park was close by, the event had
been scheduled for the convenience of FDR, who was a member of the
Happy Warrior's executive committee. "Frank Roosevelt was supposed
to be coming," Long wrote,[7] but he didn't appear. Not until the late
afternoon of September 5 in New York City did his old friend from the
Wilson days get to one of their planning sessions. "He [FDR] wants me
to take charge of activities . . . of former Republicans and Independents
and in cities like Charleston, Toledo and Minneapolis." Long's added
comment was that he'd never done anything like that before and would
much prefer to stay in the New York headquarters and send others out
to speak.

As for Republican supporters of Al Smith, the candidate himself had sent shock waves through the Democrats by putting a *Republican* in charge of the Democratic National Committee. He was John J. Raskob, the head of General Motors, a multimillionaire, but also a Catholic like Smith and a "Wet," as ardently opposed to Prohibition as the New York governor. Still, not until the middle of October did Raskob, who spent most of his time raising money, show up at the New York headquarters. "Real excitement today," Breck wrote. "I had a few minutes talk with Raskob—the Chairman! My first sight of him!"[8]

Thanks largely to Raskob and a few others, the Democrats had amassed enough funding to compete with the GOP. In the previous two presidential contests of the 1920s, they had been seriously outspent. This time, they'd raised $3.2 million to counter the Republicans' $4.1 million.[9] Besides Raskob, the big givers were Herbert Lehman, New York City contractor William Kenny, shipbuilder William Todd, and Bernard Baruch who was a boyhood friend of Al's. Breckinridge Long, while not named a major contributor, was likely among the seventy-three individuals who gave $10,000 or more to the campaign.

Radio had just begun playing an important part in political campaigns by 1928. Long worked with Henry Morgenthau Jr., who was making broadcasts on behalf of Al Smith, because the latter didn't like to use the air waves, since they intensified a New York accent that some people found vulgar or even comic. Nevertheless, Smith did go on the air from time to time and especially one night in Oklahoma City when Breck Long heard him give an electrifying speech. A fed-up Al Smith was using the occasion to blast the Ku Klux Klan, which was especially strong and especially vicious in Oklahoma. As soon as the campaign train had crossed into the Sooner State from Kansas, Smith was greeted by a burning cross, and at first he jokingly turned to his closest advisor, Judge Joseph Proskauer, a Jew (and incidentally a Southerner brought up in Alabama) and quipped, "Joe, how did they know you were on this train?"

But that evening, addressing a standing-room-only crowd in the Oklahoma City Stockyards Coliseum, the New York governor was deadly serious in his attack on bigotry. Letting out his feelings for the first time on this subject, he said, "There is no greater mockery in this world today than the burning of the cross . . . by these people who are spreading this propaganda . . . while the Christ that they are supposed to adore, love and venerate . . . taught the holy, sacred writ of brotherly love." One of Smith's closing remarks was, "Let me make myself perfectly clear. I do not want any Catholic to vote for me . . . because I am a Catholic . . . If any Catholic believes that the welfare, the wellbeing, the prosperity of the United States is best conserved and promoted by Mr. Hoover, let him vote for Mr. Hoover."[10]

How much of his eloquence fell on deaf ears? There seemed little letup in the anti-Catholicism that was hurled at Alfred E. Smith. One of the leading hatemongers, William Lloyd Clark, put out a book entitled *Three Keys To Hell; Rum, Romanism and Ruin*. A photo of Al with a group of cardinals at City Hall in New York in 1926 was used to charge that the pope had secretly made Al Smith a cardinal, and a cartoon showed the College of Cardinals forming a cabinet in the White House, presided over by Al Smith as a pope lookalike. There was a pamphlet circulated declaring, "Rome Suggests That Pope May Move Here" and "Papal Terms Placed in Cross-Word Puzzles."

Nor were the Jews spared. The claim was made how Jewish corruption was spreading in America through music published by Jewish songwriters, and a KKK handout added *corrupting movies* and *indecent fashions*, from a caricature Jew attached to a caricature priest labeled "Rome," bringing the evils of *parochial schools, world domination* and *politics*. The always-red-hot issue of immigration was also tossed into the mix by Al's opponents, as in a letter to the *Baltimore Sun* that argued, "Very little is being said about his [Smith's] proposals to abolish the quota restrictions from the immigration law, but all intelligent people know that such a policy would mean unloosing on us a horde of immigrants from such races as have already proved hardest to assimilate. It is plain that the object of this is to increase the foreign vote in the cities, which can be depended on to vote for liquor and be easily controlled by machine."[11]

The drumbeat from the religious right was having its effect on Democratic hopes, and even the usually upbeat Breck Long admitted a friend's prognosis could be right that "Smith will have a hard time to carry Missouri. Religious prejudice has been a major issue."

Openly protesting this wave of unabashed prejudice, Breck Long even took on the top leader of his own denomination, the Presbyterians. It happened after Dr. Hugh Kelso Walker, "Presbyterianism's highest eminence,"[12] the Moderator of the Presbyterian Church in the U.S., baldly stated in the *Presbyterian Magazine* that "The plain duty of every church man is to work, pray and vote for the election of Herbert Hoover." Dr. Walker, 66, was a strong Prohibitionist and buttressed his position by adding: "Let it be clearly understood that we will fight to the bitter end the election of Alfred E. Smith . . . not because he is a member of the Catholic Church . . . but because he has gone out of his way to announce himself the implacable foe of things that we count most dear."[13]

Time magazine covered the story and the opposition that Dr. Walker had encountered from certain of his own coreligionists.

> Outstanding among them [those rebutting Dr. Walker] was Presbyterian Democrat Breckinridge Long of St. Louis, onetime Assistant Secretary of State [1917–1920], now practicing international law in Washington, DC. In a long telegram (nearly 1,000 words) he expressed to Dr. Walker directly and immediately [his] entire disagreement . . . Continued Lawyer Long: "I speak not only as a member of the Presbyterian Church and baptized in that church, but as one who comes from a family the members of which the Church numbers among its devoted exponents. My grandfather, Samuel M. Breckinridge, died on the rostrum of the Presbyterian General Assembly in Detroit . . . I, for one, a member of the Presbyterian Church, am frightened, and resent your attempt, and express my entire disapproval of your course."[14]

The same *Time* magazine article also detailed the pro-Hoover moves of Baptists, Lutherans and Methodists, but emphasized that Dr. Walker's outburst was "the first direct appeal from the highest official of a denomination to all members of his communion."

October brought Breck a personal blow. His old friend and co-worker in the Democratic trenches, Rufus Hollister, whom he'd backed in the newspaper business in Jefferson City, succumbed to a lingering illness. It was hard for Long to get to the funeral in Jefferson City. But there were also some encouraging political signs. He noted on October 15 that "The campaign of 'Intolerance' is waged against the Republicans with real effect." And he mentioned Rabbi Stephen Wise, with whom he was to have many dealings in the future, and that the Rabbi would speak that evening on the topic of "Spiritual Bootlegging." Also speaking for Al Smith—on radio—in the first effort of obtaining political endorsements from sports figures, was Babe Ruth.

On October 21, Long was writing, "Smith returns from the Middle West. Great ovation everywhere." And although straw polls showed Hoover ahead, Long countered, "Our information leads to the belief he [Smith] will win."[15] Then, once more, Breckinridge Long, himself, was out on the hustings. He went up the Hudson River to Schenectady, did a half-hour radio show and came back to Manhattan via Albany, only promptly to head west. He spoke in Oberlin, Ohio, visited Smith headquarters in Cleveland and ended in St. Louis, where he was sixth in line to vote on the morning of November 6.

He had written on November 5, the day before election, "I am one of the small minority who thinks he [Smith] will win."[16] Late on November 6, having gone to Lexington, Kentucky, to stay with his cousin Desha Breckinridge, he wrote, "Badly beaten. We go to bed 11:30—disgusted."

Cousin Desha had also been a delegate to the 1928 Democratic Convention and, before then, to the 1924 and1920 events. He had been a widower since 1920, when his wife, "Madge" Breckinridge, nationally known women's suffrage leader, had died unexpectedly of a sudden heart attack. As the editor of the *Lexington Herald*, Desha (his curious surname was actually his mother's maiden name) had great visibility himself, at least in the Bluegrass State. He was not only a prominent horse owner and breeder—he would have his first entry in the Kentucky Derby the following year—but has been credited along with his late wife in "personally rescuing racing in Kentucky"[17] by pushing for the establishment of the first State Horse Racing Commission in the country, its purpose to regulate the "sport of kings" and "foster the industry of breeding thoroughbred horses."

Breckinridge Long's diary comments during this stay in Lexington focused on Desha's horses and also on his own steeds and his relations with the Laurel Park Maryland race track, founded in 1911, now that he was living at Montpelier. He specifically stated his horses *Tinita* and *Brahman* had won him about $11,000 in 1928.

The remaining less than two months of that year seemed fairly uneventful for Breck, as he doubtlessly licked his political wounds from the Al Smith campaign, which had run out his string of losses even farther. At the beginning of December, he took another trip south—to New Orleans, and then to Tucson and Nogales, where he apparently had more work to do on the complicated divorce case he was handling for Sir Charles Ross. He also noted he had bought some *mantillas* for Teenie, and his last comment, as this overall unlucky year of 1928 moved toward a close was, "Teenie develops flu—in bed."[18]

But if the truth be known, an unexpected happenstance of 1928 was to have a significant, all-encompassing, impact on the rest of Breckinridge Long's life and career. Frank Roosevelt, with whom he'd been reconnected while working for Al Smith, had been elected governor of New York State on the same day as the woeful Democratic defeat nationally!

Most Americans forget now, looking back at FDR, that he'd

experienced some pretty hair-raising elections before he'd become an American icon. In fact, until 1928, he'd been clobbered running for vice president in 1920 and badly lost in a U.S. Senate primary in 1914. Not until the very end of the campaign year of 1928 would he agree to be a candidate again.

Only four weeks before Election Day, on October 1, 1928, the New York Democrats were to choose their man for governor. Franklin had been asked—and the answer was no and his excuse not debatable—his *physical condition!* In fact, the very improvement in his paralysis at a spa he'd bought in Warm Springs, Georgia, promised that he might be walking in two more years if he concentrated on his health. Realistically, he and his sidekick, ex-newsman Louis Howe, who together had been secretly hatching plans for his future, hadn't expected to have him running for anything big until 1932, when he would go for governor, to be followed by a try for the presidency in 1936.

How FDR was convinced to run in 1928 has been debated often. Allegedly, Al Smith *didn't* want him on the ballot but gave in to the entreaties of those around him and lobbied FDR hard. So, much more subtly, did Eleanor, who supposedly wanted him to run. So too did John J. Raskob, who promised to help him financially in developing Warm Springs. In time for the state convention's decision, Franklin finally allowed his name placed in nomination. The vote for Roosevelt was resounding—and unanimous! Breck Long, who'd obviously been following these machinations from afar, was ecstatic, in a letter to FDR writing that "the present tribute of confidence in you . . . It makes New York a cinch."[19]

Not unusually, the Missourian was off the mark in one of his political pronouncements. New York was *hardly* a cinch for FDR in 1928. By all rights, the GOP should have defeated him. Their candidate was Albert Ottinger, the well-regarded attorney general of the state, an activist prosecutor who had vigorously gone after loan sharks, marketers of impure foods, and petty graft takers. Ottinger was the first Jewish person in New York nominated for governor and could expect strong support among his fellow Jews in normally Democratic New York City. Had Ottinger won, it is fair to ask if there would ever have been a New Deal.

It should also be mentioned that FDR, as a condition for running, shrewdly insisted Herbert Lehman be on the ticket with him as lieutenant governor, to help offset Ottinger's appeal to Jews. Thus it was that Lehman, a cofounder of Lehman Brothers in 1933, became the first Jewish governor of New York.

Roosevelt barnstormed by car in the four weeks he had to run. The Republican press was merciless, calling him "pathetic," pulling no bones about alluding to his physical state and using his infirmity to charge that his campaign was "unfair to himself" and "unfair to the people of New York."

Early during the night of the election, it indeed looked as if Roosevelt had lost. A few diehards remained in the headquarters at the Biltmore Hotel in downtown Manhattan. But little by little, the tide began to turn, and final results showed the country gentleman from Hyde Park had squeaked by "General" Ottinger with a margin of 25,000 out of 4 million votes cast. FDR had 2,130,995 or 48.96 percent, Ottinger 2,104,129 or 48.36 percent, and a trio of minor left-wing candidates had 125,000. Al Smith, incidentally, lost his home state by slightly more than 100,000 votes.

Fears of vote tampering by the GOP led to stringent Democratic surveillance and a two-week stall by Ottinger before he conceded. FDR took possession from the Smith family of the governor's mansion in Albany. The Happy Warrior should have been overjoyed, despite the disappointment of his own loss, that his protégé had kept control of the seat of power he had occupied for four terms. Yet unspoken was Al's idea that with his own people, Joseph Proskauer, Robert Moses and Belle Moskowitz still in key positions, the old Smith gang and himself would continue to be calling the shots. That eventually this didn't happen and Roosevelt was able to captain his own ship would lead to a clash of titans four years hence at the 1932 Democratic National Convention. The prize was the presidency, and it was a no-brainer for Breck Long to line up behind his Wilsonian buddy and fellow Ivy Leaguer, Frank Roosevelt. The only question still to be answered was: Could FDR beat Al Smith?

Chapter Twelve

The 1932 Campaign and Aftermath

A S IT HAPPENED, FRANKLIN DELANO Roosevelt did beat Alfred E.
Smith at the Chicago Democratic National Convention in 1932.
On the surface, it seemed like an easy win—only four ballots before
Roosevelt received the requisite two-thirds margin (True, the rule was
still in effect, Breckinridge Long notwithstanding) and the fight that June
turned out to be a real nail-biter, especially if you were rooting for FDR.

When it was all over and after the nominee had made his precedent-
setting airplane flight to the Windy City to address the convention in
person, a stinging post-mortem was delivered in the *Nation* magazine
by its editor, the nationally known, irascible littérateur Oswald Garrison
Villard.

Grumped Villard, a grandson of the famed fiery Abolitionist leader,
William Lloyd Garrison, "Franklin Roosevelt won in spite of the incessant
blunders and unlimited stupidity out here—managers you would not
employ to run a $10,000 a year corporation . . . Roosevelt's success is
also the triumph of cowardice and muddleheadedness—of the inability
to think any real problems through. His choice is proof positive that the
Convention was not thinking about our economic chaos and distress."

This was hardly a recommendation for Breckinridge Long, who played
an active although not commanding role as one of the floor managers for
the FDR forces. But then again, history has shown that Villard's political
analysis about the ignoring of "economic chaos and distress" turned
out to be as inaccurate as many if not most of Breckinridge Long's own
predictions about public affairs. A number of authors have stated that
Long was Roosevelt's top floor manager in 1932. Not so. The man put
in charge was Arthur F. Mullen of Nebraska, but the man *really* calling
the shots, who selected Mullen, was Jim Farley, the former Rockland
County, New York, Democratic boss, who had left Smith to become
FDR's campaign manager.

Previously, there had been a spirited fight for delegates, including a number of open primaries, and in Massachusetts FDR was trounced by Al Smith in this heavily Irish Catholic State, despite the strong support of James Michael Curley, Boston's notorious but popular mayor. Rhode Island and Connecticut, again with strong Irish Catholic influence, followed suit. The Pennsylvania primary was something of a draw. But the true shocker was the surprise victory of Texas's John Nance Garner in the California vote. Still, FDR's campaign, working through state leaders, went on quietly gathering delegates—Colorado, Iowa, Kansas, Minnesota, Michigan, Maine, Vermont, Oregon—and throughout the South. Breck Long recognized that "much of Frank's strength in the political organization comes from what is known as the dry section of the country." And of course, 1928 had shown the great reluctance of Protestants to vote for a Catholic.

The conventional wisdom was that Roosevelt would lead the pack, which also included a number of *favorite sons*, among them again Missouri's Jim Reed, but would fall considerably short of the still-needed two-thirds. So Farley knew his candidate had to keep gaining support on each subsequent vote, or his effort would falter and someone else—yet another dark horse—would take the prize.

Such a forecast soon seemed more than possible. On the first ballot, FDR was well ahead with 666 and one-quarter votes and Al Smith in second place with 201 and one-quarter, and the leader among the favorite sons was Garner with 90 and one-quarter. It was a bit scary for Breck and his fellow floor managers that while Roosevelt had done *a little better* than expected, Al Smith had done *a great deal better* than expected. On the second ballot, Roosevelt did pick up a few additional votes—and in the case of the Missouri delegation, all along there was a clear sign of Breck Long's handiwork. The earliest switch to Roosevelt came at the expense of Jim Reed, who had taken Missouri's entire 36 votes on the first ballot, but before that count was final, a dozen Missourians went over to FDR. Six more entered his column on the second ballot, making Missouri's total 18 Reed, 18 Roosevelt, as the third ballot approached. There were rumors that Tom Pendergast, Reed's boss, was also secretly helping Roosevelt.

Technically, by then Breckinridge Long was a Marylander. So he'd been assigned to focus his attentions on Governor Albert Cabell Ritchie of Maryland, one of the numerous favorite sons. Long later reported, "I was authorized to approach Ritchie and to say we would like to see him Vice President . . . It was on an *if* basis. I would make him an offer to throw our whole support to him, if he would place himself at our disposal and withdraw in Roosevelt's favor when we said the word."[1] They even cooked up an alliterative slogan for such a merger, employing three R's—"Roosevelt, Ritchie and Repeal." But it happened that Ritchie had already proved a dead end as the convention went for its third ballot, where Roosevelt picked up merely a few more votes, and Al Smith lost a few, while Garner, although still far behind, got the biggest boost, possibly supplying him with some momentum for a deadlock situation.

Rumor has it that two U.S. senators—Harry Hawes of Missouri and Key Pittman of Nevada—were the first to propose a Roosevelt-Garner ticket. The initial hard lifting was done, however, by Jim Farley, who contacted Texas Congressman Sam Rayburn, one of Garner's inner circle, and convinced Rayburn to pass on the idea to Cactus Jack. The only trouble was that Garner, then Speaker of the House in Congress, wasn't answering his telephone. Belle Moskowitz tried to get through to him for Al Smith and was rebuffed by a hotel manager who angrily told her the Texan wouldn't talk to anyone.

Except—the FDR forces learned the one exception was the powerful newspaper publisher William Randolph Hearst. But how to get Hearst to call Garner? They used Joseph P. Kennedy, an FDR supporter, in seeking to convince him, while Jim Farley also tried to enlist Hearst. And it wasn't easy. Hearst had no love for FDR, but even less for Al Smith and absolutely none for Newton D. Baker, Wilson's secretary of war, who seemed most likely to romp home a winner if the race went on.

Finally, Hearst did call Garner and got through, and Cactus Jack did seem amenable to throwing his delegates to FDR. Later, his own people would make his support a trade for the vice president's slot, but Garner's genuine motivation seemed to be to keep the Democrats from shooting themselves in the foot once more by picking another nonentity compromise like Cox or Davis. The one hurdle remaining, however, was that the bulk of Garner's delegates were from California and the man who controlled the California delegation's 44 votes was William Gibbs McAdoo.

So here precisely was where Breck Long fit in again, but playing a much more substantive role than trying to entice Maryland's governor. He was considered "close" to McAdoo, after all his hard work and financial support for him at the 1924 convention.

Throughout an all-night session, when the fourth ballot was impending, Long sought to negotiate with McAdoo. It was hard to discern what Mac wanted. Not the vice presidency for himself. Nor an ambassadorship nor a cabinet position. It struck Breck Long that the Californian was still holding out hopes for himself as the eventual nominee. Writing Key Pittman afterward, the Missourian surmised, "McAdoo was still in a trading mode, but with himself in the picture and his own future to be benefited."[2]

When everything broke, it happened very fast. After contentious caucuses, Garner's Texas and California delegates agreed to go for Roosevelt. With some difficulty, McAdoo entered the convention hall just in time when the roll call reached California. He arose and made the dramatic announcement the Golden State's 44 votes would go to Franklin Delano Roosevelt of New York and received a chorus of boos from the Smith supporters. Yet the fight was over. Mayor Anton Cermak of Chicago, leader of the Illinois delegation, announced his desertion of Smith for Roosevelt. Since he controlled Indiana, too, the Hoosiers joined the bandwagon. Jim Reed tossed in what was left of Missouri. Governor White of Ohio delivered the Buckeye State, and Governor Murray of Oklahoma next joined the bandwagon.

"Happy Days Are Here Again," the rousing Democratic theme song, was played again and again. Originally, though, Frank Roosevelt's musical identification in Chicago had started out with "Anchors Aweigh," evoking his Navy connection. Son Elliott Roosevelt, in a fine little volume he coauthored about his father and mother, called *An Untold Story*, told the till-then untold story of the melody switch. It seems Louis Howe, listening to the convention on the radio in his Chicago hotel room, was irked by the incessant choruses of "Anchors Aweigh." "For God's sakes, tell 'em to play something else," he barked in a telephone call to Ed Flynn, the Bronx Democratic boss and FDR supporter. "Like what?" Flynn barked back. Howe thought for a moment. "Tell 'em to play 'Happy Days Are Here Again,'" he responded. And the rest, as they say, is history.[3]

From the very moment he knew he was nominated, Franklin Delano Roosevelt deliberately started *making history*. No sooner did word of his victory come than FDR announced to his family in the executive mansion in Albany, "I'll fly to Chicago in the morning." He was actually breaking precedent in two ways. While no nominee had ever appeared at a major political convention before, most certainly none had ever arrived anywhere in a flying machine!

The plane, provided by American Airlines, was a tri-motor Ford, and as Elliott Roosevelt described the flight, only he and his father were able to avoid flight sickness. The trip halfway across the country was a bumpy ordeal. FDR is pictured at a folding desk set up for him, gulping hard as they'd hit an air pocket, but characteristically whenever this happened, "the smile flashed on and off around the cigarette holder clenched in his teeth"[4] Twice, the plane had to put down for fuel—in Buffalo and in Cleveland. Head winds had buffeted the craft dangerously, but the biggest danger proved to be the adoring crowd at the airfield in Chicago. FDR was swamped and almost trampled by his supporters. His arrival at the convention produced pandemonium before the crowd finally settled to hear his acceptance speech, prepared with the help of Sam Rosenman, a young lawyer inherited from Al Smith's administration.

That speech is remembered now for a single phrase, expressing a single idea, which Rosenman had borrowed from Mark Twain's *A Connecticut Yankee In King Arthur's Court*. The term was "a new deal." In his strong, mellifluous, unforgettable voice, FDR promised, "I pledge, I pledge myself to a new deal for the American people."[5]

The New Deal it was. FDR went out and swept the country, winning by a plurality of seven million votes and trouncing Herbert Hoover in the Electoral College. Ironically, the incumbent Republican president had once been a dedicated Wilsonian and later in life wrote a highly sympathetic, even worshipful, biography of Woodrow Wilson. Nevertheless, Breck Long had had a hard time warming up to Hoover, whom he had encountered during World War I, when the international engineer was the federal Food Administrator in Washington. One of Hoover's biographers, author George H. Nash, quoted Long, writing: "At the State Department, where Hoover's abrasiveness had more than once ruffled diplomatic feathers, Third Assistant Secretary Breckinridge Long hoped that McAdoo (Secretary of the Treasury) would put the Food Administration in its place. 'Hoover,' said Long, 'has a habit of blaming other people for failures in his own operations. He tried to make a written record for future reference and lay the blame for all failures on other people. He has tried it with this department and with others.'"[6]

Having helped his man win the Democratic nomination, Breck Long joined FDR on the campaign trail. We get a glimpse of the Missourian at an event in Atlanta, Georgia, as reported in the *Atlanta Constitution* on October 23, 1932, which also gives us a graphic picture of the delirium that FDR's arrival could cause and the ardor of the crowds that flocked to see him in the flesh and hear that sonorous voice unfiltered by radio.

To be sure, in Georgia FDR was in a state that could be called his second home. Warm Springs was now a going concern, and he had been spending a large amount of time there, even while carrying on his duties as governor of New York. In the past, the Georgia Democrats had tried to get him to run from the Peachtree State—as their adopted son and a Dry. Yet, something other than neighborliness was at work during that stopover in Atlanta. The parade preceding his speech to be held at the Old Armory drew 250,000 persons, "the greatest multitude ever assembled below the Mason-Dixon Line," the local newspaper declared. Their headline on the candidate's speech, itself, provided a complementary point.

HISTORY IS MADE AT OLD ARMORY IN ROOSEVELT DEMONSTRATION

The news story's byline was that of William Key, and he immediately emphasized that this was the "biggest moment in the history of the great armory." More than 7,000 Atlantans had packed themselves inside the premises and several thousands were on the sidewalks and cobblestone streets outside. The phalanx of newsmen who had accompanied the candidate on his campaign train included Jim Hagerty of the *New York Herald Tribune*, who later became President Dwight Eisenhower's press secretary, and all of these members of the fourth estate, the Atlanta reporter noted, were chewing gum "to make up for the prohibition on smoking." Warming up the crowd were police and fire department bands and a host of speakers, among them Breckinridge Long.

Rather incongruously, the musical festivities started with a rendition of "The Sidewalks of New York" ("East Side, West Side"), Al Smith's theme song, but then the musicians broke into "Dixie," and the house went wild. Hugh Howell, chairman of the Georgia Democratic State Committee, was the master of ceremonies, and he first introduced a complete lineup of Southern Democratic officeholders, ending with, "Finally, Breckinridge Long, former Secretary of State [*sic*], who is one of those fervid literary speakers to whom metaphors and hyperbole come naturally."[7]

Following Breck Long's "metaphors and hyperbole," the bands suddenly struck up "Happy Days Are Here Again," and FDR, guided by his son Jimmy, walked toward the podium while 7,000 Southerners screamed themselves hoarse for a minute and a half. A searchlight caught FDR. "You can see Roosevelt's eyes then. They are blue grey." After the audience suddenly hushed, Roosevelt spoke for fifty-five minutes. "He speaks with the logic of a man who sees things clearly, a man with a straight vision," the reporter admiringly commented. His speech given, the Democratic nominee was escorted back to his open touring car, which returned to the Terminal Station, and his seven-Pullman-car train at 10:37 left Atlanta, headed north. As a last gesture, Roosevelt had the flowers that bedecked the Old Armory sent to cheer up the children who were patients at the Grady Hospital.

Despite the euphoria that such scenes inspired—and they assuredly were repeated over and over again throughout the country—an undercurrent of anxiety could be detected among the gathering throngs. Breck Long ultimately expressed it in these words: "The people were generally quiet and undemonstrative. There was a glumness and semblance of sullenness about their faces and their demeanor. They were awestruck and in a terrible quandary."

Numerous writers have stated that Breckinridge Long financially contributed generously to FDR's 1932 campaign, but with no specific figures ever mentioned, unlike 1916, when he helped bankroll Woodrow Wilson. Bernard Baruch appears to have been the major 1932 fundraiser and donor, and topping the list with him were Joseph P. Kennedy, Ed Flynn, Henry Morgenthau Jr., Ambassador Lawrence Steinhardt, and William H. Woodin, the New Deal's original secretary of the Treasury. One can imagine that in addition to traveling on the campaign train and making warm-up speeches, Long also reached into his pocketbook and handed over unspecified funds.

The Missourian always seemed eager to be of service, actually a bit sycophantic, and often volunteering for tasks. Right after the election of 1932 and before FDR took office (in those days the president wasn't inaugurated until March), Breck Long sent a communication to Hyde Park in another of his pro-bono capacities—secretary-treasurer of the Jefferson Island Club. It was addressed to the Honorable Franklin D. Roosevelt and began, "Dear Governor." The Jefferson Island Club was, to put it bluntly, an exclusive playground resort in Chesapeake Bay for big-shot Democrats. The island had been bought in 1929, and in 1931 a clubhouse had been built on it, where members who had bought stock in the operation could meet for "political discussion and elegant entertaining." Franklin Roosevelt was a stockholder, and that's why Long was writing him. The Treasury Department through the IRS was trying to collect a tax on the purchase price of each stock certificate and also on the club dues. The president-elect owed the U.S. Government $73.83, and apparently FDR still hadn't forked over to the club $70 for his initiation fee and dues. The warning ended, "Yours very truly, Breck Long."

During this waiting period following the election of 1932, one wonders if Breckinridge Long didn't jump at the chance to put his name before his recent boss, even if only with a dunning letter. For those who work in winning political campaigns, there is at this juncture an agony of suspense for hopeful job seekers who feel their efforts should be rewarded. It is hard to know what, if anything, Breck Long wanted from FDR. With his often-overestimated sense of his own value, he may even have been dreaming of secretary of state. As it turned out, he was to render FDR a service far more exalted than reminding him about some petty monetary obligations (plus informing him the Jefferson Island Club was challenging the IRS ruling) and reap a reward, while not as high as top man at State, was high indeed—nothing less than an ambassadorship!

There is a comic-opera quality about the real truth behind this appointment to Rome, which was made in April 1933. Most references to it attribute the honor to his political contributions—especially financial—to the new president. But author Thomas B. Morgan tells a much different tale.[8]

If you remember, a minor aspect of the Democratic Convention in 1932 was the role of James Michael Curley, the scapegrace "Last Hurrah" mayor of Boston who, practically alone among Massachusetts Irish Democratic pols, supported Franklin Delano Roosevelt and not Al Smith. Shut out of being elected a delegate to the convention, he created a bit of enduring folklore by going to Puerto Rico, winning a delegate's position as *Don Jaime Curley* and coming to Chicago, where he delivered a seconding speech for FDR and, upon his man's victory, headed to the Massachusetts delegation's seats and danced an Irish jig in front of his vanquished foes.

Needless to say, Curley demanded a reward from the Rooseveltians. He told Jim Farley, who was handling appointments for the Roosevelt administration, that he wanted to be *ambassador to Italy!*

Farley was aghast. Not only was the totally unpredictable (and palpably dishonest) Curley impossible for such an important post, but there was then an unwritten rule of American diplomacy that the U.S. ambassador to Italy had to be a non-Catholic. The United States had never recognized the Vatican, and it was always feared among the Protestant majority that a Catholic in the Rome post would get too chummy with the pope. What about going to Poland, another Catholic country, Farley asked Curley. That could certainly be arranged. Curley argued instead it would be *good* to have a Catholic in Italy. Farley countered with how it was terrible politics. Nothing daunted, Curley sought out statements of support for himself from the Italian ambassador to the U.S. plus the pope's representative in DC, the Apostolic Delegate.

Thomas B. Morgan wrote:

Meanwhile the persistence of the former Boston Mayor, together with his local diplomatic incursion, had been reported to the president. He called Farley. He asked him to get Breckinridge Long of St. Louis on the telephone. Long had been Assistant Secretary of State under Wilson and had been a pal of the President when he was Undersecretary of the Navy in the same administration. The call was put through to the President. They exchanged old-time pleasantries, then the golden voice asked Long how he would like to go to Rome. Long replied as a loyal Democrat that he would do anything "the boss" asked. Long accepted. The Rome post was filled.[9]

When Curley next inquired about the job, Farley told him: "But I'm sorry, Jim . . . Rome is out. The Boss got Breckinridge Long to take Rome."[10]

A patronage position within the Roosevelt administration, needless to say, had been very much desired by Breckinridge Long. As a matter of fact, on March 29, 1933, shortly after FDR's inaugural, Long had accepted from his good friend Attorney General Homer Cummings, the rather amorphous position of a *special assistant*, prepared to work on *special cases*. Eight days later, following the president's phone call, this purported career of Long's in federal law enforcement abruptly ended with his willing if not eager resignation.

On October 21, 1933, the *St. Louis Globe-Democrat* ran the official version of the story under the headline:

ROOSEVELT NAMES BRECKINRIDGE LONG ITALIAN AMBASSADOR

The article described Long as "active in lining up the Roosevelt forces at the Chicago Convention and worked during the campaign." Also, it identified Long as "a native of St. Louis and son of a distinguished family," who had led the anti-Reed forces in 1920 and 1922; it cited aspects of his career afterward and ended by mentioning that the former Long house at 5145 Lindell Boulevard, "sold several years ago, housed one of the finest private art collections in this section of the country."

The press also carried a story of the Missourian presenting his credentials to King Victor Emmanuel III at the Quirinal Palace. His

Italian Majesty had sent four horse-drawn carriages to transport the new U.S. ambassador and embassy personnel, and Breck, rather like a boastful little kid, informed FDR that "your Ambassador to Italy has been part of a big show. The King received me yesterday and I was taken with my whole staff. A regular procession of coaches with footmen in gorgeous uniforms attended. There were four coaches, an empty carriage like a spare tire and one outrider on horseback at the head of the procession." The Missourian's intimation was that all of this fanfare was a compliment to the American president.[11]

Roosevelt's reply came a little over two weeks later. "Dear Breck, I am delighted to have your letter of June 1 and I love your description of the visit to the palace." Then, as if putting his puffed-up envoy down a peg while still being pleasant, he added humorously, "You are however mistaken in saying that there was one empty carriage. That was the vehicle occupied by GREAT CAESAR's GHOST."[12]

Chapter Thirteen

Ambassador to Italy

L IVING IN THE STYLE TO WHICH he was accustomed remained one of the hallmarks of Breckinridge Long's nearly three-year stint as U.S. ambassador extraordinary and plenipotentiary to Italy. The embassy's built-in quarters for its chief were deemed by him "too dingy" for his needs, not to mention those of his wife and teenaged daughter. "I have arranged to take the Villa Taverna as a residence with lovely gardens surrounding it, built for and used as a convent, and dates from 1560," Long wrote his friend Robert Bingham, the U.S. ambassador to Great Britain. Bought in 1920 by a Count Taverna, who refurbished it as a summer home, this splendid building has since been incorporated into the American Embassy complex in Rome.

Ambassador Bingham, by the way, soon forever endeared himself to the ladies of the Long family by arranging their inclusion among twenty-one American women to be presented to English royalty at Buckingham Palace—an event organized almost a full year before it would take place in May, 1934.

Meanwhile, comfortably installed, with his art-collecting wife obviously enthralled by the cultural atmosphere of the Eternal City, Breckinridge Long embarked upon a mission that was to plunge him right into the maelstrom of European and world politics in a way he could hardly have ever foreseen. The real power in Italy at the time, assuredly, was not the figurehead king who had welcomed him, but Benito Mussolini. Breck was soon to meet Il Duce and to convey his impressions of the dictator to FDR. "He is a man of comparatively short stature with a very soft well-modulated voice and an air of quiet and dignified elegance," Long wrote his boss. Next, after describing how he gave the Italian leader a specially-bound, autographed copy of Roosevelt's inaugural address, the characterization of Mussolini continued. "He then discussed you in a highly complimentary manner. He expressed very great personal admiration." To which the new ambassador added, perhaps gratuitously, "I told him I had your complete confidence." Eventually summing up, Breck declared he was "conscious of having been in the presence of a really unusual person."

The new ambassador had presented his credentials on May 31, 1933. His letter to FDR had been answered on June 15. Twelve days later, he had another report for the man in the White House, loaded up with first impressions.

> Mussolini is an astounding character and the effects of his organized activities are apparent throughout Italy . . . Italy today is the most interesting experience in government to come above the horizon since the formation of our Constitution 150 years ago . . . The Fascists in their black shirts are apparent in every community. They are dapper and well-dressed and standing straight and lend an atmosphere of individuality and importance to their surroundings . . . The trains are punctual, well-equipped and fast.[1]

Whether Breckinridge Long can be held responsible in his last sentence for having created the one major plaudit for the Mussolini regime still remembered—that *he made the trains run on time*—is a question up for grabs. But Long's own reputation soon suffered from the charge he was pro-Fascist. Add to this his previously quoted remark about Hitler's *Mein Kampf*, how it was "eloquent in opposition to Jews as exponents of Communism and chaos,"[2] and the impression of pro-dictatorship bias was intensified.

Professor Frederick W. Marks III, who exhibited a jaundiced view of FDR's foreign policy in his book *Wind Over Sand: The Diplomacy of Franklin Roosevelt*, pointed out that Breckinridge Long's diaries for 1933 and 1934 were missing from his papers in the Library of Congress, and he asserted that Long had withheld them to hide his early uncritical remarks about Mussolini, which Long was eventually to disavow. Marks also wrote: "Ambassador Breckinridge Long's impolitic comments on Mein Kampf have been omitted in his published diary,"[3] and that at least one page had been razored out of the documents. In the interests of full disclosure, it should be noted also that Long left the Library of Congress no diaries at all for 1930, 1931 and 1932, the three years prior to his assignment in Rome.

Long's diary production apparently resumed in 1935, a date of crucial importance in the history of modern Italy. But before advancing to the moment when our U.S. ambassador in Rome was informing his friend in the White House to equip "your diplomatic and consular officials in Europe with gas masks . . . I am satisfied Mussolini is looking forward to the certainty of war," we might first find it profitable to gain a sense of the Rooseveltian State Department for which Breck Long was now intimately working.

At the very top was the Missourian's one-time, intraparty rival Cordell Hull, named secretary of state by FDR, a courtly, silvery-haired figure from the mountains of Tennessee, well-regarded as a congressman, often mentioned for higher office and, to his critics, a bit of a smooth-talking, Southern fuddy-duddy.

But Hull was no pushover. He lasted a dozen years at the job—a record in that era. He outwitted all of the president's pals foisted on him by the "boss"—particularly Raymond Moley, Adolph Berle, and Sumner Welles—and in the case of Breck Long, Hull ultimately made him into an ally and a confidant.

The institution itself, well before the election of 1932, was deemed a bastion of Ivy League WASP snobs, notoriously self-perpetuating, who hung around exclusive clubs here and abroad and lived cushy social lives barely interrupted by brief snatches of work. In 1931, just prior to the New Deal's arrival, a sensational, anonymous tell-all book about upper-crust DC life contained one chapter on the State Department, entitled *Pink Peppermints and Protocol,* and another on our diplomatic corps, called *Starched Futility.* The title of this book itself, *Washington Merry-Go-Round,* reveals now that these hidden authors were Drew Pearson and his lesser-known sidekick Robert S. Allen.

Their description of the atmosphere inside the elegant quarters occupied by State, within the rococo office building around the corner from the White House, warrants reproduction.

Its swinging lattice doors, its wide marble mantelpieces, the carefully polished copper fixtures in its wash-rooms—all create an atmosphere of antiquity, solidarity and imperialism characteristic of the hand at the helm of American foreign affairs. Languid Negro messengers doze or work cross-word puzzles at little tables in the corridors. One of them has served the Secretary of State ever since the administration, fifty years ago, of Hamilton Fish, grandfather of the Red-baiting Congressman. Another was Theodore Roosevelt's coachman and still another is a lawyer, who receives Negro clients at his table in the corridor and discusses divorces, debts and disorderly conduct quite oblivious to worried young diplomats who rush downstairs clutching cables from London and Paris. Everything about the Department, from its deep fireplaces to its portraits of stern and ancient Secretaries of State creates the impression that not a single thing, not even a colored messenger, has been changed for a hundred years.[4]

To be fair to the Department, Pearson and Allen did try, with statistical figures, to show its tremendously increased workload since the era of Edward Livingston (secretary of state in 1831)—3,400 letters mailed out each day, 50 pouches of mail arriving daily, containing reports of 4,000 employees from 425 foreign posts and circulated to 600 employees at the home base. Still, the two authors had to lament the fact that such a beehive of activity did nothing to change the Department's reputation. "In Washington, it is called the most inefficient, dilatory, procrastinating and red-tape-bound bureaucracy in the government service," and "editors leap at opportunities to pooh-pooh the slightest tendency toward white spats and namby-pambyism on the part of its officers."[5]

Soon adding to those sealed mailbags full of confidential reports was Ambassador Breckinridge Long. By 1935 his non-confidential attitude towards the dapper Blackshirts had changed, and he would label Il Duce's Fascism in a letter to FDR as "deliberate, determined, obdurate, ruthless and vicious."

Fueling the growing tensions Mussolini was causing on the world stage was a revivified Italian nationalism. The one-time Socialist had morphed his original ideal of a "dictatorship of the proletariat" into the dream of a *new Roman Empire*. In his own words, he had declared: "For Fascism, the growth of empire, that is to say the expansion of the nation, is an essential manifestation of vitality and its opposite, a sign of decadence." In Mussolini's eyes, "the people of Italy . . . are rising again after many centuries of abasement and servitude."[6]

It was ironic that a Wilsonian like Breckinridge Long should have been sent to Italy in this period. Italy, as one of the Allies in World War I, had been infuriated by Wilson's action at the Paris Peace Conference in denying its demands for the port of Fiume on the Adriatic coast of Yugoslavia, as well as other portions of Dalmatia. Existing Italian possessions in Africa—Libya, Somalia, and Eritrea—had been grabbed at the end of the nineteenth century. But a notable Italian failure had been an earlier attempt to conquer Ethiopia in 1896, which had terminated in a humiliating defeat inflicted by spear-waving native warriors at the battle of Adowa. What Mussolini was clearly angling for in his increasingly aggressive moves toward the kingdom of Haile Selassie was revenge—as well as, speculated certain pundits, keeping a step ahead of that young upstart dictator in Germany, Adolf Hitler.

The 1935 resumption of Long's publicly deposited diaries began with an entry dated February 6 and referred to conversations conveyed to Washington that he had had with Mussolini and Foreign Under Secretary Fulvio Suvich. Also, he added an insight belying the Italians' swaggering estimation of their nation's newfound power.

> They [the Italian government] are in a very serious condition financially and economically. I dined last night with the Marchesea Casati. Volpi was there. I engaged him in conversation and discussed briefly the serious financial situation of the Italian government, but when it came to the point of commenting upon their probable future course, he shut up like a clam and wouldn't say one single word.

A week later, in his next entry, Breck Long was initially less interested in Italy's world posture than in a personnel matter at the embassy. A commercial attaché named McBride had been giving him problems—*namedropping* especially, of people who either didn't know him or have any interest in him. As a result, Long had secured his replacement, had suffered bad-mouthing from McBride, but the matter was settled.

With this minor annoyance off his back, Breck turned again to Italy. "The Abyssinian episode continues," wrote Long, "the Italian press claiming Haile Selassie couldn't go to the League of Nations because he doesn't control some areas of his country." This seemed to be Long's only mention, and without comment, of the League of Nations, as it faced its first real challenge—Mussolini's threat to Haile Selassie's Ethiopia. Despite the latter's failure to pay his League's dues, the Geneva-based organization found itself forced by its own mandate to resist such naked aggression. Breck wrote that the Italians were mobilizing their troops but ingenuously claiming it was only for the purpose of protecting Austria (from the Germans).

Germany, too, had become worrisome by this time. Long said he agreed with an (unnamed) Czech colleague who told him everyone in Europe was afraid of Hitler and the Nazis. Long was also warned by his own military attaché that the Germans were already building fourteen warplanes a day, having denounced the military strictures of the Versailles

Treaty, and had begun fashioning an army of 350,000 soldiers (soon revised upward to 600,000).

Several 1935 diary entries from Italy concerned Breck Long's relationship with Italo Balbo, one of the most prominent Fascist leaders, who was simultaneously a world famous aviator. In the transoceanic tradition of Lindbergh, Balbo had made sensational flights during 1931 and 1933, the first from Rome to Rio de Janeiro and the second from Rome to Chicago and back, leading a squadron of twenty-four flying boats. Greeted as a hero in the U.S., especially by Italo-Americans, he was invited to the White House, where President Roosevelt awarded him the U.S. Distinguished Flying Cross. How much of this fanfare Ambassador Long might have helped arrange is not known, but the two men plainly were in contact. Balbo was appointed governor of Libya at the beginning of November 1933 and rumors spread that Il Duce had put him in political exile, fearing him as a rival because of his immense popularity.

It can be seen that Balbo was clearly interested in keeping up with his American contacts. So we note in Breck Long's diary in March, 1935, that he received a request through the illustrious aristocrat Princess Colonna to have tea with Balbo, who was visiting Rome from Libya. In the course of their discreet get-together in the Colonna Palace, the Fascist hero invited the U.S. ambassador to come stay with him at his headquarters in Tripoli. Breck immediately accepted and posted an impression of his host-to-be. Balbo was as usual most gracious and virile. He is one of the most animated persons I have ever come in contact with." Breck likewise left an estimation of the Roman setting where they'd met. "The apartment of the Colonnas is the most magnificent I have ever seen, the handsomest of all the private *palazzi*."[7]

This trip of Breck's to Libya took place in May 1935. Yet, two months before, at the time of his tea party with Balbo, he had become concerned enough about his health after ten days of stomach pains to telephone his friend Dr. Cary Grayson. A long-distance diagnosis was: "Thinks it is nerves—now weigh 132 pounds, normal is 137 and a recent normal of 143."[8] But later his visit to Tripoli was timed to let him continue on to the U.S. and have his stomach X-rayed.

Lamentably, his condition worsened almost as soon as he arrived in Africa. Omitted was a whole week of trips Balbo had planned for him to places like the far-off oasis of Kufra and the world-renowned ruins at Leptis Magnis. In Tripoli, he stayed with Balbo in his governor's palace, and for outside entertainment the two men went to the cinema and saw *Little Women*, dubbed into Italian. The highlight of the visit was

Breck's presentation at a "big reception" of the actual American aviation medal Balbo had been awarded. The Italian flying ace was delighted and gave "high praise" to Franklin Delano Roosevelt. Per usual, Long expressed his admiration for Balbo—"He is a buoyant, elastic and dynamic personality." During World War II, this handsome, goateed, athletic Italian was so patently feared by Mussolini that his death, when shot down accidently by an Italian anti-aircraft gun, was rumored to have been secretly arranged by Il Duce.

At Stresa, one of the hauntingly beautiful resort lakes in northern Italy, a conference meanwhile was being held that brought together Great Britain, France and Italy, three of the major allies who had fought side-by-side in 1914–1918. Their antagonist was still the same—Germany— and in effect they were attempting a last-gasp effort to build up a solid defense against Hitler's drive to revive the Reich's war machine. Mussolini had already shown his angst that Austria could be subsumed into the Nazi orbit. Breck Long's connections with these discussions came from an unusual source—his Baltimore friend Rabbi Morris Lazaron who, to quote Long, "was quite a friend of the interpreter Signora Olivia Rosetti Engrasti." Apparently, the lady was the only other person in the Stresa conference room with three prime ministers and two foreign secretaries, and she revealed that Ramsay McDonald, the British prime minister, had pledged his help to France and Italy to halt German aggression. When that promise was later broken by a German-British naval treaty, these erstwhile partners split, and Mussolini started to tilt to the more ideologically suited (for him) dictatorial style of the Führer.

The mention of Rabbi Lazaron here brings to mind the question of an almost complete absence from Breck Long's writing in this period of any feelings about what was happening to the German Jews under the Nazis. The same was true the following year, when he recorded several conversations with another interesting Italian woman—Margharetta Sarfatti—a founder of Fascism, one of Mussolini's mistresses and a Jewess. They only seemed to talk about Italian politics. In his entries about Mme. Sarfatti, he never even identified her as Jewish.

The closest brush with the issue of anti-Semitism in his diary then occurred one month into 1936, while talking to Sir Eric Drummond, the British ambassador to Italy. It concerned Father Charles Coughlin, the virulently anti-Semitic priest in Detroit, who regularly poured out his hatred to millions of Americans over the radio and put out a news sheet every bit as Jew bashing as Henry Ford's. In their talk, Breck's nose was out of joint because Sir Eric had been speaking to Cardinals in the

Vatican about Coughlin's activities. By confronting Sir Eric, Long was asserting his belief the Englishman had shown "impertinence" through meddling in American affairs. Apparently, they'd had words before on the subject. "This time," Breck wrote, "Sir Eric said he thought Coughlin had decreased his activities." Long felt the priest had done so in order to organize politically for the 1936 election and his own conclusion was: "Think Sir Eric wanting to take the credit for disarming Coughlin."

In any case, once he left Tripoli, Breck went back to the States, was X-rayed, and to his great relief learned his stomach pains were not cancer, but an aggravated ulcer that would respond to treatment following an operation.

It was not an emergency situation and allowed him to return to Rome. But before he did, he had time to go to DC, meet FDR, and even swim with him in his pool, saying, "He is very approachable and affable in the water and is more intimately communicable than at other times." The president confided he thought his 1936 opponent would again be Hoover. A propos, Long later interjected mention of a rumor he'd heard that he was to be brought back from Italy to replace Jim Farley and head up the president's re-election campaign.

Possibly—but more than likely, this was pure wishful thinking, again. Aside from the matter of his shaky health, there was also an incident that involved Breck with Mussolini in a way sure to displease top Democratic circles in the U.S. It was quite frankly a mysterious bit of political hocus-pocus that could be seen either as brilliantly Machiavellian or just plain and simply stupid.

The scene was a private interview with Il Duce in the Palazzo Venezia on September 17, 1935, requested by Ambassador Long upon his return to Rome. At first glance, their hour-long tête-à-tête seemed to represent an unheard-of indiscretion by the American diplomat. Insisting he was speaking solely for himself, not for the American government, Breckinridge Long proposed a "deal" to Il Duce, concerning his ambitions in Ethiopia.

The nub of Long's presumptuous offer was for the Italian dictator to limit his goals in Ethiopia and leave "intact the part of the country that was the original Ethiopia,"[9] and make an arrangement with Great Britain and France for Italy to occupy the rest of the African kingdom. Breck described Mussolini as listening intently but betraying no emotion. "The expression of his face was fixed. His eyes were immovable."[10]

Once Long went on to suggest that Great Britain and France might give up the ex-German African colonies they now controlled, in return for Italy's continued protection of Austria from Hitler, Il Duce held up his hand for Long to stop. "England! Return colonies!?" Mussolini exclaimed. "It is to laugh. England would never return anything!"[11]

And soon Breck received a definitive answer to his suggestions. "It is too late," Mussolini insisted. "My plans have developed too far. My soldiers down there could not be controlled. They would act on their own account and what could I do with my army of a million?"[12] Furthermore, Il Duce vented his anger at the Ethiopians for continuing to gloat about and celebrate their 1896 victory over the Italians at Adowa, and he ended with a final point about his intentions. "I will not permit interference from any source."

Before leaving the Italian dictator's presence, Ambassador Long swore anew that this offer had been his idea exclusively. In his diary, too, he defended his action, insisting he felt "it his duty to at least make a try" for peace. His epitaph remained a belief that Mussolini was "riding into the face of a storm, which will either ruin him and [cause] lasting damage to his country, or raise him actually to that pedestal where he is sentimentally placed by his adherents."[13]

The question inevitably arises, was Breck Long prevaricating and really obeying orders in a quixotic attempt to stave off an Italo-Ethiopian war? Orders from whom? Who else but FDR. Conceivably, when the two men were swimming together in the White House pool, this gambit was concocted, a Rooseveltian peace proposal but disguised as coming from a renegade diplomat.

Yet Louis Howe might have argued differently. To the president's closest advisor, Breckinridge Long was a maverick. In a radiogram to Roosevelt, who was at sea in early October 1935 on the USS *Houston*, Howe complained, "Long has been hypnotized by Mussolini. Is sending five or six cables a day little short of absolute Italian propaganda . . . Hull tells me confidentially Long considers himself only under your authority and does not pay attention . . . Knowing Long as we do, think we can see danger if this goes unchecked."[14]

Cordell Hull's role here is murky. His memoirs contain absolutely no mention of Long's insubordinate behavior. That he knew about it was indisputable. Long himself said he had "telegraphed the Department that I had had my unauthorized interview with Mussolini." Or was the Tennessean merely being cagy, suspecting FDR had put Long up to such a breach of diplomatic protocol. In any event, he soon found himself in frequent touch with his man in Rome because the Italians were turning hostile to the U.S.

On October 3, 1935, Italian troops, these new Roman legions who were going to punish the Ethiopian barbarians, crossed the Rubicon, as it were, invading a fellow member of the League of Nations. The "civilization" the Italians brought included airplanes dropping bombs on Haile Selassie's cavalry, leaving a bad worldwide image, and it would hardly have mattered had not the Italian offensive bogged down. Before long, the League of Nations voted "sanctions" against the aggressor, but without including oil.

From Rome, Breck Long had expressed his hope to Secretary Hull that the U.S. would *not* join in any sanctions the League imposed. We didn't. Our strategy was to impose an embargo on all war materials to either belligerent—oil included. The Italians deemed such evenhandedness an unfriendly act, and Long was summoned by Foreign Under Secretary Suvich to be told of their displeasure.[15] While the Italian press berated Roosevelt for some unflattering remarks made about dictators, the real animus in Italy was against the British for trying to stymie their East African offensive. Italian students, on the rampage in Rome, chiseled off the nameplate of the Hotel Eden, and the Hotel Inglaterra was forced to change its name to Hotel Italia. In a letter to FDR, Long wrote, "They [the Italians] have worked themselves into a fury here. Every man, woman and child today hates England."[16]

A steady flow of correspondence between Long and FDR continued during these next feverish months. Breck called the Italians "a very dangerous people," whom he likened to a blind Samson pulling down the temple on his own head, and he predicted they would try to capture the Suez Canal if hostilities broke out. Also Breck foresaw that British-Italian enmity could only lead to "an aggrandizement of the power and importance of Germany." And at the time he debunked various rumors that "Mussolini is mad," calling Il Duce "cool, calm and deliberate."

Roosevelt wrote back, stating that Long and Ambassador Dodd in Germany had been "far more accurate in their pessimism than other friends in Europe." One whole subsequent Long-FDR letter was concerned with oil. Long maintained that British oil companies were still doing business with Italy and at the Suez Canal were actually pumping oil into Italian troopships en route to Ethiopia. "The British do not miss one chance to earn an honest penny." Additionally, he had seen the practical effect of an oil stoppage threat when his wife Christine's automobile was halted while driving in Rome and a sign placed on it that cars were only to be used for emergencies. Daughter Teenie was told not to drive to the Golf Club, and Mrs. Long had to curtail her excursions.

One new complication in the tense international situation occurred when Hitler announced on March 7, 1936, his intention to re-militarize the Rhineland. This action drew another vote of censure from the League of Nations, which proved equally as ineffective as its protesting the Italian aggression in Ethiopia.

Three days later, according to Breck Long's diary, his own personal circumstances underwent a significant transformation. He wrote, "This morning, I had a letter from the President saying he wanted me to come home during the spring and resign and engage in the campaign. So I will plan to do that, leaving here probably in the neighborhood of the first of May."[17]

But in a handwritten postscript almost ten years later, dated 8/6/45, Long changed this story, stating he had first notified FDR that "my health might not permit me to continue working in Rome and that I would like to protect it and resign,"[18] although not immediately, and "would stick it out until spring." The president had *then* written to him, he claimed.

Mulling over his circumstances at the time, Long did write in his diary in March 1936 that "the climate and the food [in Italy] apparently do not agree with me" and that "I lack the association of friends and all in all I will be pleased to go home."[19] On the other hand, were war suddenly to break out, it would not look good for him to abandon his position, he thought.

Finally, a letter went from Long to the president, announcing he would take up FDR's suggestion and return to the U.S. "My tummy is gladder," he wrote facetiously and he would leave Europe in May, but because of his need for an ulcer operation would not be able to partake in the Democratic Convention in Philadelphia, not that it mattered since FDR would be unanimously re-nominated.

On April 16, 1936, he telegraphed the State Department, asking for a leave of absence, which was granted forthwith. He made arrangements to leave via Germany, stopping first in Berlin, before proceeding to Hamburg. Concurrently, he entered an odd comment in his diary regarding the Führer. "I see no indication of a pathological condition in Hitler's recent speeches and actions, which would indicate that he was not acting in a very sane and able manner."[20]

On April 30, Breckinridge Long arrived in the U.S. and by May 9 was back at Montpelier—"Home again and glad to be here." Following a stop in Washington and lunch with Secretary Hull and Bill Phillips, his replacement in Rome, he was off to Rochester, Minnesota, and the Mayo Clinic, where he underwent surgery for his stomach problems.

The pen-pal exchange with the president continued. On June 15, Breck wrote from his hospital bed that a good part of his stomach had been removed, "just an old ulcer that had been irritating" him for years and he would now be in better health.[21] After two or three weeks of rest, he figured, he could start going to their campaign headquarters.

A sidelight of this back-and-forth letter writing showed Long's tendency, on occasion, to show off. He wanted FDR to know he had established an "off the record" tie with the Vatican, particularly through Cardinal Eugenio Pacelli, the papal secretary of state (and later Pope Pius XII). Therefore, he declared, he was closing his official position with "the revelation of an unofficial relationship with the authorities of the Vatican, which is not of record anywhere, but of which I think you should be advised." Here, perhaps, was a further argument that his unorthodox approach to Mussolini had been truly self-generated.

Roosevelt's responses were unfailingly solicitous.

> Dear Breck,
>   I have followed your progress at the Mayo's first with alarm and later with deep satisfaction that the operation was wholly successful . . . I do not need to tell you how proud I am of the splendid record you made in Rome.[22]

> My dear Mr. Ambassador,
>   I wish to express not only my deep regret that for considerations of health, you are obliged to resign, but also my most sincere appreciation of your splendid work in Rome.

Long was equally effusive. He signed one letter: "Affectionately and respectfully," another "Yours as ever," still another, "Most sincerely, your friend and servant," and an ultimate P.S.: "You are a good friend as well as being a great chief."

Roosevelt had the last word in encomiums. He wrote to Breck: "You are a grand fellow and you know my devotion to you."[23]

Chapter Fourteen

The 1936 Campaign and Aftermath

ABOUT ALL THAT BRECKINRIDGE LONG could contribute by way of personal service to FDR's 1936 campaign was to join a "victory train" trip to the west in the month of October. His ulcer operation at the Mayo Clinic had been far more strenuous than he'd foreseen. But on October 8, he joined the president's party and traveled with them beyond the Mississippi and back to Albany by October 17. It was an ebullient experience. Everywhere, gigantic crowds exploded into "wild enthusiasm." Breck was struck by the contrast with 1932.

"It was an astonishing experience to travel through much of the territory we had traveled through four years ago when I was also on the President's train," he wrote, naming a string of states: Minnesota, Iowa, Wyoming, Colorado, Nebraska, Kansas, Missouri, Illinois, Michigan, Ohio, New York—where the crowds then had been big "but quiet and undemonstrative, glum, even sullen," and now in 1936 were greeting the incumbent with unbounded excitement.[1]

Long spoke of "excellent speeches," penned mostly by Judge (Samuel) Rosenman, and how he and Senators Key Pittman, Burt Wheeler, and Joe O'Mahoney made their contributions with "ideas, paragraphs and other suggestions." Roosevelt would do a bit of editing, himself, reducing the message "to the simple language of the man in the street." No new ideas were promoted, Breck explained, since it was obvious to everyone that the campaign was already won. A million people showed up in Chicago; an even bigger crowd turned out in Detroit, and in Long's home town of St. Louis, the attendance was "very large," and he especially cited the "wildness of the crowd" at Rochester, New York.

The Missourian rode in Car number 4, which was furnished with a "very comfortable drawing room," while the Roosevelt family was in the rear car. Breck lunched twice with the president and Mrs. Roosevelt and dined with them twice, once while crossing the Mississippi River. Joining them in Missouri were U.S. Senators Bennett Clark (son of Champ Clark), Harry Truman, and Governor Guy B. Park. Breck also reported an "intimate" talk he had with FDR, just before they reached Albany on the return trip—how he had told the president he wished all Americans could have been on the train and of the responsibility of arousing such hope in the electorate and that Roosevelt countered by saying he wished "every Republican chairman of the boards of big corporations could have been on hand to "see something of the human side of America." Long added how at every crossroad, a crowd had gathered, standing alongside their cars, hats off, waving.

A pool betting on the outcome of the election was established. How many electoral votes would FDR garner? Breck Long ventured 472, and never a flawless prognosticator, claimed Governor Alf Landon, the Republican candidate, would carry his own state of Kansas and possibly Iowa and Wyoming. As it turned out, only Democratic Party chair James Farley had the right answer—i.e., that FDR would capture 46 States, all except Maine and Vermont. While on the train, Breckinridge Long did make some short speeches—in his native Missouri and in Iowa and Detroit, even at a Republican gathering in New York, and in his adopted state of Maryland at Towson on the Friday night before the voting. He also spoke for FDR in the GOP stronghold of Nantucket, where he had been recuperating from his surgery. The final outcome on Nantucket was Roosevelt 548 and Landon 1,969, drawing a remark from Breck that Woodrow Wilson was the only Democrat ever to have carried the Massachusetts island.

Following FDR's landslide win, Breck Long reported to Jim Farley at Democratic headquarters. He was to take over work that Senator O'Mahoney had been doing and was named a vice-chairman of the Democratic National Committee. His office connected with Farley's, and nearby were the offices of Forbes Morgan and Frank Walker, respectively the party treasurer and the chair of the DNC's finance committee. Clearly, Breckinridge Long was still valued by the Democrats for his financial capability.

What was to be his reward for all of his voluntary service? Long's diary writings during this immediate post-election period are full of speculations. His attendance at a dinner on January 19, 1937, for "the key men and women of his [FDR's] campaign organization" seemed to bode well that a place would be found for him in the second Roosevelt administration. There were about sixty to seventy persons present. He himself was seated next to Sara Delano Roosevelt, the president's mother.

"The headquarters crowd was there," he stated—Jim Farley, Maurice Tobin, Sam Rayburn." He had no chance to hold a private conversation with the president, who left early to work on the inaugural speech, but Breck's hopes were high.

The foreign policy arena would be his first choice. Along the way, another ambassadorship for him seemed in the offing. Germany was mentioned. He'd have liked that. So also was Chile. However, wife Christine thought it too far from their daughter, who was in school in the U.S. Continuing to work for the Democratic National Committee was one thing, but hardly a career move upward.

The first really tantalizing possibility Long mentioned surfaced in his writings on January 24, 1937, only three days after FDR's inauguration, which Breck attended with his old law partner from St. Louis, Frank Thompson. Wrote the Missourian, "Farley gave me the impression that the President would consider me in connection with the Cabinet or some other similar high post." An impression he had was that it involved the War Department, mainly because Farley had "dwelt so long on that position."

But as time went on and no such political plum appeared, the Missourian admitted he'd better start looking for a job. His rationale was,

> I am tired of loafing. For the first four or five months after my operation, I had the object of regaining my health. My activity in the campaign helped a lot to re-establish my mental activity. Since then I have been quiescent and want either to open my own office or to be active with the Administration.[2]

However, he hesitated to set up a law office if he then had to turn around and close it to take a government post. He enlisted the help of Senator Key Pittman, hoping the Nevada Democrat would get the president to give him a job—maybe ambassador to England, although he had informed Pittman he preferred to stay in DC. It seems that Pittman did mention Long for ambassador to England but that FDR "very promptly told him he had other ideas about London." When Pittman next had brought up the notion of under secretary of state for Breckinridge Long, he'd been told the decision was strictly up to Cordell Hull.

This latter intelligence was hardly good news. Sixteen years had passed since 1921 and the Democratic National Committee meeting in St. Louis when Cordell Hull had assumed chairmanship of the

Democratic Party. In his own interpretation of what had happened, Breck now confessed,

> I have felt that Cordell has a sort of antipathy to me . . . Not since the episode of 1921 when I was chosen to be Chairman of the National Committee at the time George White resigned—and when I was unable to qualify because of the obtrusiveness of Ed Goltra, Hull was chosen in my stead.[3]

Adding to this unpleasantness of old, Breck felt sure, was his disagreement with Hull on the "oil embargo and supplies to Italy during the Ethiopian War." Besides, under secretary of state was the *number two* position in the State Department, and rumor had it that Hull's favorite for the job was his old friend R. Walton Moore, a career man, while the president wanted to install Sumner Welles, Groton and Harvard, who was like family to him and who had been a participant in his wedding to Eleanor.

In the end, as always, FDR had his way. Despite Hull's distaste for Welles and lack of trust in him, the latter did receive the under secretary appointment. Moore, seventy-six years old, well beyond the age of seventy, which the president had made an issue of in his Supreme Court-packing scheme, had a special State Department position created for him, and the compromise settled the matter, with Breckinridge Long still left out in the cold.

Long said he was reluctant to lobby Roosevelt. "Our personal relations have been very happy and warm and intimate and I thought it would be inconsistent to try to force him to take me into his Cabinet."

Nevertheless, Breck *was* offered one job he wasn't too eager to accept. A group of Democratic senators had, as he put it, "conspired against me to become again the Treasurer of the Jefferson Island Club." Running this recreation project for Democratic elite had been a headache before he'd been able to turn the task over to Joseph Davies, except now Davies was off to Moscow as ambassador to the U.S.S.R., and "they have picked on me again."

But in his fashion of making himself useful, he took on the pro-bono work. Likewise, he let it be known to Jimmy Roosevelt that he'd be willing to help his father with the controversial—to say the least—Court-packing attempt.

On the positive side for Breck, in the first month of 1937 was the honor of being nominated to the Princeton board of trustees, representing the Alumni Association. Despite some doubts he would be elected, he did become a member of that prestigious body. The president of the DC Princeton Club, which had put forward his name, had shown signs of wanting to practice law with Long, who was still ambivalent about opening an office, not to mention practicing alongside someone else. The law would be tough for him, he thought. He hadn't done a trial in twenty years. It was plain he yearned for another chance at government service, and he wrote ruefully, "Being without employment in the public service, I am too young and too active to retire or to withdraw from the activities of life." He thought possibly of writing but reasoned that he had "no contacts with magazines or publications of any kind."

The limbo in which Breckinridge Long found himself seemingly lasted for another year and a half until on September 30, 1938, he was asked to do a favor for President Roosevelt. The person who contacted him on FDR's behalf was George S. Messersmith of the State Department, the man currently in charge of administering the Department.

Messersmith, a rural Pennsylvanian of German descent, was sort of a legend in the Department, a veteran of the consular service, who was to cross the once-unbreachable boundary to ambassadorial rank and whose record as consul general in Berlin during the rise of the Nazis had stamped him as Hitler's most outspoken foe among American diplomats. He had wanted to be ambassador to Germany, but the top brass at State had brought him back to DC in 1937, when a shake-up had taken place, and certain old-time fixtures like Wilbur J. Carr were shunted off (to be ambassador to Czechoslovakia) and Bill Phillips eased out as under secretary to make way for Sumner Welles.

Whether Messersmith, who liked Breckinridge Long, had recommended him to head up a special mission isn't known—only that he phoned the Missourian and said the president wanted him to lead an official goodwill trip to South America. He was to take his wife with him, all expenses paid, and the group would leave within a week and visit Rio de Janeiro, Buenos Aires, and Montevideo on the first boat of a new mercantile service initiated by the U.S. Shipping Board. Once Breck had obtained Christine's assent, he went to see the president and thanked him. They talked briefly, with FDR questioning him about the recent New England hurricane and what damage it might have caused on Nantucket. Also, regarding the trip to South America,

> he wanted me to go, thought I would enjoy it, was to give messages from him to the presidents of Brazil, Argentina and Uruguay,

make as many friends as possible, etc . . . We had a pleasant short
visit and on leaving, I congratulated him on his notes to Hitler,
especially the last one.[4]

Here it is appropriate to backtrack a bit into Long's diary entries
earlier in 1938 because they deal with an apparent metamorphosis in
Breck's thinking about the German dictator. Since accusations of anti-
Semitism hang so heavily over Breckinridge Long's reputation, his
attitudes towards the Nazis, as he expressed them may offer clues to his
inner feelings. At any rate, they vary. His entry for February 18, 1938
concerns the question of a continued independent existence for Austria.
The Hitlerians had been infiltrating their neighboring country—Hitler's
birthplace—ever since taking power in Germany in 1933 and a year later,
Austrian Nazis had assassinated Engelbert Dollfuss, Austria's fascist but
anti-Nazi Chancellor. The successor to him was Kurt von Schuschnigg,
a much weaker man. On February 18, 1938, Breck was commenting on
a recent meeting between Hitler and Schuschnigg and predicting that
Austrian independence was guaranteed. He called upon his experiences in Italy,
a country vitally interested in German-Austrian affairs, as background
for his opinion.

> I know that Mussolini does not want a war in Europe . . . I am sure
> he must have persuaded Hitler to his philosophy. Consequently, I
> am sure that Austria's independence will continue, that she will be
> a buffer state between Italy and Germany.[5]

Besides being dead wrong yet again, he added this rather astonishing
postscript:

> I also know that if the State Department thought I entertained
> any such radical views and could look upon any action of either
> Mussolini or Hitler with equanimity to say nothing of approval,
> that I would be carried on their blacklist forever. It is almost
> heresy to mention the name of Hitler or Mussolini to anyone
> in the State Department . . . unless criticism, condemnation or
> vilification are expressed.

And finishing up the thought, he seemed to echo some of the
noise that Charles Lindbergh was making publicly, especially about
German power and its advances in aviation. Lindbergh, invited by

Reichsmarschall Göring, and working through the U.S. military attaché in Berlin—an openly pro-Nazi U.S. Air Force officer named Truman Smith—had been allowed in October of 1937 to attend the super-secret Lilienthal Aeronautical Society meeting in Munich. One result—and after the American aviator-hero had toured many Luftwaffe sites throughout Germany—was a report from him to our State Department, entitled "The General Estimate of Germany's Air Power of November 1, 1937." Lindbergh, who was to accept a highly-coveted decoration from Hitler, emphasized the Third Reich's aerial might, which was growing every day from a base he estimated at 175 to 225 squadrons and 2,400 first-line airplanes.[6]

So Breck Long underlined his belief, seemingly based on common sense, that anti-Axis sentiment should not get in the way of realpolitik. "It warps our international point of view," he argued. "They [Germany and Italy] are real powers and they have to be dealt with. We have no other persons in Germany or Italy to deal with . . . I try to see situations as they are and not as we would like them to be."[7] Long's crystal ball on this occasion was a bit more accurate than usual. He actually foresaw the four-power Munich conference that took place in September 1938, involving Germany, Italy, Great Britain and France, after Austria had been absorbed by Germany, and Hitler was turning his attention to Czechoslovakia and the Sudetenland. Yet Breck was also much too ready to accept Hitler as reasonable. He wrote on February 18, 1938,

Hitler's speech is a very able presentation of the German point of view. There is a good deal of bombast about it, but there is no mailed fist and I am inclined to accept it at its face value. I believe he desires an extension of German influence to the east and southeast, but that does not mean military or political control or domination or annexation.

One rather cryptic remark of Long's refers to England's role in 1938 and Neville Chamberlain's assuming control of His Majesty's foreign policy. Without explaining himself, Breck argued, referring to the Brits, "But if they had followed my advice and had adopted policy based upon my recommendations, they would be in a better shape today than they have found themselves."[8]

Next, it appeared, Breck Long could also chide Hitler for not having followed Long's own scenario for the Nazi leader. On September 26, 1938, in the midst of the Munich get-together, his diary entry reads:

Hitler made a damned fool speech today. He took an intransigent position. That, coupled with his enlarged demands, as now learned, create a situation of grave danger—and for the first time, I am apprehensive. He had his war won without a fight. But now he is near causing a fight to get what he has already won. I listened to him over the radio and he seemed like a madman.

Thus we go full circle in estimating what Breckinridge Long's private feelings were like in that tempestuous year of 1938. Certainly, he felt left out of things. Nothing really had opened up for him in government. At age fifty-seven, was any meaningful professional life on his own terms—and not just racing his stable of horses—left for him? He followed the news and what was happening politically, both domestically and on the international scene. There are indications he stuck his neck out in Maryland, in an effort to defeat U.S. Senator Millard Tydings in a Democratic Primary, as part of a presidential purge of fellow party members who had not supported the New Deal program. The utter failure of this effort was never mentioned by Long. But it showed his devotion to FDR.

In fact, the single event he highlighted in his diary after those February 18, 1938, disquisitions was the marriage of his daughter, Teenie. She was wed at Montpelier on April 18, 1938. Her bridegroom was Arnold Augur Willcox, a Midwesterner born in Illinois, who'd gone east to school (Yale, Class of 1932), later becoming employed as an economist by the Department of Justice and, like his father-in-law, a breeder and racer of horses. Breck's description of the event is interestingly perfunctory. Not a word about his only child's intended, not even his name.

Teenie was married at home in the Library this afternoon in a very pretty wedding before a company of relatives and close friends. [There is something of a contradiction here, since he ends his one paragraph by intimating there were five hundred people present.] I gave her away (raining—had to do it in the house).

And then he saw fit to cloak Teenie's wedding within the framework of a gallery of ancestors, musing,

The ceremony was in the room from the walls of which portraits and pictures of her ancestors looked down: Samuel and Sarah Miller, Alexander Breckinridge, John Breckinridge, John Cabell

Breckinridge, and the Webbs and old Jonathan Dickinson . . . After the cake was cut, I proposed a toast to the bride and groom and the wedding party . . . in Madeira imported by Teenie's great grandfather, Francis P. Blair, Sr.

Notable among the guests was U.S. Senator Key Pittman. Breck also mentioned that three of his 1903 Princeton classmates were present.

Either Breck Long was very busy in 1938 or too dispirited by his own lack of meaningful involvement in affairs to attend much to his diary. A perusal of his separate correspondence in 1938 until September shows only a smattering of efforts worth keeping on record. Possibly the most important was a deal he was trying to cook up, with the help of Bernard Baruch, to have Woodrow Wilson's papers become the property of Princeton University. "Bernie" was close to Mrs. Wilson, who controlled the late president's effects. In January 1938, Breck took a special trip to Baruch's plantation, Hobcaw Barony in South Carolina, and also spent time bird-hunting with the famed Jewish financier. He was hoping to get Baruch's papers, too, for Princeton, which he did. (Bernie Baruch had attended the City College of New York).

Invitations to social events were always part of Breck and Christine Long's lives. One of note in May 1938 was from Ambassador and Mrs. Robert Woods Bliss to a musical evening of Bach and Stravinsky, the orchestra conducted by Nadia Boulanger, a world-renowned French teacher of classical musicians. It was neither the program nor the performers that later would resonate here but the irony of the location— the Bliss estate in DC's Georgetown section, Dumbarton Oaks, where the United Nations was to be conceived, with the active participation of Breckinridge Long.

Favors were as always being asked of people with "connections," as Breck Long was considered. A Princeton classmate (one of the three at Teenie's wedding) and "very good friend," Howard Ameli, who worked for the Department of Justice, was looking for a better job. Breck gave him a letter of introduction to the second-in-command at the Department of the Treasury. Another friend, Billy Collins, was working at the U.S. Court for China in Shanghai and wanted to get transferred. Breck was asked, as well, to delve into visa work and procure one for the sister of Nikita Carpenko, owner of the Norwegian Pottery Shop on Nantucket.

Some law work was coming Breck's way. He wrote his diplomat friend Jefferson Caffrey, then ambassador to Brazil, how he had finally decided, once his health had returned, "to begin again my erstwhile professional activity in international law." And he let Caffrey know he was representing the Spanish government (presumably that of the legally elected republic, not the Franco insurgents), while simultaneously inviting Caffrey and his wife to come stay with the Longs at Nantucket during the summer.

There were little triumphs for the Breckinridge Long ego. One was to be invited by the president of Rutgers to join him, in Long's capacity as a Princeton trustee, for lunch in the Rutgers gymnasium before the Princeton-Rutgers football game. In another venue, ex-Ambassador Long was presented with a prestigious decoration from the king of Italy, making him a Grand Officer of the Saints Mauritius and Lazarus Society.

Yet another kudos that came Breck's way concerned the Jefferson Island Club, once he had resumed the financial reins as treasurer. He could triumphantly report in July 1938 that "the Club has received subscriptions of $29,675, which insures operations for this year and they hope for some years to come." There followed a totally mysterious, never explained notation, presented solely as: "The matter of the colored baseball team."

But from the end of September on, Breck Long may have felt a turn in his fortunes that he could sense if not articulate. Munich was happening, and the whole world was applauding a seeming march towards peace. Indeed, it was on the very date the Munich pact was made public, September 30, 1938, that Breck's phone rang, and George Messersmith was on the line, officially asking Breck to do a favor for FDR.

Weren't there hints that his acceptance could lead to doors later opening in the administration?

Anyway, who could turn down such an inviting junket?

Chapter Fifteen

Special Mission to Latin America
and the
Evian Conference

TO A LARGE DEGREE, THE fun trip in the autumn of 1938 that Breck Long headed up was simply a *vacation interlude* for himself and Christine. There was no way of knowing that the rest of this decade of the 1930s and most of the following one would be overflowing with strife—at least in his professional career. On shipboard to and from the southern continent, it was dressing for dinner, sumptuous meals, dancing, and on shore in Argentina and Uruguay and Brazil, official rah-rah speeches at black- or white-tie and gown events, on behalf of his superiors back home about something that sounded just swell—good neighbor policy—with words of warm welcome from his friendly, eager-to-please hosts.

Thus, for example, we have the effusive rhetoric of the "Remarks of His Excellency, Barros, Intervenor of the State of São Paulo, Brazil, at Luncheon, November 1, 1938." These were addressed to: "Your Excellency, Ambassador Breckinridge Long and Your Excellency, Admiral E. S. Land, President of the U.S. Maritime Commission." Speaking in the name of the São Paulo people and as chief of the government of the state of São Paulo, Barros praised, "Your great enterprise you have just realized, inaugurating the new line of navigation that is binding the United States of America with the big coast of Atlantico and Brazil," and he spoke of "the firm reaction of the government of President Roosevelt approaching more these two peoples, whose ethnic and geographic formation demanded the same strength in the colonization work and the same sacrifice for the political emancipation."[1]

In other words, despite Senhor Barros's slightly fractured English, the

theme was: *We are all Americans.* So it was throughout the trip, which had
started with the arrival at the port of Buenos Aires on October 26, 1938,
aboard the *S.S. Brazil,* and a white-tie reception October 28. The foreign
minister of Argentina, José María Cantilo, whom Breck Long had known
overseas, took time in his remarks to say to the ex-ambassador to Italy:
"You had the kindness to recall a personal relationship which dates back
to our common stay in Rome at the head of our respective embassies."[2]

Long talked of President Roosevelt's previous visit in December
1936 for the Buenos Aires Conference of American States, where FDR
had felt the need for better communications, resulting in this voyage
of the first of "a line of ships" to begin "an additional means of
communication—the Good Neighbor fleet—of subsidized ships . . .
subsidized by the Government of the United States." After mentioning
Foreign Minister Cantilo, "who was my colleague in Rome and . . . where
we were good friends," and "it is most pleasing to see him again in a seat
of even greater authority," he ended on a ringing note by promising the
United States would "cultivate the spirit of peaceful and reciprocal Good
Neighbor Policy in its relations with its friend, Argentina."

Left unsaid was any reference to the fact that in the past, Argentina
had been a constant opponent, if not rival, to the U.S. in Latin American
affairs and that his friend Cantilo was regarded as much more pro-North
American, or at least neutral, than his predecessor, Carlos Saavedra
Lamas, with whom Cordell Hull had had a good deal of trouble.

The realities behind all the friendly words were, if consciously in Breck
Long's mind, ignored. For instance, the title of *Intervenor* given to Barros
in São Paulo meant—and Long no doubt knew this—that he wasn't an
elected governor but had been placed there by Brazil's strongman and
dictator, President Getulio Vargas, who had removed state executives
reluctant to kowtow to his regime.

Unlike the Argentines, however, the Brazilian leaders were strongly
pro-U.S., and these included the Foreign Minister Oswaldo Aranha, who
with Vargas had led a revolution in 1930, when they had taken power
together. In Rio de Janeiro, at that time the capital of the country, Long
met with Aranha, and because the U.S. ambassador to Brazil, Jefferson
Caffrey, was on vacation, Long was given a letter addressed to Cordell
Hull, highly confidential, and asked to deliver it to the secretary of state.

Part of this classified document was diplomatic boiler plate. "My
dear Mr. Cordell Hull, I wish to express to you and ask you to convey
to the President, the appreciation of the Brazilian government for the
visit of Ambassador Breckinridge Long and for the mission of good

will he brought from President Roosevelt to President Getulio Vargas and the people of Brazil." But finally, there was a serious note. Calling Long's visit "very opportune" and explaining that Ambassador Caffrey had departed for Europe, he revealed the discovery in Brazil of

> unmistakable evidence of a large and well-planned underground organization directed by a German general and aimed at the establishment of a Nazist [*sic*] regime in Brazil . . . I asked Ambassador Long to be kind enough to inform you of the details of this disclosure, which I am sure cannot fail to impress you of its dangerous character . . . The Brazilian government feels it to be its duty to inform you of this grave fact.[3]

The foreign minister's letter was dated November 3, 1938. This alarming information was later to have a significant impact on Breckinridge Long in his subsequent career at the Department of State.

The return trip to the U.S. had the SS *Brazil* passing through Trinidad, the Virgin Islands, and Puerto Rico, and reaching New York City on November 15, 1938. Two days later, Long met with FDR and gave him Aranha's message, which he subsequently also relayed to Under Secretary Sumner Welles and Cordell Hull, to whom it had been addressed.

The idea of an Axis threat in Latin America took hold forthwith, strongly endorsed by FDR, and adding credence to restrictions on refugees, even Jews, who as Nazi agents could theoretically slip into the U.S. through our neighbors to the south.

Less than a week after Aranha had dated his letter and while Breck Long was on his way home, the steady build-up of official anti-Semitism in Germany furiously exploded into full view. The Nazi government orchestrated a countrywide pogrom on the night of November 9, 1938, which was promptly dubbed *Kristallnacht*—Night of Broken Glass.

This unprecedented super-rampage continued on into the next day, and the brutality of the Germans against their fellow Germans of Jewish origin created headlines and shock waves throughout the world. Its excuse was that in the city of Paris a teenage Polish-Jewish refugee, outraged by Nazi treatment of his parents who had been living in Germany, entered the Third Reich's French Embassy and shot to death one of the staff, who ironically, it turned out, was a closet anti-Nazi. But evidence existed the Hitlerites had been merely looking for any pretext to strike. Camouflaging the Third Reich's involvement, the *Führer* had insisted the Nazi Party play no role.

More than one thousand synagogues were burned that night, countless Jewish-owned stores were ransacked and destroyed, the constant shattering of windows creating an unforgettable impression of continuously shattering glass. At least ninety-one Jews met their deaths during the riots and thirty thousand Jewish men were marched off to concentration camps. Also inflicted was the confiscation of all German Jewish property and wealth, and the Nazis finished by cynically fining the Jewish community one billion marks for the damage the storm troopers had caused.

In some cases, this hideous event was a wake-up call to the German Jews, themselves. To my in-laws, for example. They were more German than Germans. My father-in-law, Ludwig Florsheim of Munich, was a World War I veteran of the German army, an industrialist who owned an important electronics factory, who with his workers had fought a Communist takeover of Munich in the early 1920s, and who stubbornly had rejected any thoughts of leaving his beloved *Heimat*.*

On *Kristallnacht*, he was carted off to Dachau. But possibly the truest horror of that evening was expressed by my mother-in-law, Charlotte Rulf Florsheim, telling us years afterward how the Gestapo had come to their Munich apartment, and she'd been told she had twenty-four hours to vacate it with her two young children.

My father-in-law never spoke about his experiences nor what atrocities he had witnessed at Dachau. My mother-in-law, though, did relate two stories I've never forgotten. One, to illustrate her utter helplessness, was how the youthful Gestapo officer in charge of telling her to leave kept eyeing a lovely antique porcelain box on her parlor table and ended up just putting it into his pocket. The other tale concerned her husband, whom we called Lou—on his way home after release from the Dachau concentration camp. When she told us that instead of coming straight back, he stopped first to buy milk for the children, sure there was none at home, her eyes filled with tears.

My in-laws were lucky. In her youth, my mother-in-law had gone to art school in the United States and become an American citizen, before marrying Lou and going back to live in Germany. Although by 1938 she had been out of our country for more than five years, she convinced the American consuls to honor her citizenship. The Florsheims were thus able to leave Germany at the end of 1938, basically bereft of all their possessions, reach Holland and, just before the war broke out

*No direct translation: cultural and regional milieu.

in September 1939, manage to emigrate to the U.S. Sadly, they were a distinct exception in relation to the ever-increasing numbers who had to flee as Hitler conquered most of Europe.

Well before *Kristallnacht,* the Roosevelt administration had been confronted by this slowly burgeoning problem of Jewish persecution. A mere three weeks after Hitler took power on March 27, 1933, a mass protest rally was held at Madison Square Garden and a boycott of German goods proposed, an idea vigorously opposed by the U.S. State Department. To Hull and the bureaucrats around him (they would not include Breckinridge Long until 1939) "the plight of the German Jews was considered to be a domestic German affair and hence above intervention."[4]

In Cabinet meetings during these early days of 1933, the sole person to raise a voice in favor—if not of intervention—at least of lessening the restrictions these victims faced, was Labor Secretary Frances Perkins. On April 18, 1933, she pushed for an executive order from FDR to countermand President Herbert Hoover's 1930 order promulgating extensive use of a major technique for denying visas—that the applicant *might become* a "public charge." Strong—and effective—opposition followed from Secretary Hull and Under Secretary Phillps. It has also been written that a small coterie of anti-Semites in the State Department successfully fought against another idea favored by Mme. Perkins—filling the unused quota for German emigrants with German-Jewish refugees.

Such a mindset in the Department could be traced back even to before the restrictionists' victory in 1924 that clamped down on "non-Nordic" immigration into the U.S. East European Jews were among the main targets then, and apparently from 1933 on, so were German Jews. While charges of anti-Semitism have been made against top-ranking State Department officials like Wilbur J. Carr and William Phillips, many of the rank and file exhibited identical feelings, as characterized by a division officer, C. Paul Fletcher, who stated that when and if "ships begin to arrive in New York City laden with Jewish immigrants, the sleeping State Department would be blamed for betraying the interests of the United States."[5] Another staff person named Wilkinson expressed a common opinion among the WASP denizens of Foggy Bottom:

Experience has taught that Jews are persistent in their endeavors to obtain immigration visas, that Jews have a strong tendency—no matter where they are—to allege that they are the subjects of either religious or political persecution, that Jews have constantly endeavored to find means of entering the U.S. despite the barriers set up by our immigration laws.[6]

One could say, then, the die had been cast as soon as the Nazis began their persecutions. In 1933, certainly, nobody could discern that all of this was headed one day towards Auschwitz. Most assuredly, FDR had far more pressing matters on his plate, and he could smugly bask in the knowledge that fifteen percent of his appointees were Jewish-Americans. No other president had even come close.

As with the proverbial frog in the slowly heating pot, the temperature rose against the Jews in Germany in the 1930s but was greeted at first without undue alarm. In 1935, after the Nuremberg laws went into effect, Jewish leaders tried to enlist James G. McDonald, an ex-Indiana University professor who had just resigned as the League of Nations High Commissioner for Refugees, to use his influence with President Roosevelt to do something. McDonald's diaries relate a woeful story of failed effort after failed effort to mobilize support, not just with FDR, but even among well-to-do Jews all over the world.

By the onset of 1938, Franklin Roosevelt at last felt a need to bestir himself on this issue. After Hitler's absorption of Austria, he called for an international conference on the refugee situation and had his State Department organize one in July 1938. The site chosen was a resort town in eastern France, the famous Evian-les-Bains, noted for its curative (and bottled) waters. There, on the French shore of Lake Geneva, in the spa's glitziest hotel, *Le Royal*, delegates assembled from thirty-two countries and observers from twenty-four volunteer organizations. Despite American sponsorship, no big names from Washington were included, and the U.S. delegation was headed by a friend of FDR's, businessman Myron C. Taylor. His title was Ambassador on a Special Mission, much like Long's official nomenclature in South America. After nine days of debate, everyone packed up and left, essentially having done nothing.

A novel later written by one of the attendees, a Hungarian journalist with the German pen name of Hans Habe, caught well the spirit of hopelessness that pervaded this lovely setting. The book was called *The Mission*,[7] and its tragic central character was based on a real-life person at Evian, a Viennese Jew, Dr. Heinrich Von Neumann (in the book he was Heinrich Von Benda), sent by the Nazis to pull off a diabolical deal. It was nothing less than ransoming forty thousand Jews for a blackmail price of $2,500 per person. No Surprise—there were no takers, and the exultant Nazis crowed: *See, no one wants to take Jews off our hands.* Actually,

Hitler expressed it as, "See, anti-Semitism is merely a matter of degree." The sense of prevalent despair was well characterized by author Habe when his hero was told towards the end of the proceedings, "perhaps tomorrow 32 lifeboats would put out to sea again, without having taken a single shipwrecked person aboard."[8] The novel also quotes a Munich newspaper article that ended with,

> If they care so much about the Jews in Germany, they can have them. We shall be glad to get rid of them and won't ask anything in return.[9]

Unfortunately, no nation really came forward.

Nazi mouthpieces openly gloated over the fact the delegates even failed to pass a resolution condemning German treatment of the Jews. Moreover some delegates did nothing to hide their own anti-Semitic sentiments. Prominent among them was the chief of the Swiss federal police, Dr. Heinrich H. Rothmund, who defiantly stated:

> Switzerland, which has as little use for the Jews as Nazi Germany, will herself take measures to protect Switzerland from being swamped by Jews with the connivance of the Viennese police.

Three years earlier, High Commissioner McDonald had met with Rothmund and, no doubt, received a preview of such views. The following year, he entered the very inner sanctum of those directing the German handling of the Jews and met with SS leaders Heinrich Himmler and Reinhard Heydrich, the future architects of the Final Solution. At that point in time—1936—the Nazi goal was still simply to force all Jews into exile, and McDonald was received by them because his mission was "specifically to give help to the Jews of Germany to assist them in leaving Germany."

McDonald has given an impression of these two men, who in time were to become among history's worst mass murderers. Himmler, he wrote,

> at first glance appeared to be like a title searcher in the office of the Recorder of Deeds of a country county seat. No pomp, etc. He sat there with three SS officers around him, but those eyes of his, those beady, button eyes, cruel as he was cunning, cunning as he was cruel.[10]

Conversely, Heydrich struck McDonald as having the makings of a great tackle on a professional football team. "He was a blond gorilla, big shoulders, long arms, powerful legs."[11]

McDonald, who had also had a meeting with Hitler and experienced his ranting on the *Jewish Question*, was to become the chair of FDR's Advisory Committee on Refugees. In the run-up to the Evian Conference, this group and the State Department locked horns, with the latter entity enforcing its position that the U.S. Government would not participate in any emigration or settlement projects.

The "high point" of the Evian Conference, as McDonald put it, was an offer by Dominican Republic dictator Rafael Trujillo to take in one hundred thousand refugees and the "low point," the refusal of Central American republics to accept "traders or intellectuals." In any case, very few refugees were to go to these nations.

What was posited to be a helpful accomplishment was the agreement to create an Intergovernmental Committee on Governmental Refugees, whose initial chairman was the Washington lawyer George Rublee, the first graduate of Groton, FDR's prep school alma mater. Its usefulness, too, proved illusory.

A reviewer of Hans Habe's book expressed the feeling in sardonic terms: "The figure of Habe's protagonist . . . is so overwhelmed with the mantle of tragedy that his death, of a heart attack in the train bearing him back to occupied Vienna, comes as a kind of comic relief."[12]

One of the few outspoken voices to be heard at Evian was that of the delegate from Colombia, Professor J. M. Yepes, and he referred to the Evian Conference as a "modern Wailing Wall." More importantly, he put his finger on what the Nazis were doing and its deleterious effect on all countries.

> Can a State without upsetting the bases of our civilization, and indeed of all civilization, arbitrarily withdraw nationality from a whole class of its citizens, thereby making them stateless . . . ? Can a State, acting in this way, flood other countries with citizens of whom it wishes to get rid of and can it thrust upon others the consequences of an evil policy?

That there was to be no answer until World War II, underscored the futility of those efforts of FDR in the summer of 1938—a *quasi-fiasco* that dovetailed logically into Munich, the Sudeten takeover, and *Kristallnacht*.

Incidentally, one of the observers at the event was Golda Meir, representing the *Yishuv*, the Jewish population of Palestine, and one can well imagine the future prime minister of Israel's frustration.

Once the world had been jolted by the German barbarity of *Kristallnacht*, Roosevelt knew he had to do something else. Unfortunately, the only act that seemed available to him was another mere gesture. He recalled Hugh Wilson, the U.S. ambassador from Berlin. Nor would the U.S. be represented again in Germany by a full-fledged ambassador until 1955.

Meanwhile, one American did have hopes that he would be picked to succeed Hugh Wilson.

Lest we forget, by November 1938, Breckinridge Long still hadn't landed a permanent position at the U.S. State Department. There is no indication he had ever been involved with refugees, Jewish or non-Jewish. The closest he had come was to deliver Brazilian Foreign Minister Aranha's warning letter to the president. On *Kristallnacht* itself, he was actually sailing home from his South American goodwill trip.

In the new year, 1939, still job hunting, Breck was encouraged by a conversation with Sumner Welles in which he'd been told the president did now want him to reactivate the ambassadorship in Germany. Until then, the U.S. was merely represented in the Berlin embassy by a lower-level chargé d'affaires, in this case the highly competent Alexander Kirk. Welles told Long that Hugh Wilson would be sent to Chile as ambassador, but the reassignment would not occur for several months. Soon, however, Breck reported a new complication. The Chile post was going instead to Claude Bowers, who had been the envoy to the now defunct Spanish Republic, and Hugh Wilson was consequently slated for Canada, since the Ottawa embassy was due for a change. Yet ever hopeful, Long had actually begun taking German lessons. At a British embassy reception in June 1939, on the occasion of the English king and queen's famous visit to the U.S., Breck talked with Jimmy Roosevelt, who thought the German ambassadorship would happen for the Missourian in September.

On the first of September 1939, World War II broke out, following Hitler's surprise invasion of Poland. The Roosevelt administration, if it *had* intended to have Breckinridge Long in Berlin, suddenly had a different plan for him.

On the second of September, Long was summoned to the State Department. There, he met with Sumner Welles and George Messersmith. They asked him to take charge of a special division being created at the State Department to deal with the emergencies caused by the outbreak of war. Primarily, this would involve repatriating Americans caught in the war zones and providing relief for them until they could be transported home. Associated in this effort was ex-Ambassador Hugh Wilson, to serve as Breck's assistant, and former Consul General George Brandt, who had been part of the American delegation at Evian, to act as the division's administrator. Welles told Breck there was no longer any question of his being ambassador to Germany, since there would be no ambassador to the Hitler regime for the foreseeable future. To emphasize the fact, Hugh Wilson officially resigned as the ambassador to Germany.

The "establishment of a new division in the Department" to bring Americans abroad to safety had been in preparation for more than three years, under the supervision of Assistant Secretary of State George Messersmith. It was ready to go into operation by the onset of the Munich negotiations. So immediately following the announcement of his appointment, Breckinridge Long lost no time getting to work.

In response to a querying memo from the president, he started his report to FDR: "We have warned all Americans out of the Balkan countries, as well as Turkey, Palestine, Egypt and the North African coast . . . Those in Tunisia and points west to go to Casablanca in Morocco, which is accessible by motor and rail," with one American ship already there and another on the way. Genoa, Italy, was the rendezvous for Americans in Switzerland, Yugoslavia, Hungary and Italy. "The *Washington* sailed from Genoa yesterday with 1,076 passengers . . . We are waiting to hear from Pell" (Herbert Pell, a State Department staffer who was the father of Rhode Island Senator Claiborne Pell) at Lisbon in order to ascertain how many Americans needed evacuation. The *Washington* was scheduled to reach Gibraltar the next day and, if necessary, could go to the Portuguese capital. Another U.S. ship, the *Manhattan*, was heading east and could be diverted to Lisbon also, if war broke out in the Mediterranean, and "perhaps proceed to Bilbao (Spain) and pick up Americans warned out of England and France and who are collecting in the neighborhood of Bordeaux." If Italy joined the war and Genoa was closed, the Americans directed there would have to go to Bordeaux. This would cause problems for Americans in Greece, Bulgaria, Rumania, and Turkey, but there were American ships currently in the eastern Mediterranean. They could pick up passengers at Piraeus (Greece), and Tel Aviv and Jaffa (Palestine).

Stating that some people always ignore warnings, Breck added that contingencies would be made for them to exit Europe through Vladivostok, and the same would be true for Americans in Sweden.

"We have communicated to Kennedy [U.S. ambassador in London], and Grey in Dublin your desires about Bantry Bay. As you know, Kennedy wired that Ireland may be a trouble spot . . . But Bantry Bay may be the best evacuation spot."

The undated communication was signed, "Faithfully yours, Breckinridge Long."

His *new career* at the State Department had begun in earnest.

Chapter Sixteen

War and Return to Service

WOULD THAT A TOCSIN MIGHT sound now. Or Shakespearean weird sisters appear, gazing into a steaming cauldron and cackling dire forecasts. Or a chorus of Athenian alarms erupt . . . some notice of dramatic warning prefacing the protagonist's first step onto a fatal path about to lead him ineluctably, impelled by an innate flaw, towards—what else but tragedy!

Had Breckinridge Long received another ambassadorship prior to September 1939, would his doleful record during World War II have been entirely different?

As things stood, the specialized task that Breckinridge Long now oversaw of repatriating Americans from the war zones was "right up his alley." It was busy work with a sense of urgency, demanding certain kinds of fussiness in attention to detail, the type of thing—making arrangements—that had absorbed so much of his time as third assistant secretary of state throughout World War I. His private wealth also helped when he waded into the troubleshooting he had to do. Paying ship owners for the loan of their private vessels was an initial problem, and on the first of the commandeered vessels, The *Orizaba*, Long had to guarantee a $50,000 fee, saying he'd back it up with his own funds if the State Department balked.

Having ironed out problems of "jurisdiction, authority and funds" to move ships to their destinations, he was also forced to deal with labor troubles—American sailors calling for bonuses and forty percent wage increases and life insurance carrying $25,000 premiums. He called these demands essentially a *strike*, with five American ships tied up at docks. There was also further anger on his part towards Ambassador William Bullitt in France, who refused to ask the French not to intern sailors of foreign ancestry on American ships as enemy aliens, plus resentment over the explosive Ambassador Joseph Kennedy in England, who was screaming about getting Americans out of Great Britain.

His second day on the job, the sinking of the SS *Athenia*, a 14,000 ton British ocean liner, became Breck's first big crisis. This ship, which had 1,104 persons on board, 300 of them Americans, was torpedoed by a U-Boat 250 miles off the coast of Ireland. Only 112 passengers and crew were lost, including 28 Americans. The rescue of the others occurred in good order, despite the attack's having been carried out with no warning.

In record speed, Breck Long soon had 20,000 berths available for transporting his fellow countrymen and possibly did not feel he needed ad hoc suggestions from other cabinet members, such as Treasury Secretary Henry Morgenthau Jr. In his diary, he complained, "Morgenthau threw a bomb into the Cabinet Session by proposing we take over the *Normandie* [a French luxury liner] and the *Queen Mary* [a British luxury liner] now in our ports and charge it up to their war debt to operate these ships."[1]

By the beginning of October, Long could report 50,000 Americans had returned, and his division had enough boats to accommodate all who wanted to be repatriated. Some boats had not been fully utilized, and Breck blamed his two *bête noires*, Ambassadors Kennedy and Bullitt, for saying they were "unsafe," although certified by the Maritime Commission. Simultaneously, Breck was taking part in various ancillary discussions at the State Department, especially what to do about various U.S. consulates abroad. These were ticklish problems he aired in the following diary entry on the subject.

Some like Stuttgart have to be abandoned temporarily. Some like Calais might be abandoned except that there is a Negro consul there and we don't know what to do with him if we take him out of Calais . . . also problems in Tallinn [the capital of Estonia] where some of the clerks are White Russians who may be killed if the Russians occupy Estonia.[2]

At the end of October, Special Division Director Breckinridge Long could affirm that 75,000 Americans were home safe and sound.

Breck was already receiving hints that FDR wanted to talk to him about something. Dreams of an important posting overseas were back in his mind—ambassador to Germany? And if that post were not to be reinstated, Belgium was a possibility and itself a highly prestigious diplomatic plum.

At this juncture, the Nazis' conduct towards the Jewish citizens of their country and the refugee problem thus deliberately created did not figure in Breckinridge Long's diaries. His feelings towards Jews, whatever they were, did not go into his writings, except for his closeness to "Bernie" Baruch.

But in describing a group formed to raise funds for an FDR library at Hyde Park, a number of prominent Jewish Democrats were mentioned as participants. "Uncle" Henry Morgenthau Sr. was one of the speakers. "I had not seen him in years," Breck wrote. "We had a nice chat and sat in the café a while after adjournment." Another old friend there whom he had not seen for years was Felix Frankfurter, and the Supreme Court justice was "most effusive," according to Breck. "He wanted me to say 'Felix,' not 'Mr. Justice'—but I told him I could only do that in private." Without comment of any kind, Long mentioned he sat near well-known Jews closely attached to FDR—Sam Rosenman, Donald Richberg, and Sol Rosenblatt. A final report of that evening included an excerpt from the Morgenthau speech, how the old gentleman had "predicated his remarks in support of the project upon the great championship of the President for the Jews, although he did not use the noun. He simply referred to them as 'the oppressed people.'"[3] During other dinners for the Library attended by Long, more Jewish supporters were cited, including Sidney Weinberg, Nathan Straus Jr., Lewis Rosenstiel, and one of the few Jewish diplomats in the State Department, Laurence Steinhardt, with whom Long would become quite chummy in future years.

A further reference to Jews that he recorded occurred amidst a conversation he had with Jim Farley, who was contemplating a run for president in 1940, if Roosevelt did not go for a third term. The New Yorker was arguing with Breck that his Catholicism wouldn't hurt him in the way it had hurt Al Smith. His thesis was that religious prejudice in the U.S. had been softened due to what was happening in Germany, and "the sympathy expressed in America for the persecuted Jews." Yet Breck strongly disagreed, saying,

> On the contrary, I begin to feel that intolerance, particularly as regards the Jews and secondarily as regards the Catholics will develop and be more strong than it is today . . . I am sorry to feel so but I do.[4]

Before he had any promise from the administration of a more permanent job, Long did append a diary notation that "England published a White Paper this morning on the treatment of Jews by Germany in internment camps, a very bad picture." This White Paper was not to be confused with another from His Majesty's Government about six months earlier—the infamous White Paper that repudiated Great Britain's promise to create a Jewish homeland in Palestine and severely restricted Jewish immigration into the Mandated Territory England held.

Was Breckinridge Long guessing the problem of Jewish escape from the Nazis might be his responsibility in whatever new position they gave him? The issue was growing hotter all the time. The Evian Conference had garnered considerable press. *Kristallnacht* even more. The past spring and summer of 1939 had seen the saga of the *St. Louis*, a German ship full of German Jewish refugees bound for Cuba and, while once docked in Havana harbor, prevented from landing these refugees, who all had legitimate Cuban documents—quite probably because not a big enough bribe was being paid to the Cuban president. They were sent back to Germany and also refused admittance to the U.S., and in the end, allowed into countries like France that were later invaded by the Germans. About half of these people were to perish in the death camps.

Was Breckinridge Long involved at all in the *St. Louis* episode? Did he find it incongruous that the foreign vessel should bear the name of his hometown? This "Voyage of the Damned" still reverberates to this day. But at the time, Long had not even been offered his later post at the State Department.

In November 1939, while his stint at the Special Division for repatriating Americans was winding down, he did write about aspects of the refugee problem that had entered the task of rescuing his countrymen, declaring, "I am still wrestling with pressure from persons who want the State Department to act on behalf of non-Americans to obtain the release of their friends or relatives abroad." His adamant position on that score was he would only act on behalf of American citizens. One of his superiors, Judge R. Walton Moore, the legal counsel of the Department, actually sent him a memo to take positive not negative action on a certain case, but Long sent it back "through Messersmith, who promised to support my position."5

One Jewish refugee he did go to bat for, albeit halfheartedly, was Madame Margherita Sarfatti, Mussolini's ex-mistress, with whom he had been so friendly in Rome. Currently, she was living in exile in France. He explained she was

now forced to accept her own decision that she can no longer live in Italy because she has some Jewish blood . . . despite her position as a pioneer founder of Fascism and one of its ablest exponents.[6]

Long asked Bernie Baruch to find her a job in the U.S.

Through Baruch, too, Breck at the end of October 1939 received two memoranda—written by a man named C. J. Gass—and these had to do with

> the whole program of visas from abroad, very careful inspection upon immigration, history of persons coming into the country, inspection of ships . . . examinations of the memberships of crews of ingoing and outgoing ships, etc.[7]

Possibly, since he was a confidant of FDR's, Baruch knew something of what was in store for Breckinridge Long and that the information from Gass might be useful to him eventually.

Less than two months afterward, this hint of prophecy became a reality for Long. Secretary of State Hull called him into his office and asked him—nay, really told him—that it was the president's wish and his own for Long to become an assistant secretary of state.

Whether the courtly Tennessean added *once again* is unlikely. It would have occurred to Hull, as it most certainly did to Breck Long, here was the same position, if altered in its duties, held by him almost a quarter of a century earlier.

The new job, it was made plain to Breck, was no longer mainly ceremonial, as it had been during his first assistant secretaryship. In essence, he would be the State Department's administrator, taking over the work that George Messersmith had been handling. The former consul general in Berlin was to become an *ambassador*—crossing the line that Wilbur J. Carr had fought so hard to erase. The Department was sending him as the top envoy to Cuba.

George Messersmith, it must be said, was a complex individual. Everyone agreed that while he was the consul general in Germany during Hitler's rise to power, he was the most vocal anti-Nazi in the American diplomatic service. In 1937 he was brought back to Washington to handle the administrative duties of running the State Department. Supreme Court Justice Louis Brandeis remarked that he was the Jews' "only actual friend among the higher-ups at the State Department." But Messersmith's biographer Jesse Stiller, to round out the picture of this Pennsylvania Dutch country boy, added:

His visceral Americanism, source of much that was admirable in him, had a selfish side that favored selective immigration policies even in good times . . . Applicants for visas at the Berlin consulate general during his tenure found abundant sympathy and no disposition whatever to bend the rules in their favor.[8]

Moreover, during the short period he held his administrative position in DC, he proved to be a *tiger* at fighting every effort to loosen the restrictions on allowing those fleeing Hitlerian persecution to enter the U.S. When Labor Secretary Frances Perkins said it would be possible to ease a Hoover area requirement that two affidavits were needed to vouch for each refugee, Messersmith countered that the move would cause "a storm of protest." Equally insistent, he called her plan illegal to extend visas for German Jews in the U.S. so they wouldn't have to go back to Nazi Germany, but he was overruled by FDR. Nevertheless, he kept loudly insisting members of Congress were telling him that any attempts to increase quotas would result in existing quotas being cut and he used this argument to try to dissuade James G. McDonald and the President's Advisory Committee from asking for a legislative increase.

One might sum up Messersmith's attitude by quoting several excerpts from a letter he wrote to John Wiley, the American consul in Vienna:

> I have had some of the most extraordinary letters from professors and others who seem to be very resentful that we are not giving them on a golden platter a position which native-born Americans would be glad to get at the end of a long and hard fought career . . . I get other letters from persons who have been admitted into this country and who are not yet American citizens who tell us just how we ought to run the country, how we ought to change our laws and what we owe to the rest of the world . . . I am glad to say that the country still belongs to native-born Americans and I am hopeful that the ideals of our native-born Americans may continue to control.[9]

No doubt Messersmith's complaint about the *arrogance* and/or *ingratitude* of people the U.S. *did* save would have found favor with most of the State Department personnel. Although never publicly voiced in a similar manner by Breckinridge Long, he must have acquiesced in such feelings while speaking privately to the man he was to replace. In departing, Messersmith openly announced that he considered Breck

Long to be "one of the finest men that I know and that if I could have selected my own successor (he *had* recommended the Missourian to his superiors) I could not have chosen one in whom I have more confidence."[10]

Yet Messersmith's letter to Consul Wiley ended with a seemingly contradictory nod to his sympathy for the German-Jewish victims. "It is really unspeakable what Germany is doing to these people," which was followed by his own thoughts on a solution: "I am one of those who believe that this movement toward discrimination will not be eliminated until the regime in Germany is eliminated."[11]

When Messersmith made this statement, the U.S. was not at war with Hitler's Third Reich. Once we were in the war, the theme became official policy—i.e., that the only salvation for the Jews trapped in Nazi-occupied Europe was for the Allies to win the war. Over and over again, this mantra was used to avoid any direct rescue action.

Long took his time before agreeing to accept the post. He spoke first with Messersmith, expressing his need, if he did agree, to retain the services of his faithful secretary, Miss Winifred Aderton, who had been with him since his international law days. "No problem," Messersmith assured Breck. He would arrange to have Miss Aderton transferred from the Special Division, where she'd been working for Long, and in addition the new assistant secretary of state would have a bigger and better office. A talk with Sumner Welles added another dimension to this new job. Long's political experience and contacts would be of great service to the Department. Breck was told he would be an ideal lobbyist to help Cordell Hull get his beloved reciprocal trade agreements approved by Congress. Under Secretary Welles confided that "the Skipper," FDR, was not going to run for president in 1940, that he, himself, would back Hull's nomination and that the successful passage of the trade agreements were essential to Hull's campaign. A veteran politico like Breck Long could readily see that staying in Hull's good graces might pay enormous benefits for his own future.

Long mused to himself in his diary, "So it looks like I was to stay here. I would love to be in Berlin [as ambassador to Germany]. But I will stay here and do a work which is new to me."[12]

Still, on December 19, 1939, a frank discussion with Hull let both men put their cards on the table. Long asked for more time to think over their job offer, stating his fear of so many duties and areas unfamiliar to him, such as economics and finances, and that it would "exclude him from actual participation in the field of foreign affairs [i.e., an ambassadorship again]," while Hull circumspectly alluded to possible future rewards if he pleased his superiors by accepting. Long wrote of Hull:

> He was friendly and in every way indicated the placing of entire confidence. He did not urge me to do it. He said do what I thought and what I wanted but hoped I would understand they all really hoped I would.[13]

Although Breck Long had written after his initial discussions with Hull, Welles and Messersmith, "They wanted me. He [Hull] made that emphatic. Would I? Of course, I would do whatever they wanted. This was no time to pursue pet ambitions,"[14] he could not refrain from adding a wry comment of, "I had never considered returning to the status I occupied 25 years ago."

Nevertheless, on December 21, 1939, Breck laconically wrote: "Saw Hull and agreed to accept." Having already gone right to work on his boss's highest priority, he added he'd been in touch with Speaker of the House William Bankhead about the trade agreements issue.

Note there was no mention here of visas, immigrants or refugees. An impression has been left by the emphasis of various writers that Breck Long's sole responsibility in his wartime job at State was dealing with Jews, inferring, too, that he sought out this duty due to his innate anti-Semitism as the place where he could do the most harm to the objects of his bias.

In point of fact, except for the consular service, the Department of State did not at this time (December 1939 to January 1940) have jurisdiction over immigration as such. That responsibility still lay with the Department of Labor and its liberal-minded secretary, Frances Perkins. As much as she could, until the Immigration Bureau was stripped from her Department, Madam Secretary served as a foil to the prevailing State Department ethos of clamping down on *undesirable immigration*, which had always included scruffy, poverty-stricken Eastern European Jews but now, after 1933, extended to highly cultivated once-rich German Jews, like my father-in-law, robbed of their wealth by the Nazis.

Such a course, even under Cordell Hull, had actually been articulated by one of the careerists at the State Department with the very striped pants name of Jay Pierrepont Moffat. This was back in September 1933 when the German-Jewish problem was just beginning. The thesis of his memo, written in collaboration with the Department's Legal Advisor

Green H. Hackworth, was that if they did anything for these persecuted people, it would

reverse the policy for which we have fought for twelve years.[15]

In other words, undo all their restrictionist work contained in the Johnson-Reed law. It was something they absolutely couldn't allow to happen. Those quotas were set in stone.

Six years later, with the European refugee problem worsening every day, the baton was being handed on—inside the State Department's quarters—as if on a relay. It had been passed from Wilbur J. Carr to Jay Pierrepont Moffat to William Phillips to George Messersmith and now finally, in full confidence, put into the grip of the new guy on the block, Breckinridge Long.

Chapter Seventeen

Assistant Secretary of State Again

I T WAS ONLY IN THE new year, 1940, that Breckinridge Long was confirmed for his second try at the job of assistant secretary of state. The press had published a notice on January 2, 1940, about his appointment but without official confirmation from the Roosevelt administration. Actually, Breck did not take the oath of office until three weeks later, January 23, while his diary shows he had already begun working on State Department business at Congress, especially on Hull's trade agreements. Some senators, he discovered, were miffed these negotiated deals could only be treated like legislation and not treaties, which would require a two-thirds favorable vote. To counter an adverse position taken by William Green, president of the American Federation of Labor, Long brought in Dan Tobin, head of the Teamsters Union, the AF of L's largest member, and won his loud and enthusiastic support.

So far, at least as documented in his published *War Diary*,[1] Long had not encountered the refugee problem, nor was he to mention the subject specifically until *May 8, 1940*.

This was two days after the Nazis' surprise takeover of Norway and Denmark and two days before Breck stayed up all night with Hull, Welles, Moffat, and other State Department officials, as the Nazi war machine continued its rampage, invading the neutral Low Countries and outflanking France's highly touted but ultimately ineffectual Maginot Line defense.

The May 8 concern with refugees started with Long's own statement:

At the request of the President, Welles called in a few of us this morning to consider ways and means of preventing the further inflow of German and Russian propagandists and agents and of attempting to attend to those who had filtered through.[2]

Paranoia was running high. The swift success of the Germans' spring offensive was attributed to the diabolically clever actions of Nazi "fifth columnists," who borrowed a term from the Spanish Civil War, and who had infiltrated the ranks of the European democracies. Long insisted that among the sixteen thousand aliens in the U.S. who had forfeited their bonds were a number of known German agents. "The Department of Labor is very non-cooperative," he complained. State's visa section and Passport Division and the FBI were working together splendidly, but Frances Perkins's crew at Labor had offered no help, except through the commissioner of immigration, who was sympathetic. This official, by the way, was James H. Houghteling, married to President Roosevelt's cousin, the former Elizabeth Delano, who was an active member of the Daughters of the American Revolution and highly outspoken about her anti-immigrant and anti-refugee sentiments.

Mrs. Houghteling, incidentally, had earned some notoriety during the debate in Congress from February to June 1939 (before Breckinridge Long was back in the State Department) over a bill that would have allowed twenty thousand Jewish children from Germany to come to the U.S. outside the quota. This was the Wagner-Rogers Bill, cosponsored by Senator Robert Wagner (D), of New York and Congresswoman Edith Nourse Rogers (R) of Massachusetts. Elizabeth Delano Houghteling's contribution to the fierce opposition that kept the bill from even getting out of committee was to make the snotty point that "20,000 charming children would grow up to become 20,000 ugly adults."

In this same diary excerpt attacking the Labor Department, Long introduced the name of Avra Warren, the man in charge of the visa section, who was just as prejudiced if not as vocal as Mrs. Houghteling. Long claimed he *had* given this matter "considerable attention for three or four months but very little of it comes under my jurisdiction." Well aware of the Soviet-Nazi pact of August 1939 and the apparent cooperation between these two dictators, he opined that "if we have any trouble with Germany every Russian agent will become a German agent"[3]—a doubtful thesis but one on which he would later seek to act.

During this hectic period, Long had an interesting head-to-head conversation with Cordell Hull that had nothing to do with the dramatic and disturbing events in Europe. As Breck wrote on May 10, 1940, Cordell (as he called him)

took the opportunity that was afforded by the absence of other ranking officers from the Department to revert to the political aspect, which has recently invested his prospects for the Presidency with real importance. It has developed to the point where he now recognizes that there is a practical unanimity of unofficial agreement upon him to be nominated in case Roosevelt is not.[4]

If Breck needed any further stimulus, in addition to his own predilection, for adopting the State Department view on "aliens" coming to the U.S., this would have been it. Play ball with Cordell Hull . . . he was now very possibly destined for higher office. Rise with him.

Avra Warren had already been set in motion. According to Long, he was preparing a letter and memo "making certain proposals for additional legislation so as to authorize a more strict control. We used the word 'supervisor' instead of 'control.'"

At the same time, Avra's boss was writing a letter of his own, but for Hull's signature, telling FDR that even the legislation they wanted wouldn't be enough, and neither would the administrative changes they had requested. There were two more "important elements." They were informing the president of the need for "concentration in an official of authority" (could that be Breckinridge Long?) and dealing with "the lack of coordination among the interested Departments." Then followed another slam at the Labor Department and another harangue about espionage on the part of Germany and Russia.

By May 13, 1940, the assistant secretary was reporting in his diary that there was "more talk about an influx of aliens" and that Avra Warren's "long report, which has my entire approval," had been sent to FDR, who had approved it but with one exception. As Breck told it, "he wants the Bureau of Immigration taken out of Labor and put in Justice."[5] Breck left unanswered the surmise that Avra Warren might have originally suggested the Bureau of Immigration should be transferred to the State Department.

Let loose on *aliens*, Breck and his cohorts swung into action. Claiming that "'our big ships' sailing to the Mediterranean were so booked up with foreigners proceeding to the U.S." that Americans seeking to escape the war zone were finding it hard to leave, Long sought a legal way to cancel those passages,[6] but was having a hard time finding the authority to do so. Undiscouraged, he began pushing for a bill to *register* all aliens in the country and all aliens in the future, making them report regularly and be subject to deportation if "illegally entering or illegally overstaying." He talked about having visa control shifted to Washington, DC and taken out of the hands of the consuls overseas—gave a grudging nod to the

Constitution and declared, "It is a necessary requirement that we have authority to handle any 'fourth army' or 'fifth army' there may be in the United States."[7]

In an attempt to lighten the atmosphere in this time of crisis, Long told officials at Hull's meeting about a bit of real-life comedy that had occurred at the American consulate in Salvador, Bahia, Brazil. The vice consul, it seems, had been gambling heavily, borrowing money from a fellow American, bouncing his check to pay the debt back, then had the consul lend him the same sum, which was placed in a safe at the consulate, only to have it stolen by the very vice consul who, when caught, jumped in a nearby river and unsuccessfully tried to drown himself. Then the consul learned that an Englishman had tried to rape his wife and threatened the offender with physical harm, when it was discovered that the consul himself had been trifling with the wife of a local Brazilian resident. This charge was followed by the accusation of another Englishman that the consul had been after his wife and that if he met the consul he would "dispose of him immediately."[8]

Breck Long ended by suggesting, tongue-in-cheek, that "when the file is complete . . . the papers all be sent to me and I would bundle them up and send them to Hollywood where it would form the basis for a most interesting melodrama."

Another tale out of the State Department occurred about this time that proved anything but amusing. It was an out-and-out case of espionage at the London embassy, called "one of the most serious breaches of security in World War II," and the culprit was neither an alien nor a refugee nor a blackmailed Jew in exile, but a WASP of impeccable credentials from an old Virginia family whose father had been a career Foreign Service officer. Young Tyler Kent, who had been recommended to the State Department by Senator Harry Byrd, had attended the prestigious St. Albans prep school in Washington, DC, and—this must have caused Breckinridge Long some heartburn—was a Princeton graduate. What Kent had done in London, after having been transferred there from Moscow with the blessing of Ambassador Laurence Steinhardt, was to steal top-secret documents and have them end up in the hands of the *Abwehr*, Hitler's primary intelligence agency. Among them were highly classified exchanges between Roosevelt and Winston Churchill, who had recently supplanted Neville Chamberlain as Great Britain's prime minister, and the necessity for keeping them under wraps was that they revealed Roosevelt's hush-hush efforts of violating the U.S. Neutrality Act in order to help the English resist the Nazis.

It was MI6, British intelligence, which arrested Kent while a no-doubt embarrassed U.S. State Department looked the other way. The apprehended spy received a seven-year prison sentence. Before his arrest, he had been notably active in a vocal anti-Semitic group led by a member of parliament. It is worth divulging that in his voluminous two volumes of memoirs, Cordell Hull never refers to this incident, but Breckinridge Long in his diaries does several times.

He apparently took no lesson from the fact that a Princetonian had betrayed the U.S., while he continued devising his plan for further and further restrictions on the refugee flow. "Supervision of aliens would be in a board consisting of State, Treasury, Justice, Post Office and one other agency he would name," he wrote on May 13, 1940. It would be "under the Chair of the representative of the Secretary of State." Guess who that was supposed to be.

In the next paragraph, he added some facts he had since learned about the "fifth columnist" apprehended in London, but again left out that the man was a Princeton grad.

On May 21, 1940, another step was taken towards the realization of Breckinridge Long's goals. The Bureau of Immigration was, by executive order of the president, removed from the Department of Labor and given to the Department of Justice. Under Secretary of State Sumner Welles had been pushing the move for several months, despite the opposition not only of Labor Secretary Frances Perkins but also of the Justice Department head, himself, Attorney General Robert Jackson. Perkins, who had survived an impeachment attempt by Congress because of her liberalism, was being strongly attacked for refusing to initiate a wholesale effort to fingerprint all aliens. Jackson merely didn't want the additional headache of dealing with immigration. Welles conceivably was trying to keep the government's entire immigration program from accruing to Breckinridge Long, whom he by now perhaps believed was after his own position.

Was Breckinridge Long, indeed, "empire building" right out of the gate? His energy, bordering on obsessive fanaticism vis-à-vis the refugee issue would have caught anybody's eye, certainly that of an experienced bureaucratic in-fighter like Sumner Welles, and the question would naturally arise: where did the Missourian think he was headed? Some historians have attributed Long's zeal to pure anti-Semitism. Or was it pure self-serving? Or both?

With Frances Perkins out of the way, the fingerprinting of all aliens began under Attorney General Jackson and continued after he was elevated to the Supreme Court and replaced by Francis Biddle. FDR's political advisors saw the move as crucial to winning his third term 1940 campaign. Even Madam Secretary Perkins, who was unhappy to see immigration leave her shop, reconciled herself to the loss. As her most recent biographer Kirstin Downey has written, "With the world at war, she accepted FDR's decision and understood why the move was made."[9] Her enemies were pleased but still grumbled that Roosevelt should have fired Perkins at the same time.

Overseas, simultaneously, Long's efforts in the middle of 1940 were having a serious impact. Describing these deleterious results was an American Quaker woman named Margaret E. Jones, who was working with Europeans trying to emigrate to the U.S. Ms. Jones sent a memo to a fellow Quaker, Clarence E. Pickett, headed: "Visa Situation in Vienna," and she began it, using the Quaker form of address: "Because I am deeply disturbed over present visa difficulties in Vienna, I want thee to have this memorandum for thy information."

She proceeded to say how she had been trying to find out the reason for the recent orders from Washington to U.S. consulates to "severely limit the number of visas ordinarily issued month by month." Giving the State Department the benefit of the doubt, she had phrased her question in a way that could be favorable to this move, i.e., State was instituting the cut to forestall Congress from stopping all immigration. No answer was given her, and then in August, back in Vienna, she met with Avra Warren who'd been sent abroad to visit consulates. After telling her *no more aliens* would be coming to the U.S., he answered her particular question by saying "not Congress but the President just did not want any more aliens coming to the U.S. and would like to have it closed, especially for aliens from Germany." Slickly, he added that the State Department had "asked to be allowed to taper it [the total ban] off gradually and he, Warren, was touring Europe as far out as Moscow to check up with the consulates and to make plans accordingly." The motives he gave for this draconian action were familiar: "anti-Semitism in the U.S., refugees traced to fifth column activities, the need for more visas for the English." But his whole idea was that emigration for German Jews coming from Germany was practically finished."[10]

Warren's instructions, Ms. Jones elaborated, were that each candidate had to be evaluated by the criterion: "What outstanding contribution can he make to the U.S.A?" She detailed the incredible effort it took to get through the interview process at the consulates—the weeks it took, the expenditures in Deutschmarks it cost, getting two friends to say you were upright and not engaged in espionage, obtaining a police certificate, facing a board of consuls for questioning of forty minutes duration and having to speak to German employees of the consulate, probably members of the Gestapo on the lookout for anti-Nazi remarks, yet if you didn't express anti-Nazi sentiments, being taken for a fifth columnist.

Finally, Ms. Jones emphasized the *mental* suffering of those who had to go through this excruciating sieve, which under the new (Breckinridge Long) rules made acceptance well nigh impossible. She concluded: "We could alleviate a lot of mental suffering, of course, by restoring the normal visa program for the applicants in Germany."[11]

During those months of May and June 1940, Breckinridge Long had been a busy boy. His diary entries that late spring *were* dominated by the refugee issue. On June 29, 1940, he could write,

The cables practically stopping immigration went!

A notable break from Breck's obsession appeared on June 20 when he highlighted that "one pleasant occurrence" interrupting this workload was the victory of his horse Nasca in her first racing start. Not only could he savor his success as a racehorse owner but also enjoy the fact that Bernie Baruch, when told earlier in the day by Long that his mare would run, bet $50 on her. Other notables who profited were Steve Early, FDR's press secretary, who bet $10, and the president, himself, who bet $2. "They were all very happy," Long reported, "and I telegraphed Bernie back in New York that I was glad I could contribute to his expenses on his trip to Washington."

There had been zigs and zags for Breck on the way to his triumph in blocking aliens. On May 28, 1940, he openly voiced his fear the administration might be getting cold feet or, as he put it, "the President and the Cabinet are hesitating on the alien clampdown" and he added a complaint that his office could exclude from the country foreign *visitors* "who hold views inimical to the welfare of our country and government but we cannot do this for *immigrants*."

Long had a special bone to pick with William Bullitt, the American ambassador to now beleaguered France, as to who should be evacuated. Americans, of course, could come home, but Bullitt, a scandalized Long protested, "wanted alien nurses and maids" to accompany their employers. Also, former Americans who had married foreigners and lost their citizenship should be allowed to reclaim it, Bullitt insisted. No way, said Long, and he stated the general rules: American citizens first, but some provision made for alien members of their *immediate* family (no aunts or brothers, but solely fathers, mothers and children). Alien nurses would only be allowed in if it were a *medical necessity*. Otherwise, as Long declared: "Mothers can look after their own children and leave alien nurses there."

At the beginning of June, he was still working on tightening the regulations, drafting several executive orders for the president to issue and preparing "telegrams to restrict the granting of visas and to stop up the holes of unauthorized immigration into the U.S." He also mentioned that specific approval would be required for the entry of "any journalists of any category, lecturers, propagandists, etc."

The Tyler Kent case was commented upon again. Long now tried to turn it to his advantage, claiming that Kent must have had accomplices, moles in other embassies, so he was working out a system with military intelligence of infiltrating moles of their own, disguised as State Department couriers.

On June 22, 1940, Long joined Sumner Welles in meeting with the president's Advisory Committee on Refugees—the group with which Long was to lock horns in the future. The discussion he reported from this meeting concerned *political refugees*. A list had been sent from the Foreign Affairs Council of those who should be allowed into the United States; men like Manuel Azaña, the last president of the Spanish Republic before it succumbed to Franco, Count Carlo Sforza, the famed Italian anti-Fascist, and various professors, scientists, writers, etc, of note. The group settled on authorizing visas for those not "objectionable to the interests of this country." Breck Long showed his political colors in wanting to keep out Juan Negrin, the leftist former prime minister of Spain and "others of his ilk who want to go to Mexico—or other places where they can continue their activities possibly against this country."

In any case, his opinion about these anti-Nazis and anti-Fascists was that "the chances are they—or at most only a few—will not get away from the clutches of Hitler and Mussolini."*[12]

Long's apparent paranoia about spies slipping into the U.S. via the immigration route was such that he even wanted to go after individuals who had had the fortitude to get through the torturous process he'd

*Juan Negrin did get to Mexico; Manuel Azana died in France in November 1940; and Count Sforza spent three years in the U.S., 1940 to 1943, before going back to a distinguished career in liberated Italy.

devised and had received visas. On June 26, 1940, the day he sent out his messages shutting all doors, he nevertheless wrote:

> Discussed *further* restriction of immigration, including those who have visas. It is very apparent that the Germans are using visitor visas to send agents and documents through the United States.[13]

How real *was* his paranoia? As we have seen, he liked to play the political pundit and make prognostications. In his comments on the Tyler Kent espionage case, he could project a possible damaging political effect, writing,

> It is a terrible blow—almost a major catastrophe. No doubt the Germans will publish another White Book during our political campaign, which will have as its purpose the defeat of Roosevelt and the election of a ticket opposed to him and presumably in sympathy with Hitler—an appeasement ticket—an administration to succeed ours which will play ball with Germany or surrender America.[14]

Sounding anti-Axis to the core. Or was he? In almost the same breath, in June 1940 he would protest, following FDR's famous attack on Mussolini for invading France, that his boss shouldn't have used such a strong metaphor as, *the hand that held the dagger has struck it into the back of its neighbor.* According to Breck:

> In my opinion, we have gone a little farther than we should go not only in attacking the heads of other Governments but in making gestures to the Allies. If we are not very careful, we are going to find ourselves the champions of a defeated cause.

This remark can certainly be cited as pro-Axis—and has been.

The main factor, in any case, that does stand out about this man at this time was his visible hysteria and—if there is such a word—the "totalitarianizing" of his approach to the issue. Exhibit A is Long's behavior over the *Quanza* incident of September 1940.

In this instance, a Portuguese vessel, the *Quanza*, was carrying a shipload of Jewish refugees to Mexico. There were eighty-three of these asylum seekers on board, and all had transit visas into Mexico, for which they had paid $100 apiece. But as with the *St. Louis,* they were turned back and not allowed to land by local authorities. Once more, the spectacle of another "doomed voyage" appeared to be in the offing. Rejected at Vera Cruz, the Captain made for Nicaragua, but again their travel documents were not accepted, and so the ship with nowhere else to go headed back to Portugal.

Here is Breckinridge Long's view of this matter, as expressed in his diary.

> September 9, 1940—a refugee ship from Lisbon at Vera Cruz refused permission to land its passengers and putting in at Norfolk for coal on its way back to Portugal and the refugees want to land. Rabbi Wise pleads as many others do—Sol Bloom [Congressman and Chair of the House Foreign Affairs Committee] and many more—but to do so would be a violation of the spirit of the law if not the letter. We have been generous but there are limitations.[15]

On September 18, 1940, there was a further entry about this incident, and Breck was decidedly testy now in discussing what he called the "visit" of the *Quanza* to Norfolk, referring to the passengers—"They all were Jewish. They all had money," documenting how much they'd paid for the visas sold to them by South American and Central American consuls and huffily complaining about the ship that was proceeding "ostensibly for Portugal and then conveniently discovered that they would have to put in at Norfolk for fuel."

Breck goes on to write:

> I was flooded with pressure groups and telegrams and telephone and personal visits to permit the landing of the persons off the boat. I consistently declined to deviate from the procedure which we had adopted and said that the fact that the people were on the boat and were nearing the American shores did not constitute an emergency of any kind.[16]

Eleanor Roosevelt was one of those who telephoned Breckinridge Long and expressed particular concern about the children on board. Ultimately Long reached the president, who told him to call back the next day, by which time FDR would have returned to DC. Breck did, but commented that the president did not want to talk to him about this subject. The conclusion the assistant secretary drew was a no-brainer for him: "I inferred—and it now seems correctly—that he would leave the matter entirely within my hands."

But others were getting into the act. Patrick Malin, an employee of the President's Advisory Committee on Refugees, arrived in Norfolk. Still in force was an agreement Long had said he would honor of accepting this committee's recommendations to allow in *refugees in danger and leading intellectuals of the liberal movement in Europe*. What Breck finally said he would do was let off the boat anyone with authentic documents for the purpose of traveling through the United States to another destination.

No doubt, his thought had been that this very narrowly drawn concession would apply to only a small handful of the passengers, if even that.

Imagine his surprise, which turned to fury, when Patrick Malin phoned to say that he had found three children and two mothers and thirty-five persons in all who had valid travel documents to travel in the U.S., plus that everyone else on board was deemed a *political refugee* by the President's Advisory Committee and eligible for entry.

Breck Long's first response was to harrumph that this result "was due to a very generous interpretation of the validity of the documents" and that the inclusion of everyone else as a *political refugee* did not comply with the conditions he had agreed to accept.

Under Malin's interpretation, all eighty-three of the passengers were allowed in.

Breckinridge Long went ballistic and wrote,

> I remonstrated violently. Said that I thought it was a violation of the law, that it was not in accordance with my understanding with them, that it was not a proper interpretation of my agreement, that I could not be a party to it, that I will not give my consent to it, that I would not have any responsibility for it and that if they did it that I would have to take the matter up some other way.[17]

Hell hath no fury like a bureaucrat outflanked, one might say. In this case, Long's high dudgeon and fierce imprecations and threats got him nowhere. The *fix was in*, so to speak. Eleanor had gotten to Franklin this one time. FDR, it can be surmised, had a tough election coming up within less than two months. Here he was, running for a third term, against Wendell Willkie, a formidable opponent. He had taken a lot of grief for the *St. Louis* incident because he had declined to intervene. Let

Breck Long huff and puff—the president was a politician first and a past master at shifting strategies when convenient.

That it was Roosevelt who determined the *Quanza* outcome, there seems to be no doubt. Rabbi Stephen Wise stated definitively in a letter about the *Quanza* victory that "of course it could not have been done unless the Skipper had taken the needful step."[18]

Breckinridge Long didn't give up but set his sights on the President's Advisory Committee as target number one. After the *Quanza* denouement, he wrote to the president at the suggestion of Cordell Hull and

> asked his consent to a change in the procedure, which would place in our consuls abroad *rather than in the President's Advisory Committee* the final determination as to whether the person was entitled to entry to the U.S.

In this letter, he cited "generosity"—his term for the State Department's actions in bringing in "persons in imminent danger and rabbis and leaders of rabbinical schools and colleges and labor union leaders," as well as "certain individuals" guaranteed by McDonald's group. His next goal, he made it plain, now that the lists of rabbis and labor union leaders had been closed, was further to curb the President's Advisory Committee.

The die was cast on September 28, 1940, at a meeting of Long and Sumner Welles with James G. McDonald and his executive director, George Warren. Long was quite blunt in his description of this confrontation.

> McDonald is very wroth at the limitations upon the activities of his committee, which where set out in a letter sent to him by the Secretary [Hull]. He looks upon me as an obstructionist and was very bitter and somewhat denunciatory. There were a few warm words between us.

Yet Breck claimed they got things straightened out, although ended by saying McDonald planned to speak to the president. And he wrote:

> In the meantime, I am tightening up on immigrants and visitors. I have the support of the Attorney-General [Robert Jackson] but not the support I would like from some of his subordinates.

Long called them too soft-hearted and sympathetic to refugees. By the beginning of October, he was asking Jackson to close a loophole in the law that didn't allow those on permanent visas, as opposed to temporary visas, to be deported if deemed a risk to public safety.

A talk with FDR a few days later brought another diatribe against McDonald, who Long claimed

> has developed a very definite and violent antagonism to me . . .
> In a recent conversation in Mr. Welles' office, he indicated that he had a superlative ego and a vindicative [*sic*] mentality added to his disregard, to put it lightly, of me.

Later, in October, Breckinridge Long's stubbornness and single-mindedness seemed to be paying off for him. After a meeting with FDR, he could declare: "I left him with the satisfactory thought that he was wholeheartedly in support of the policy which resolves in favor of the U.S. any doubts about admissibility of any individual." Furthermore, Breck was almost gleeful in describing a "dressing down" that FDR gave to McDonald, breaking in when the chair of the Advisory Committee criticized Assistant Secretary Long, saying, "Don't pull any sob stuff on me" and that he wouldn't have anyone admitted to the U.S. by any organization—Rabbi Wise or McDonald or William Green [of the AFof L] and that "any person not seen by a consul would not be admitted."

This last admonition was subsequently carried out in an agreement between Long, Welles and Francis Biddle, the new attorney general, stating that consuls had full authority to withhold visas, even if the President's Advisory Committee recommended that person.

One secret to Long's successful counterattack could be seen as due to the fact that since this was an election year, the Missourian's Democratic bona fides—and cash—still gave him more clout than the ordinary bureaucrat. He went to the Democratic Convention and saw FDR re-nominated by acclamation. He visited campaign headquarters and financially contributed.

So, once the third term was assured, Breck found himself in a strong position, although there were still challenges to his authority ahead.

Chapter Eighteen

Further Tightening the Screws on Refugees

H AROLD L. ICKES, FDR'S SECRETARY of the interior, was soon to be the next bane of Breckinridge Long's existence in the latter's attempt to achieve a total blockage of "aliens" into the U.S. An ex-Republican from Illinois, Ickes had already earned a reputation as one of the most liberal of FDR's cabinet members, as well as the sobriquet of the "Curmudgeon," for his gruff and seemingly ill-tempered plain speaking.

Almost a year before Breck Long's return to the State Department, Ickes had shown an interest in the refugee problem—specifically of the German Jews and their plight after *Kristallnacht*. In November 1938, in his capacity as the administrator of the Alaska Territory, he proposed to set off part of this vast nearly empty land as a sanctuary for Jews fleeing Hitler's Reich. That his idea eventually didn't fly was not due ostensibly to any furious resistance from Long's predecessors in the State Department and visa sector, but most of all to the objections of Rabbi Stephen Wise, who disliked the notion that Jews would be "taking over some part of the country for themselves." Nor did FDR back up his interior secretary, proposing much smaller numbers than Ickes wanted and then quietly abandoning the proposal altogether.

Two years afterward, following the November 1940 election, Breck Long barely had time to savor his recent successes in closing off most emigration into the U.S., when a new challenge arose from Secretary Ickes.

Like Alaska, the Virgin Islands Territory in the Caribbean constituted a U.S. *possession* not yet converted to statehood. Its governor, and Alaska's then, too, was appointed by the president, instead of being elected by the citizenry. On November 13, 1940, Breck Long would write with alarm in his diary:

Virgin Islands problem. Governor Cramer [Lawrence William Cramer] with the advice of the solicitor in the Department of the Interior and Mr. Hart of Justice issued a proclamation allowing refugees into the Virgin Islands.[1]

The horrors, in his view, were then delineated:

After a short period of residence in the Virgin Islands and an affidavit that they are bona fide residents they may proceed without visas or other formalities to the U.S. There is no consular investigation of the individual prior to their arrival in the U.S.[2]

The bugaboo of German agents hiding among anti-Nazi refugees was equally harped upon as further ammunition for shooting down this end-around move. Long declared there were 12,000 refugees in Portugal with many German agents among them, and all could come to the U.S. if they had the money. Avra Warren had just spent two weeks in Lisbon and presumably could verify and quantify his boss's anxiety. The proclamation of the Virgin Islands governor had been publicly issued on November 12, 1940. Breck's condemnation one day later continued in the vein that "It constitutes a pipeline to siphon refugees out of Portugal into the U.S. and is part of a program which Mr. Hart has indulged in in connection with the President's Advisory Committee," adding, "Biddle, as Solicitor General, has been associated with him, but I think he has not quite understood the purpose and objectives."[3]

Frantically, Breckinridge Long tried to reach FDR, but the president was in his swimming pool. Only that evening was he able to contact Roosevelt by phone. FDR told him to talk to Ickes.

The result was a far from satisfactory conversation. The Curmudgeon did not yield an inch to the assistant secretary of state. "I talked to Ickes and found that he knew of the order and had authorized it and that he was an advocate of the whole scheme," Long stated, almost in disbelief. Ickes, he claimed, had insisted the holes in the State Department's sieve were too small and should be enlarged. Moreover, Ickes "was rather obdurate and a little sarcastic."[4]

However, Long's own obduracy and no doubt his constant stress on the German agent scare won the day. Informed of the discussions with Ickes, FDR promised Breck he would issue an executive order, suspending Governor Cramer's proclamation.

An interesting footnote to Breck Long's priorities at this juncture followed immediately in his diary. There was the cursory announcement, "Teenie had a baby girl this morning." No first-time grandpa exaltation. The focus remained on refugees.

Within a week of having bested Ickes, Breck was bemoaning, "In the meantime, I still have a good deal of trouble with refugees." Cited was the case of a man given a visa, who allegedly was "an *expert dynamiter* with subversive intent." (Conceivably an ex-Spanish Loyalist from Asturias, whose militant miners were renowned for their expertise with explosives.) This snafu led him to muse on how difficult it seemed "to draw the line and get the other agencies of the Government to cooperate."[5] Despite the switch of the immigration bureau to the Department of Justice, he continued to encounter resistance from that quarter. And further defining his aggravation, he wrote of thousands in Europe, in South America, in Shanghai . . . wanting to get into the United States. In rather convoluted language, he described his dilemma as needing "to admit outside the quota persons who really ought to be admitted and to hold over for the regular quota of immigration those who should come in the ordinary way."[6]

Subsequently, the Department of Justice at a meeting with Long agreed to accept his proposals, except that its Bureau of Immigration did not want the FBI involved. By then Breck was boasting how his office had "so cleared up the visa question in Europe that the quotas are now practically current or will be in the near future." He credited Avra Warren with having accomplished this feat by *taking off* the lists refugees who had quota numbers yet couldn't get exit permits or steamship tickets to use them, and so were "bumped" for those who did have means of travel, making these latter able to "avail themselves of visas."

His delight over this neat arrangement—with no expressed sense of playing chess with human lives—was perhaps diminished upon his learning that one of his colleagues, Robert T. Pell of the State Department's European Division, knew of Secretary Ickes's Virgin Islands scheme and "was apparently *parties ex criminus* to the plot that the president quashed." Pell, who was an uncle of future U.S. Senator Claiborne Pell and part of the U.S. delegation to the Evian Conference, also later worked in secret helping to bring an important rabbi out of German-occupied Poland and into the United States. This was a member of the famous Schneersohn family, the Rebbe Joseph Isaac Schneersohn. Breck Long bided his time to get even with Robert Pell, and in 1941 was able to effect his resignation as the State Department's liaison with the Intergovernmental Committee on Refugees, created at Evian.

Be that as it may, by November 1940, Long's hard and fast position on immigration was beginning to attract attention—and criticism. On November 25th of that year, the *Washington Post* ran a scathing story that involved him. The writers were Joseph Alsop and Robert Kinter, and it was titled "The Bureaucrats are Pouting," and ostensibly dealt with the failure of the Justice Department and State Department to cooperate in cracking down on the misdeeds of German and Italian diplomats in the U.S. The authors' first mention of Breckinridge Long was his leading role in handling the matter, "which has produced nothing to date but a fit of pout on both sides." Then, eventually, they really laid into the assistant secretary of state, declaring it was no surprise nothing had been done, seeing Long had been put in charge.

> Those who worked for earlier admission of the English children to this country saw him [Long] use every resource of his position to obstruct their project and know he would have succeeded if the president had not rapped him smartly over the official knuckles. Those who tried to help the European political refugees heard him argue visas could not be issued to these unfortunates except in the discretion of the "independent consuls" despite several indications that the independent consuls had received informal instructions [to reject almost all visas] from Washington. Long seems to have a knack for these imbroglios.

Thus, a year before the U.S. entered the war, Breck Long was already experiencing a hostile press. To the privacy of his diary, he openly expressed what was in his heart, or his mind, including definite paranoia, regarding the turn of events.

> The pressure that has been brought to bear on me in the last two months has been astonishing. The opposition is now using me as a fulcrum to pry open the door. I antagonized Ickes irreparably by opposing his Virgin Islands scheme and he is aligned with certain persons in the Department of Justice and on other branches of Government in an effort to unseat me officially.[7]

As if for proof, he soon noted he had lost a fight against the Department of Justice. Permanent immigrants admitted on visas to the U.S. would be allowed to exercise the rights of Americans citizens and participate in political activity. Apparently, Long had sought a different ruling but had been overruled by Attorney General Francis Biddle.

In December 1940, we find Long meeting a delegation of Jewish leaders—Rabbis Teitlebaum and Wise, a Mr. Leavitt of the American-Jewish Joint Distribution Committee, Mr. Bisgyer of B'nai Brith and Dr. Nahum Goldmann of the World Jewish Congress. They had come to ask the assistant secretary of state to accept 3,800 additional names of Jewish religious figures from Lithuania and Russian-occupied Eastern Europe for admittance to the U.S. In his diary, Long declared he had been noncommittal with them concerning what he would do, only to unveil his real feelings through the following touch of self-pity: "but feel it is just a part of the movement to place me and the Department in general in an embarrassing position."[8]

Long's introspection eventually brought him an explanation for what was transpiring, i.e. that the attacks on the State Department and

> the unpleasant situation in the press over the refugee matter are more widespread than before and seem to be joined up with the small element in the country which wants to push us into this war. Those persons are largely concentrated along the Atlantic seaboard, principally around New York. There are elements of them in the Government here. They are all woven together in the barrage of opposition against the State Department, which makes me the bull's eye.

Such a statement might easily be labeled "unspoken anti-Semitism." One might also facetiously consider it the prejudice of a Midwestern Missourian against the East Coast establishment. Or both. Or neither—maybe just the maunderings of an ambitious public official taking his lumps.

Rabbis were again in Breck's office before the end of the year—their spokesman, Mr. Schenkalewski, with a Rabbi Hyman and a Rabbi Heschel. They were looking to bring in a new list of their coreligionists from Europe on visitors visas. Breck told them to apply for immigration visas.

The last week and a half of December 1940 found the assistant secretary of state in better fettle. With FDR's third term about to start the following March, the pro forma request was made to all of the administration's appointed upper-level staff to submit their resignations. Breck Long was pleased to report to his diary that his had been declined (but not that of Bill Bullitt, which no doubt made him all the happier). Then to his surprise he was informed the president had named him to the Commission for Celebrating Thomas Jefferson's 200th Birthday—"a designation quite unexpected by me." And finally, a rumor was floating about that Judge R. Walton Moore, the State Department's top lawyer, would resign and he, Breckinridge Long, would become his replacement.

The climactic year of 1941 commenced. Two major events during the next twelve months—in time—were to have a special effect on Breck Long's career and history. One was Hitler's sudden invasion of Soviet Russia in June 1941 and the other December 7, 1941, the Pearl Harbor attack.

Arno J. Mayer, a professor of European History at Princeton, has written an intriguing book about the Holocaust entitled *Why Did The Heavens Not Darken?* In it he zeroes in on the June 1941 event as the critical moment in turning Hitler's anti-Semitism into wholesale mechanized slaughter. "Without Operation Barbarossa," Mayer insists, "there would and could have been no Jewish catastrophe, no 'Final Solution.'"[9] And, he further alleges, it was not the launched blitzkrieg against Hitler's erstwhile allies in the Soviet Union that led to the gas chambers, but the *failure* of that lightning attack to defeat Stalin. Mayer contends it was "the desperate but unsuccessful race to Moscow in November-December 1941 [that] precipitated the rush to the 'Final Solution.'"[10] Actually, he points out, not until October 1941 were Jews forbidden to emigrate from Germany and territories controlled by the Reich.

True, Hitler in an infamous speech at the Reichstag in January 1939, nine months before the start of World War II, had threatened "the destruction of the Jewish race in Europe" if hostilities did break out, but Professor Mayer would write, concerning the Führer's adventure on the eastern front,

> accordingly, the escalation and systemization of the assault on the Jews was an expression not of soaring hubris on the eve of victory, but of bewilderment and fear in the face of possible defeat. Indeed, the decision to exterminate the Jews marked the incipient debacle of the Nazi Behemoth, not its imminent triumph.[11]

How does this bit of opinion relate to Breckinridge Long? It might seem appropriate to ask at what date the assistant secretary of state took note of the Nazi atrocities against the Jews in Eastern Europe. Other scholars like David S. Wyman, the non-Jewish, Harvard-trained historian of the Holocaust and strong critic of the Roosevelt administration, have disputed Mayer, contending that the wholesale slaughter of Jews began with the *Einsatzgruppen* killings by shooting in Russian territory right at the start of the June 1941 invasion. The first gas chamber—at Chelmno—did not go into operation until "late 1941," Wyman wrote.[12] In any event, Long had already been at his job for close to two years before the Nazis turned on the Soviets.

He has not given many hints of his feelings about what was happening to the Jews in Europe. Although called a "self-avowed anti-Semite" by one historian, such a *self-avowal* is absent in the hundreds of his diary pages and letters I have perused. Indeed, Breck Long always took pains openly to deny the charge of anti-Semitism whenever it was leveled against him.

By the fall of 1941, thanks in large degree to Breckinridge Long's energy and stubborn doggedness, the remaining Jews in Germany and Europe really did have nowhere to go (certainly not to the United States). Whatever exodus there had been—almost half of Germany's Jews had left and a large percentage of Austrian Jews as well—the gates were closed. Forced emigration was no longer a Nazi option.

Earlier that year, it *had* seemed likely that President Roosevelt's friend Breck might occupy another job in the State Department, one relieving him of all the administrative work he had to do and, in particular, the perennial headaches of the immigration controversies causing him a bad press.

On January 3, 1941, he wrote that Secretary of State Hull had sent for him and handed him

a little penciled memorandum written on a White House memorandum pad and signed FDR.

It was a confirmation of the rumor the president wanted him to replace the ailing Judge R. Walton Moore as the State Department's counsel and that Dean Acheson would be appointed an assistant secretary to replace Henry F. Grady, who was departing: "It is very gratifying to me to feel that I shall be relieved of some of the excessive work that has crowded my desk and made broader thinking very difficult," wrote Breck, and he called the counsel job "much more appealing than the tense detailed executive activity I have been confronted with for a year."[13] He actually ruminated aloud on the inconsequential coincidence that this appointment would take place in January, as had his previous assistant secretary appointments—in January, 1940, and January 1917 and, in both cases, around the 25th to 27th of the month.

Except well before the 25th of January 1941, this neat arrangement had unraveled. One of the other assistant secretaries, Adolph Berle Jr., who was very close to FDR, had made a big fuss. He wanted the counsel job for himself and claimed he had seniority over Long, having been an assistant secretary for a longer time. Breck disagreed with this argument, pointing out that "in length of service [back to 1917]," as he told Hull, "I was far in front of Mr. Berle." But being a good soldier, he also added he would do whatever the secretary of state suggested, namely, not to have a new counsel at all but adding one more assistant secretary, who could take over many of Long's administrative duties since the latter would also assume the work of the now vacant counsel's post. Thus it was that G. Howland Shaw, who'd been chief of the Foreign Service Personnel Division, became the fourth assistant secretary.

The "calm before the storm" was one way to describe those early months of 1941. The Nazis were focused on consolidating their 1940 gains, which included the occupation of Denmark, Norway, Holland, Belgium, Luxembourg, and a goodly chunk of France to add to previously conquered Poland, Austria and Czechoslovakia. They also still sought to drive Great Britain out of the war with their relentless although ultimately ineffectual bombing campaign. The *refugee problems*—primarily of Jews and anti-Nazis fleeing the Germans—while not as acute as they once had been, nevertheless posed continuous headaches for Breck Long. Among others, he was wrestling with the conundrum that the American quota for German immigrants was 37,000 annually, that all who could receive visas and leave the Reich had to have exit permits, and those permits were issued by the Gestapo, who were now sending two trainloads of 500 persons each via France and Spain to Portugal every week. Through transportation charges that Germany was demanding—mostly paid for by "Jewish aid societies and friends in the U.S."[14]—the Nazis were collecting $235,000 in foreign exchange every week. Yet Long's real complaint went beyond the fact that Hitler's coffers were being filled. He emphatically stated,

> there is no doubt in operation a systematic traffic in private hands with the connivance of the German Government. It is sinister because the German Government only gives permits to the persons they want to come to the U.S. It is a perfect opening for Germany to load the U.S. with agents.[15]

This articulation of a fear that sounded quite plausible was an opinion he tirelessly expressed and conceivably believed in fiercely. It was so to color his thinking in the years to come that more than ever he fought to keep *all* aliens out of the country. In Congress, he worked alongside Senator Richard Russell of Georgia for a bill, in his words, "to exclude immigrants who are considered to be inimical to our welfare," quite possibly an issue of *free speech*, since Breckinridge Long objected to immigrants voicing their positions on political issues before they became American citizens.

On June 17, 1941, Long further elaborated his thoughts on this subject, mixed in with complaints about the Justice Department, which he hadn't bought into his thinking entirely. He contended, "I cannot accept the philosophy that [in] some segment of our Constitution guarantees of liberty attach to an alien outside the U.S. the moment he applies for a visa to come here."[16] And then the assistant secretary went on to express doubt that such a person can be allowed to say or even entertain privately anything derogatory about the U.S. or its government.

This June 17 diary entry was a long one and began innocuously enough with the news that Breck would be spending his last weekend at Princeton as a member of its board of trustees, his term having ended. But curiously, one part of his June 17 deliberations never made it into the collection of Long's *Wartime Diaries*. Here, he reaffirmed his strong belief in a policy of

> excluding all persons whether they had relatives in Germany or not and denying visas to any immigrant in Germany, Russia, Italy or any of their occupied territories.

And he added: "I had come to the point where I thought it should be done and I am going to recommend it."

His mention of persons who "had relatives in Germany" had become a sore point after he had earlier tried to institute as State Department policy that no visa be given to any person escaping Nazi Germany who still had family members left behind there, on the theory that the Gestapo would blackmail them into working for the Germans. Such logic was devastating, since Long now essentially said that no one who had escaped the Axis, but left relatives in the old country, could ever come to the United States of America.

Moreover, five days later on June 22, 1941, the Nazis invaded the Soviet Union, closed off all borders and placed millions more Jews and others undesirable in their eyes under the Swastika's iron control.

But before examining Breckinridge Long's actions following Hitler's earth-shaking attack on his former ally Stalin, it is well to take a look at his new revised position in the State Department, which had a bearing on subsequent events that involved him. There seemed to be no hurry by his superiors to put those agreed-upon arrangements into effect. In the middle of February 1941, Long was complaining that the workload relief he'd been promised had been repeatedly stalled. To quote him:

> When I first spoke of it last fall I was asked to wait till the first of the year. The first of the year, I was asked to wait till Inauguration. At Inauguration, I was asked to wait till the first of February . . . All of this I assented to do, though the drain on me has been terrific. My physical and nervous resources have been taxed to the point of exhaustion.[17]

Of the forty-one divisions in the State Department, Long had twenty-three under his direct supervision. Of these, thirteen were administrative divisions, and the ten others included passports, visas, the Special Division (which provided overseas relief and the rescue of Americans), and international communications. In an apparently final discussion with Under Secretary Sumner Welles, the redistribution arrangement was at last hammered out. Long *would* take over the counsel's job, with special emphasis on congressional liaison; he would keep three of his twenty-three divisions—those he most wanted, it seems, like the Special Division "with its extra war work" (which Breck himself had created), the Visa Division and its refugee responsibilities, and international communications (which also handled shipping). "Shaw will have all the purely administrative duties and the other seven Divisions I have carried are to be divided between Berle and Acheson."[18]

By the second week in March 1941, Long could report to his diary that the "readjustment of labors" had occurred and that he had vacated his former office and taken the one Judge Moore had occupied. He would now be more formally active in the halls of Congress, had also somehow gotten responsibility for the Philippines and fisheries and yet, withal, no longer felt as he'd once expressed it, "at the end of my rope."

The onset of the German invasion of the Soviet Union found Breckinridge Long already well ensconced in his new position. It seemed that Long's prestige within the organization had risen. He had moved closer to Cordell Hull, just as in his first tour of duty starting in World War I he had ended up close to Secretary of State Robert Lansing.

As for the refugee/alien situation, he was gradually making ever more progress, as he saw it. Towards the end of April 1941, he was reporting: "The President has approved the proposal to concentrate visa control in Washington and has directed the allocation of space near the Department for that purpose."[19] Simultaneously, the secretary of war had presented a recommendation from the various branches of military intelligence and the FBI to control all immigration into the U.S. through visas and to set up an exit permit system as well. Long said he had been "gradually moving in that direction for a year." Within a month, he could write that FDR had approved "my bill," calling it a reenactment of a 1918 statute to control "the exit and entry from and into the United States of all persons, including American citizens." Passport control and control of exit permits would accomplish this rigid restriction, he explained. Long was conferring with the attorney general on the proposed bill and preparing to have it introduced in Congress.

Presumably this effort was well under way when the news of the Nazi thrust into Russia made headlines. In reaction, with his penchant for foreign policy analysis, Breck Long tried to account for the Führer's bold move, which bordered on recklessness. Long saw Hitler's objectives as threefold:

1. To liquidate Communism
2. To obtain food in the Ukraine and oil in the Caucasus
3. To "enlist the decent opinion of the world by fighting Communism"

Strongly anti-Communist himself, Long nonetheless declared, "We cannot waver in our opposition to Hitler just because somebody else, in this case even Communistic Russia, is opposing Hitler. We cannot change our stand because he happens to have picked on another Party for which I personally have the greatest dislike."[20]

Three days later, we hear from Breckinridge Long that "the immigration issue is very hot," no doubt due to the changed war situation. All U.S. consulates in Germany and Italy were to be closed by July 15. "Everyone wants their friends out now. Pressure is very bad." Then, in line with his fifth-column paranoia, "Germany sees her last chance to get her agents out."

Long heard from his friend Laurence Steinhardt, the U.S. ambassador in Moscow, that it looked like the Stalin regime was about to fall. A litany of the increased demands this Russo-German clash heaped upon the assistant secretary's new office ran the gamut from transporting U.S.

consuls home from Germany and Italy (and sending Axis diplomats back), to a rush of immigrants "pushing to get under the wire before July," to overseeing a presidential proclamation on passport and visa control, and even having to fill in for FDR and make a speech at Gettysburg.

A special concern was Long's belief that the Vatican, because of its intense opposition to Communism, would now move closer to Hitler and—as a special worry for the U.S.—the Catholics of Latin America would become pro-Nazi. Signs of this had begun appearing in Colombia and Argentina.

During early July 1941, American military authorities were predicting that Russia would collapse by October and that Moscow would be captured within a week. Then it was "six weeks," then "eight weeks," but with Long still believing that Operation Barbarossa would succeed. In the meantime, he had taken almost a month of vacation, spending it at the family summer home on Nantucket. This respite from work left him "considerably rested."

On the last day of August 1941, the second anniversary of the eve of the start of World War II, the situation in the Soviet Union had brought forth a less negative attitude towards Stalin's prospects. Long wrote,

> The Russians are holding pretty well . . . inflicting terrible losses in men and machines and causing an enormous unexpected effort. And the weather there will get worse and make it still more difficult for Hitler.[21]

Meanwhile Breck Long was finding himself besieged at home—on the immigration question. He took part in a rancorous conference with FDR, Attorney General Biddle, and members of James McDonald's President's Advisory Committee, including Rabbi Stephen Wise and the Archbishop of New Orleans. Rabbi Wise, especially, got under his skin: "Wise always assumes such a sanctimonious air." And in rebuttal to the Jewish leader's plea for "the intellectuals and brave spirits, refugees from the tortures of dictators," was Long's retort that "only an infinitesimal fraction of the immigrants" were of that category, "and some are certainly German agents and others are sympathizers, the last named coming here because it is away from the scene of combat and looks like a safe place."[22]

Apparently Long became quite heated in expressing his views. Of those who opposed him, he opined, "Each of these men hates me. I am to them the embodiment of a nemesis." He then stated he deliberately had held back from alluding to the horrible conditions aboard a refugee ship, the *Navemar*, carrying Jews who had had to pay extravagant prices, saying they were "victims of the greed of their fellows," implying Jewish ship owners, "not of Germany or the United States policy."[23]

Once the Russian winter began in 1941, and the German juggernaut creaked to a halt inside Russia, something else was happening within Germany—the ratcheting up of the ultimate, unsurpassed example in world history of man's inhumanity to humanity—the *Shoah*, in Hebrew—the Holocaust!

Chapter Nineteen

The Shoah

A LTHOUGH THERE IS NO SIGNED document that could be Exhibit A in any trial of the instigator of the Final Solution, no one can doubt the order came from the Führer, Adolf Hitler. Holocaust deniers may try to hang one of their main specious arguments on the absence of a paper trail, but such fanatics are nothing more than shills for keeping Nazi propaganda alive. The real question is *when* did Hitler ultimately give the word to proceed with wholesale extermination.

We have already encountered the argument of Arno Mayer that this diabolic scenario was not fully implemented until the Führer's blitzkrieg against the Soviet Union failed to accomplish its goal of a quick knockout punch. One argument for this supposition was that between June 22, 1941, the launch date for Operation Barbarossa, and October 23, 1941, when Jewish emigration was frozen, Jews had still been able to leave the Third Reich.

A surviving Nazi document has been cited by Mayer as an important milestone on the road to the Holocaust. It was dated July 31, 1941, *more than a month after the invasion of the U.S.S.R.*, and there was a sneaky sleight of hand in its creation. On the surface, it was a letter from Reichsmarschall Hermann Göring, the number-two man in the Nazi regime, to Reinhard Heydrich, who was the number-two man in the SS command. According to Mayer, the letter to Heydrich was actually instigated by Heydrich, himself, who dictated it to one of his underlings, the later-to-be notorious Adolf Eichmann, and then had it presented to Göring for his initials and signature. What the letter said—or what Heydrich had Göring say—was to order Heydrich to prepare an update to a previous 1939 plan "to solve the Jewish question by emigration or evacuation," which now needed revision due to the vastly increased numbers of Jews suddenly in German hands. The letter's final paragraph stated—and here's the really chilling part:

I further commission you to submit to me, before long, a master plan of the administrative, practical and financial measures that need to be taken *zur Durchführung* [to carry out] the sought-after *Endlösung* [final definitive solution] of the Jewish question.[1]

Another version seemingly of this same scenario is that "Göring empowered Himmler and Heydrich 'to solve the Jewish Problem'" on January 24, 1939, two and a half years before the date given by Mayer and eight months before the Nazis started World War II. The same source also stated that on July 31, 1939, "he [Göring] requested them to prepare plans that would once and for all liquidate the Jewish Question." Mayer's date for such a command from the Reichsmarschall was, interestingly enough, July 31, 1941, two years later to the day, and as noted above, was an update to an earlier 1939 plan for settling *the Jewish Question by emigration or evacuation*. A September 21, 1939, Heydrich order known as PS-3363 at the Nuremberg trial is also cited as a veiled reference and prelude to an extermination intent. Another much later document, NG-2586F, dated December 12, 1941, from the German foreign ministry buttresses an argument that the Final Solution was adopted well prior to the now much-publicized Wannsee Conference of January 1942.[2]

Professor David S. Wyman, one of the world's foremost experts on the Holocaust, has, as we have seen, his own dates for the timing of the Nazi mass-murder initiative. His prize-winning book, *The Abandonment of the Jews*,[3] opens by declaring, "During the spring of 1941, while planning the invasion of Russia, the Nazis made the decision to annihilate the Jews in the territories to be taken from the USSR."[4] Right from the start, then, SS *Einsatzgruppen* (literally "action groups") followed immediately behind the Wehrmacht's shock troops that crossed the Soviet borders on June 22, 1941. They rounded up Jews and shot them en masse, mowing down men, women and children. These were really like old-fashioned pogroms but on a modern, totalitarian scale.

Half a million Jews were massacred between June and December 1941, according to Wyman. Soon added to the death toll exacted by Himmler's special forces were another nine hundred thousand of Eastern European Jewry. What appeared to have changed afterward in the Nazi mind was that shooting was too slow a process, wasted too much ammunition and caused morale problems among the executioners. The goal still remained the same—all Yids everywhere had to die—but poison gas was the way to go!

Whatever the timetable and methodology, the role of Adolf

Eichmann was pivotal. Expert at organizing deportations, tireless in his own inner war against the Jews, this runty, German-born ex-salesman-turned-bureaucrat, who grew up in Hitler's own Austrian home city of Linz, was to become world-famous because of his sensational capture, trial and execution in 1960–61.

That Eichmann's name is often linked to a phrase, "the banality of evil," follows from a famous reportage in the *New Yorker* by the German Jewish émigré writer-philosopher Hannah Arendt, who used the term in the subtitle of her book, *Eichmann in Jerusalem.*[5] The very idea—that such *evil* as that conducted by Eichmann could be judged *banal*—caused a firestorm of protest. Even fifty years later in a *New York Times* book review, Arendt was being tweaked as Nazi-inspired by the pro-Hitler German intellectual Martin Heidegger, her professor (and lover) in Weimar Germany. "Arendt's thinking about the Holocaust and her famous formulation, 'the banality of evil,' were contaminated by Heidegger" is a statement from that review.[6]

Thus with a good deal of trepidation I decided to employ Arendt's construct, as I viewed it, for part of the title of this biography of Breckinridge Long: *An American Eichmann???* (And please note the question marks.) I've been told I was over the top in doing so. Yet I did not intend to be sensational, but in following Long's second career at the State Department, I saw parallels between the two men. Quasi-faceless bureaucrats, embedded high within a government structure, and the harm they can cause—that was a start. One might jokingly say no one ever had to call Adolf Eichmann an anti-Semite, since he so obviously was one. Indeed, the only person who ever claimed he wasn't anti-Jewish was Eichmann, himself, who professed great interest in all things Jewish and protested how well he always worked with Jewish leaders. On the other hand, Breckinridge Long has frequently been described as an outright if not fanatical Jew-hater, which he would always deny and perhaps, if challenged, point to his long-time strong personal friendship with "Bernie" Baruch, a man who would certainly not tolerate an openly anti-Semitic pal.

Possibly the most bristly hackle Hannah Arendt raised in her coverage of the Jerusalem trial was a single sentence, that "*Eichmann never realized what he was doing.*"[7] Without going into my own disagreement with this statement of hers as it baldly stands, I would amend it to mean that this SS apparatchik never thought about what he was doing as he did it, yet if and when he did, his self-justification was always overwhelming, crowned by the catch-all: *orders are orders*. Breck Long, I believe, trod a similar if not identical path. There had to be no doubt he eventually knew the fate of those he helped keep trapped in Europe. But he had a concept of duty that precluded any such self-searching. To bolster his ego in this regard, he was also prone to self-congratulation on how "generous" the State Department had been in its admissions of refugees.

Then, there is the question of ambition. Neither man was that far from the top of his profession. Eichmann had reached *Obersturmbannführer* (Lieutenant Colonel) and could easily envision before long an ascent to *SS-Obergruppenführer* (General). He was close to Lieutenant General Reinhard Heydrich, who might someday even take over the SS from Heinrich Himmler. Like Breckinridge Long, Eichmann headed a key bureau, Section IV B4, under the Gestapo, handling "Evacuation and Jewish Affairs," and, in addition, he bore the special designation of *Referent*, a title given to select experts who could consult on any level. Eichmann's expertise rating was in Jewish Affairs. Obversely, Breck Long liked to consider himself a high flyer, too. He'd already been an ambassador. But now he was in Washington, DC, at the heart of the action. He was close to Cordell Hull, who conceivably might someday be president. FDR was an old friend who supported, even applauded, his actions, he believed. Was it not possible to dream of a further upward advancement—under secretary, at least, but never discounting the absolute pinnacle of being named U.S. secretary of state?

Another characteristic Long and Eichmann shared was their blind devotion to their jobs and a reputation for getting things done. Breck Long had impressed his superiors with the efficiency he'd shown in evacuating Americans from Europe at the outbreak of World War II. This display of talent may well have secured him his further employment some months later. Roosevelt found him useful, not just for his loyalty and financial support of the Democratic Party, but also as the fall guy for a refugee policy that drew continual criticism. Eichmann, too, was noted for his loyalty and for his utter dedication to the Nazi cause. He apparently first cemented his reputation by a display of skill in deporting the Jews out of conquered Austria and Czechoslovakia. Heydrich found him useful for doing secretarial chores. His energy in carrying out the Führer's orders actually led him during the closing months of the war to keep the deportations to the death camps going even after Himmler had shut them down. Breckinridge Long had displayed similar fanaticism in the *Quanza* incident, raising an unholy stink, and carrying on an unending political battle to diminish those who were pushing for a more liberal and humane treatment of refugees.

It is highly unlikely these two men ever knew of each other. Long's death in 1958 preceded by two years Eichmann's explosive reentry on the international scene. Until then, the Holocaust itself had not made the stark impression it has today. The newsreels from the liberated concentration camps early on had shocked consciences, opening the pages of a hideous book, but had remained somewhat muted in their impact. The Eichmann case, with its film noir-like drama, was a needed breakthrough.

The chronology of the *Shoah* has since been thoroughly covered in print and media. Its first major planning kick-off, the Wannsee Conference in a Berlin suburb on January 20, 1942, was actually re-created as a British television drama. Eichmann attended as Heydrich's flunky and did much of the scut work, including taking minutes, of this gathering of major German governmental unit heads, brought together to coordinate history's greatest premeditated mass murder. It seemed a signal honor to Eichmann that he was allowed to stay afterward in the lakeside mansion where they'd met and drink expensive French brandy with these Nazi big shots. For all Eichmann cared, they might have been discussing coal shipments instead of people shipments in their unprecedented effort to rid the world of eleven million Jews.

On the other side of the Atlantic, Breck Long was naturally unmindful of this giant war-crime coordinating conclave on January 20, 1942. Nonetheless, reacting to the turmoil of his job immediately following Pearl Harbor the previous month, he allowed himself an indulgence in self-pity through a diary entry that was to color his public persona for years to come. His words have often been quoted by those who would answer the question marks of his comparison to Eichmann in the affirmative.

January 13, 1942, referring to his boss Cordell Hull, Long writes,

He looks tired, thin, disheartened and has no present zest for his work. He is awaiting the blow. The blow may come—to him and to me, for I have incurred the enmity of various powerful and vengeful elements: the Communists, extreme radicals, Jewish professional agitators, refugee enthusiasts who blindly seek the admission of persons under the guise of refugees and their sympathetic agents in the Government service who are their spokesmen and agents. They all hate me—and are opposed to Hull because he has supported me.[8]

Two days after Wannsee, on January 22, 1942, Breckinridge Long was documenting some of the frustrations he was encountering in his line of work. Once more, there was commiseration with poor Cordell Hull—in this case because of a report Long had to make to Congress on a conference in Rio de Janeiro, where twenty-one Latin American Republics were being urged to break off all relations with the Axis powers. From the secretary of state's point of view (and no doubt Long's), the meeting had ended badly, seeing that Under Secretary Sumner Welles had let Argentina off the hook through a compromise, conceding them their ties with Germany, Italy and Japan. The normally unflappable Hull became practically apoplectic when he learned what had happened.

Vichy France was also causing headaches in the hierarchy of the State Department at this period. That is, U.S. support for the rump government the Nazis had allowed to stay in control of a zone left unoccupied in France, once the German juggernaut had forced a French surrender. Rooseveltian policy was to recognize the Pétain regime as the legal ruler of this truncated France and its empire, and Cordell Hull had been in a tizzy ever since the opposing forces of General Charles de Gaulle had captured two small French islands, St. Pierre and Miquelon, just off the Atlantic coast of Canada. Vichy was screaming that this was an invasion of French soil and the U.S. should expel the intruders.

Breck Long had had his own problems with Vichy—not because the government, centered in the old health spa city famed for its waters, was soft on refugees. Just the opposite—with its own extensive, grim internment camps. But for a time, a small group of Americans in Marseilles had been able to work at cross-purposes to Long's Visa Division instructions, enabling prominent Jews and anti-Nazis to get to safety. Spearheading this courageous effort were a Harvard graduate, Varian Fry, and a Yale graduate, Hiram Bingham IV.

The latter was actually a consular official, and the honor roll of those the Fry-Bingham team enabled to flee included such names as Hannah Arendt, Marc Chagall, Marcel Duchamp, Andre Breton, Lion Feuchtwanger, Wanda Landowska, Jacques Lipschitz, Heinrich and Golo Mann, Anna Seghers, and Franz Werfel. It might be argued that Breckinridge Long himself would have approved of these renowned writers, artists, musicians, etc., who fit the image of *notables who might be helpful to the U.S.*

Yet it wasn't long before Fry was arrested and deported by the Vichyites, and most indicative of the State Department's ire, Hiram Bingham was transferred first to Portugal and then to Argentina. No doubt he would have been summarily dismissed from the consular corps had his father not once been a powerful U.S. senator from Connecticut. What role if any Breck Long played in his removal from Marseilles remains undiscovered.

The fatal clock had now started ticking in earnest for Jews all over Europe, and other enemies of the Nazis. It should be cited that among the attendees at the Wannsee conference was one Dr. Rudolf Erwin Lange, head of the *Einsatzgruppe* in Latvia, the only person present with hands-on experience in killing Jews on a large scale. Some discussion of extermination methods did occur, and if Professor Wyman is correct, by then the deadly gas routine with Zyklon B had already come into use at Chelmno—and the rapid appearance during early 1942 of death camps like Treblinka, Sobibor, Belzec, etc., and the beginning of the Auschwitz camps seem to bear this out.

How long could the macabre secret of these places be kept from the world at large? The Nazi cover story for the deportations was that all Jews were being moved to the east for work details. No one had heard the bit of dialogue that Eichmann later revealed to his interrogators in Israel: When Heydrich came to him and said, "The Führer, well, on emigration (of Jews) . . . the Führer has ordered physical extermination."[9]—an exchange allegedly occurring during the fall of 1941.

By the summer of 1942, once the trains had been rolling under Eichmann's energetic supervision, the first concrete effort was made to alert the Allies.

It began with a courageous German businessman named Eduard Schulte. Secretly an anti-Nazi, he held a high position in the Giesche Company, the largest producer of zinc in Europe, and was trusted by the Nazis because of the firm's importance to the German war effort. The headquarters of this mining and manufacturing operation was in Breslau, a German city close to the Polish border and, incidentally, to Auschwitz (Oswiecim in Polish). On July 17, 1942, SS Commander Heinrich Himmler visited the budding death camp and witnessed the gassing of 449 Jews—and the story got back to Eduard Schulte of what the *Reichsführer* had seen and, particularly, how he had gone *weak in the knees*, watching the ghastly procedure. Twelve days later, Schulte unobtrusively took a train to Switzerland.

His underground contact there was Gerhart Riegner, a German-Jewish lawyer who had fled Germany in 1933 and had a job in Geneva representing the World Jewish Congress. Schulte and Riegner met prior to August 8, 1942, at which time the latter sent an alarming telegram to his office in the U.S. Its wording had the formalized sentence structure that one might expect from a German trained in the law, with slight alterations necessary for telegraphic purposes. Its import was grim and horrific.

> In Führer's headquarters plan discussed and under consideration all Jews in countries occupied or controlled by Germany number three and a half to four million should after deportation and concentration in East at one blow be exterminated to resolve once and for all Jewish question in Europe.

But this was wartime, and the only way Riegner could get his message delivered to the U.S. was to transmit it through the American Embassy in Bern. Only diplomatic messages, protected by secrecy, could be wired. Riegner's terrible news was addressed to his boss at the World Jewish Congress, Rabbi Stephen S. Wise. Instead, the American minister in Switzerland, Leland Harrison, on his own, had it diverted to Under Secretary of State Sumner Welles, commenting that an unnamed German businessman had given the information to Riegner.

Thereupon a mystery ensued that has never been unraveled. The State Department's immediate reaction was to dismiss the report by calling it "a fantastic rumor," and on those grounds the telegram was withheld from Rabbi Wise. Who was responsible? Did Breck Long have a hand in this charade? Poor Riegner was soon aware that no one believed him. But he had also taken the step of sending an identically worded cable through the British Foreign Office to a Jewish member of parliament in London, Sidney Silverman. On August 28, 1942, the MP did receive it and at once had a copy sent to Rabbi Wise.

Immediately, Wise informed Under Secretary Sumner Welles of its contents, no doubt demanding an explanation of why he'd never received the original communication. Rather than pooh-pooh the revelation as his unnamed subordinates had done, Welles simply asked Wise not to make the information known until it could be confirmed. So Wise held off and two months later was summoned by Welles, who produced four sworn statements relayed from Switzerland via Leland Harrison, all validating Riegner's telegram.

In his autobiography, Rabbi Wise graphically described the moment of truth. Welles said to him:

> I regret to tell you, Doctor Wise, that these statements confirm and justify your deepest fears.

Wise further wrote:

> He handed me the original documents from Berne . . . The
> documents' red seals suggested the blood of my people pouring
> forth in rivers.

Then, the under secretary ended the interview by telling the Jewish
leader that although he himself couldn't release this material to the
public, Wise could and should.[10]

On November 24, 1942, the Rabbi held a press conference and finally
revealed the awful story to the world, yet it did not become a sensation.
The print media buried it on the back pages. The war dominated the
headlines, especially the Allies' takeover of French North Africa, their first
major offensive thrust towards the European theater. Still, Rabbi Wise
managed to arrange a meeting with President Roosevelt on December
8, 1942, where he and several other rabbis talked to FDR about what
would eventually be called the Holocaust. At this point, the only concrete
step that resulted was a declaration issued by the United States, Great
Britain, and ten Allied governments-in-exile denouncing the Nazis'
implementation of "Hitler's oft-repeated intention to exterminate the
Jewish people in Europe." No immediate rescue plans were developed
and quite possibly weren't even mentioned. Pressure to do something
merely slowly mounted throughout 1943.

It is interesting to look at Breck Long's diaries during this period,
since they do reflect that the ripple effect of the Nazis' murderous Jew-
baiting activities had entered his consciousness. On September 12, 1942,
while the Riegner telegram was still being kept under wraps—did Long
have access to it?—the assistant secretary of state was writing:

> I have accepted a proposal to facilitate the reception here of
> 1,000 Jewish children from France. Another effort will be made
> to move 6,000 or 8,000 to this hemisphere. They are derelicts.
> Their elders are being herded like cattle and deported to Poland
> or to German workshops. [This seems to argue that he did know
> what was going on.] The appeal for asylum is irresistible to any
> human instinct and the act of barbarity just as repulsive as the
> result is appalling. But we can not receive into our own midst
> *all*—or even a large fraction of the oppressed—and no other
> country will receive them.

And here he made a caveat of the Dominican Republic dictator Rafael Trujillo's offer to take in 3,500 refugee children.[11]

On September 26, 1942, Breck Long added to these comments:

> We have agreed to take 1,000 Jewish children out of France. Their families are to be deported to Poland. We have a request to make it 5,000—backed by Mrs. Roosevelt.

But he wanted FDR to be consulted before they finally acted, and the president could not be reached on that particular day.[12]

Three days later, Long was working on another proposal to help Jews in Europe, this time to send food to Jews in Warsaw. Rabbi Wise's son and Rabbi Nahum Goldmann of the Jewish Agency for Palestine had come to see him. Long agreed to $12,000 a month to buy food in Portugal, which would be transshipped, and he received approval from Secretary Hull, who said he would present the idea to FDR.[13]

Whether this latter project ever was activated isn't recorded in Long's writings, nor is the fact that the Allied invasion of French North Africa and the subsequent occupation of Vichy by the Nazis put an end to the plan to bring abandoned Polish Jewish children from France to the U.S.

The pressures to do much more about the Nazis' extermination policies continued to intensify during 1943, presenting additional problems for Breckinridge Long.

His predictable solution was to settle upon a typical bureaucratic stalling device—a *Conference.*

Just as at the previous Evian confab on Nazi anti-Semitism in 1938, this get-together scheduled for the island of Bermuda in April 1943 was surrounded with a lot of hullabaloo. But it was deliberately devised—under Breckinridge Long—not to produce very much, if anything, in the way of action.

More on its details will follow in the next chapter, primarily because one of the unintended consequences of this nine-day meeting on the exclusive British semi-tropical Atlantic island was how ultimately it would prove most harmful to Breck Long's State Department career.

Chapter Twenty

The Bermuda Conference

B RECK LONG WAS QUITE CHARY about discussing the Bermuda Conference in his diaries, although by all accounts he was the U.S. point man in arranging this tawdry affair. It was a joint British-American effort, and Long was credited with having chosen Bermuda for the site—isolated, out-of-bounds to visitors, and ensuring that no hostile demonstrations by uninvited pressure groups could take place. Furthermore, just so any snoopy media didn't play up its deliberations, the discussions in their entirety were kept top secret.

The actual impetus for the gathering had come from the British. *Pressure* was mounting on Parliament and the Churchill government to take some action, as news of the Germans' Final Solution and the massacre of Europe's Jews continued to increase during the early months of 1943. On March 23, 1943, William Temple, the Archbishop of Canterbury, titular head of the Church of England, told the House of Lords: "We stand at the bar of history, of humanity and of God," and he was demanding that something be done to arrest Hitler's diabolical plan of annihilation.

There are two versions of who actually proposed the conference—one, that the British did; the other, that because the British were boasting they had done so much more than the Yanks in saving refugees (numerically they had), the State Department rushed to preempt them.

Ex post facto, many commentators have stressed how this hastily thrown together wingding was simply the bureaucrats' time-honored stratagem of appearing to do something, while really doing not much of anything—and in this case, certainly nothing about trying to interfere with the Nazi murder machine.

In fact, one of the most egregious statements ever issued by a civilized governmental body was included in an *aide-memoire* (British for "memorandum") issued by His Majesty's Foreign Service. A copy was included among Breckinridge Long's papers, and it's implications are simply staggering.

The document was titled: BERMUDA CONFERENCE TO CONSIDER THE REFUGEE PROBLEM, APRIL 19-28, 1943, AND THE IMPLEMENTATION OF CERTAIN OF THE CONFERENCE RECOMMENDATIONS, and it was sent from "The British Embassy [in DC] to the Department of State."

Subparagraph C expressed certain "complicating factors" pertaining to the proposed "consultation and joint effort" to take place in Bermuda. One incredible sentence contained therein describes one "complication" as follows.

> There is a possibility that the Germans or their satellites may change over from the policy of extermination to one of extrusion and aim as they did before the war at embarrassing other countries by flooding them with alien immigrants.

David S. Wyman, in his book *The Abandonment of the Jews* reproduced the same statement and signified its "cold words," as he put it, italicizing this appalling fear expressed by the British that: the Germans might stop killing the Jews and instead "embarrass" the Allies by freeing them all.

It was as if the British Foreign Office were cheering on the Nazis to keep the gas chambers busy, lest the poor Allies be burdened with the problem of dealing with so many captive innocents made stateless and destitute by dictatorial fiat—now condemned to death for simply being themselves. So hurry up Himmler and Eichmann, and get the job finished. We'll try to give you as much time as you need to do so.

As for Breckinridge Long, his first mention of the Bermuda Conference was on April 3, 1943. He began his diary entry for that day with the news he had been in bed because of a virus in his lungs but had gotten a lot of work done over the phone. Then, the admission: "Had a hard time getting a proper person to head the delegation to the Bermuda Conference."

His first choice had been the Evian delegation head, Myron C. Taylor, that former president of U.S. Steel, who also had been FDR's personal representative to the Vatican, but Taylor had said no. Next on the list was Supreme Court Justice Owen Roberts, but he said that Chief Justice Harlan Stone wouldn't give him the time off. Charles Seymour, president of Yale, did accept but soon withdrew his name after some trustees objected. In the end, Breck Long used his Princeton connection to persuade his friend Harold Dodds, president of Princeton, to take the job. Another of Long's choices for delegate, Congressman Sol Bloom of New York City, drew objections from "Rabbi Stephen Wise and a few of his colleagues": that Bloom, a Yiddish-speaking, show-business type—before he entered politics and became chair of the House Foreign Affairs Committee—was not "a representative of Jewry." Long tartly rejoined that Bloom "was a representative of America."[1]

Jewish groups were already concerned that very little, if anything, would come out of the Bermuda meeting and that their point of view would be ignored, notwithstanding Sol Bloom's presence. On April 10, 1943, a "Meeting of the Emergency Committee of European Jewish Affairs" brought together a number of Jewish-American leaders, with Rabbi Wise presiding. The first to speak was Congressman Emanuel Celler, already known as much more of a hawk than Bloom on the refugee issue. Manny Celler described his meeting with FDR at which the president had arranged for three Jewish congressmen—Bloom, Celler, and Samuel Dickstein—to talk to Breckinridge Long and other State Department personnel about simplifying the visa rules. Some possibilities were raised, Celler reported, but no progress had resulted.

Then the group went into the main topic of conversation, the Bermuda Conference, scheduled to open in nine days. Judge Joseph M. Proskauer, the New York lawyer close to Al Smith and FDR, took the floor to speak about a get-together he'd had with Myron Taylor and Sumner Welles the previous day. The upshot of their discussion had been that a delegation would be formed to try to see the president, and names would be sent to Welles suggesting Jewish experts who should be included in the Bermuda talks. However, Dr. Nahum Goldmann, co-chair of the World Jewish Congress, argued that Bermuda was only going to deal with Bulgarian Jews and Jewish refugees already in Spain and Turkey and that it would be "unnecessary" to have experts there. "These experts would only be an alibi like the designation of Sol Bloom," he scathingly stated.[2]

Judge Proskauer did also report that Sumner Welles had told him he would consider Bermuda a success "if 50,000 people could be saved."[3] Motions then made and accepted included asking that the Joint Emergency Committee be allowed to send a delegation to Bermuda. Unsurprisingly, nothing of the kind ever happened. Breckinridge Long neglected to forward their request, and on April 20, 1943, the day after the conference opened, he was writing in his diary, "The Bermuda Conference on Refugees has been born. It has taken a lot of nursing, but is now in existence," whereupon he promptly excoriated "one Jewish faction under the leadership of Rabbi Stephen Wise" for being so assiduous in pushing their particular cause in letters and telegrams to the president, the secretary and Welles—in public meetings to arouse emotions—in full page newspaper advertisements—in resolutions to be presented to the conference . . . they are apt to produce a reaction against their interest.

Long's *raison d'être* for not listening to these folks and denying their request for inclusion was baldly put forth—an argument no doubt often used for doing nothing about imperiled Jews—and, in light of the mounting evidence of gassings and the Final Solution now merrily underway, of dubious validity. But Breck said it, anyway:

> One danger in all this is that their activities may lend color to the charges of Hitler that we are fighting this war on account of and at the instigation and direction of our Jewish citizens.[4]

But if Breckinridge Long was displeased or annoyed or alarmed by Rabbi Wise's pressure and unwillingness to be silenced, imagine his chagrin on May 4, 1943, after Bermuda had terminated, when a full-page advertisement on page 17 of *The New York Times* proclaimed in huge headline type:

TO 5,000,000 JEWS IN THE NAZI DEATH TRAP, BERMUDA WAS A "CRUEL MOCKERY"

The mammoth protest was not the work of Rabbi Wise and his cohorts. Its sponsors called themselves The Committee For a Jewish Army of Stateless and Palestinian Jews, with an address at 535 Fifth Avenue, New York City. They were in actuality the Bergson Group, named for their fiery leader Peter Bergson, and a bitter rivalry existed between them and Rabbi Wise's people.

Even before the Bermuda Conference took place—and perhaps contributing to the pressure for a gesture from the British and American governments—was the Bergson Group's great rally at Madison Square Garden on March 9, 1943, staged around a pageant called, *We Will Never Die*. Hollywood stars Edward G. Robinson and Paul Muni played major roles in it; Kurt Weill provided the music; Ben Hecht fashioned the drama, and Moss Hart directed. An audience of forty thousand was in attendance, and the show later went on the road to major cities. Their performance in Washington, DC, was attended by Eleanor Roosevelt, although her husband had been persuaded by his advisors not to send a message to the opening night. Mrs. Roosevelt called the musical play "one of the most impressive and moving pageants I have ever seen," and she especially remarked on the haunting refrain, "remember us"— one of whose stanzas recorded the fate of the deportees Eichmann was shipping to their deaths even as the words were being sung:

> Remember us, who were put in the freight trains that left France and Belgium, who rode across Europe . . . standing up, we died in the freight trains, standing up . . . Remember us.

Unfortunately, even Sumner Welles's minimal hope that Bermuda might save fifty thousand Jews did not materialize. The Bergson Group's May 4 advertisement phrased the matter in highly emotional terms in its opening paragraphs.

> Somehow through invisible underground channels, one ray of shining hope might have penetrated the ghettoes of Europe. A rumor might have spread among the agonized Jews of Hitler's hell. A whisper telling of deliverance from torture, death, starvation and agony in slaughter-houses. This ray of hope and this whisper were expressed in one word: "Bermuda!"

The text goes on to say that "Men and women of good will everywhere at last believed that the United Nations had decided to do something about the unprecedented disaster of a people put to death." And next, this final stinging paragraph:

> Wretched, doomed victims of Hitler's tyranny! Poor men and women of good faith the world over! You have cherished an illusion. Your hopes have been in vain. Bermuda was not the dawn of a new era, of an era of humanity and compassion, of translating pity into deed. Bermuda was a mockery and a cruel jest.

These deliberations at Bermuda were kept classified, thus allowing those on both sides of the argument to make their own points with little fear of contradiction. Sol Bloom came back and addressed a session of the Hebrew Immigrant Aid Society (HIAS) and chastised critics who had spoken out. "No one can criticize what we did in Bermuda without knowing what we did," he began. Yet instead of telling his audience what they did do, he merely stated, "But as a Jew, I am perfectly satisfied with the results." As if to illustrate an example of those results, he read a letter from President Roosevelt to himself as a delegate, asking him to try to get the Intergovernmental Committee on Refugees to act, with Bloom boasting that "We got it into action . . . and it is in action now."

That Intergovernmental Committee, set up at Evian in 1938, had done nothing much afterward and been moribund ever since. To bureaucrats, the resurrection of such an entity might seem like a piece of action in and of itself and indeed was hailed as the crowning achievement of Bermuda. It should be noted, on the other hand, that James G. McDonald, one-time chair of the President's Advisory Committee on Refugees, turned down an offer to become vice-director of this so-called revitalized Intergovernmental Committee on Refugees. Actually, he was quite scornful about the whole business, stating,

> Thus having reached negative conclusions on most of the issues raised, the Bermuda Conference made the unoriginal and not very helpful suggestion that additional wartime refugee problems be handled by a revived and strengthened Intergovernmental Committee.[5]

Attacks on Bermuda continued apace. The Synagogue Council of America declared:

> We cannot believe that the Bermuda Conference on Refugees is the answer to the agonizing cry of millions of innocent victims.[6]

The National Conference on Palestine denounced the Bermuda Conference as "ineffective." The American Federation of Polish Jews adopted a resolution expressing "disappointment at the failure of the Bermuda Conference to make constructive efforts to feed or rescue the remnants of Jews still alive in Poland."[7] The Sunday *New York Times* in its "News of the Week in Review" section carried a story by Julian Meltzer, datelined Jerusalem, that Zionists in Palestine found the "outlook dark," and now were facing the "most acute and baffling deadlock" since the Zionist movement had started fifty years before and that "the recent Anglo-American conference held in Bermuda brought about that deadlock."[8]

Rebuttals to such a chorus of negative reaction were made by Sol

Bloom and his fellow delegate, U.S. Senator Scott W. Lucas (D) of Illinois, chairman of the Senate Foreign Relations Committee. Lucas even went after the Bergson Group's *New York Times* ad, making a floor speech in which he claimed that its list of dignitaries contained two senators who hadn't given permission to have their names printed: Albert (Happy) Chandler of Kentucky and Harry S. Truman of Missouri. The latter, as a result, asked to have his name removed. But the Bergson Group came right back and stated that the listings objected to were in a separate box of their ad, under the heading of "Proclamation of the Moral Rights of the Stateless and Palestinian Jews," and that all of the senators named *had* signed that document, which declared:

> We shall no longer witness with pity alone, and with passive sympathy, the calculated extermination of the ancient Jewish people by the barbarous Nazis.

The retreat from passivity, it could be said, had already begun. An effort was on to create a new U.S. governmental agency, separate from the State Department, to focus on rescuing Jewish victims yet surviving in Europe. Breck Long commented in his diary entry of April 20, 1943, that "U.S. Senator Johnson of Colorado" had submitted a resolution calling for an action operation that would be out of State's control. To those who knew "Big Ed" Johnson, the conservative Democrat might have seemed an odd person to be backing the "radical" cause of saving Jews. He had made his reputation in his western home base by clamping down on immigrants and strongly supporting the internment of Japanese-Americans. But here he was, national chairman of the Committee for a Jewish Army. His resolution to have the Bermuda Conference take "swift action to save the remaining European Jews" did not even reach the Senate floor. But future efforts of similar ilk were soon to follow.

It was also not noted by Breck at the time that the day the Bermuda Conference convened, something dramatic happened among the beleaguered Jews in Eastern Europe. The Warsaw Ghetto uprising broke out and continued for a heroic three weeks, embarrassing the SS general sent to suppress it. Other Jewish revolts had occurred earlier, but this one resounded worldwide and created a whole new psychology among Jews everywhere. Passivity was no longer acceptable.

On May 7, 1943, a complacent Breckinridge Long was reporting in his diary, "The Bermuda Conference adjourned and the delegates back. They met with the Secretary yesterday and me—went over their report."

Action at his end consisted of recommending to the president that he "grant certain authority" to Myron Taylor who was representing the U.S. on the Intergovernmental Committee. Positive spin was added in the sphere of moving those refugees who had escaped the Nazis into possibly less precarious sanctuaries—"out of Spain to North Africa— out of Greece etc. [i.e., the Balkans] to Cirenaica [Libya]—some to Palestine—possibly more to Ethiopia and to Madagascar."[9]

Then, Long went on to highlight what seemingly interested him much more—Cordell Hull's beloved trade agreements, one of which was coming out of committee and onto the House floor and that he feared (quite rightly, it turned out) would be amended.

One rather piquant sidebar to all the dithering in 1943 over immigration appeared in Breck Long's diary about a week after the conclusion of the Bermuda Conference. It pertained to America's oldest anti-immigrant law, the Chinese Exclusion Act, signed by President Chester A. Arthur in May 1882, which had become an embarrassment. China was now a staunch U.S. ally in the battle against Japan, and to Chinese leaders the continued existence of such a discriminatory law was an insult of the highest order. Breck Long did concede that it was "a little inconsistent to claim China as one of our principal allies in war and to deny its citizens admission to the United States." Ironically, it now became *his* task to remove a restrictive immigration law from the books and allow in *aliens* and "yellow Peril" ones, no less.

With his usual circumspection, Long proceeded to approach Speaker of the House Sam Rayburn. What he sought was the Texan's assurance that if a repeal bill were introduced, they'd have enough votes to pass it. "The international effect of defeat would be unfortunate," he insisted. "We do not want to offend by an adverse vote in Congress." Before the end of 1943, the skids in Congress had been greased well enough to allow Senator Warren Magnuson's bill to pass, ending the complete exclusion. Under the new dispensation, 105 Chinese could be admitted to the U.S. every year. No doubt Breck Long thought that generous.

As for Bermuda, it struck the assistant secretary the big fuss had quickly dampened. On June 23, 1943, he wrote,

> The refugee question has died down. The pressure groups have temporarily withdrawn from the assertion of pressure. Information which we have received indicates very plainly that they now see the correctness of the position which we have maintained from the beginning, which is that we will be glad to help such refugees

as find their way out of the clutches of Germany but that we cannot deal with the enemy on the account of refugees any more than we can deal with them on any other account.[10]

Once again, Breck was mostly wrong in his forecasting, except for commenting that the pressure groups on the issue of the extermination of the Jews had withdrawn *temporarily*.

He also was honest enough to admit in this entry that "the recommendations of the Bermuda Conference [skimpy as they were] have not been carried forward."[11]

Chapter Twenty-One

The Paper Walls Finished

WHILE FLIMFLAM LIKE THE BERMUDA Conference was being perpetrated by the State Department in the name of cover-your-butt politics, the atrocities wrought by Hitler and company in Europe continued without much hindrance. The experiences of the rare survivors thus reach our later generations as cautionary and poignant reminders of the human tragedies wreaked by distorted thinking.

There are might-have-beens among us also. My wife's family has already been mentioned, and the awakening that Kristallnacht was for my in-laws. Happily for them, they made their move to leave Germany before Breckinridge Long assumed the reins at the State Department's Visa Division. At that, they still had to go through tough enough pre-Long procedures, which included having a sponsor ensure you would have enough money never to become a public charge. The Florsheims—father, mother, my wife Carlotta (Carla), and older brother Robert (Bob)—spent a year in Holland, sailed for the U.S. in 1939, on one of the last voyages of the Holland-America Line before the outbreak of World War II, and settled amidst an informal enclave of fellow German-Jewish émigrés in Kew Gardens, Queens, New York.

I have to admit that as a second-generation American of Eastern European Jewish descent, growing up in a suburb of Boston in the 1930s and 1940s, I'd never had knowledge of places like Kew Gardens. The only concrete connection to the European Jews' plight in our neighborhood of South Brookline was the appearance of two German-Jewish brothers, taken in by a local family. Neither Peter nor Werner Gossels were in my grade, so I did not know them very well. Many years later, I was to see a film, made by Peter's daughter, called *The Children of Chabannes*, and learn that her father and uncle had gone first to Vichy France and somehow, with three hundred other Jewish youngsters— thanks to a Quaker organization and allegedly with the help of Eleanor

Roosevelt—had been able to reach the U.S. Both these brothers, one a Harvard grad, one a Yale grad, are today pillars of the town of Wayland, Massachusetts.

During my years of working in New York City, I befriended two other German-born refugees of my generation—Michael Roemer, later to achieve distinction as a movie director, and Hans Ashbourne, an international businessman. Here was another angle on those who'd escaped the Nazi net in time. They had been part of a *Kindertransport*—a children's train, allowed to leave Germany for eventual asylum in England, where these Jewish kids went to school. Neither of my pals were specific about how they'd come to America. But Mike Roemer's one story that did stick in my mind concerned their train trip out of Germany. With a movie man's talent for visuals, he graphically described this exit, passing stop after stop in *Deutschland*, facing hard-eyed, hate-filled faces of Germans watching to see them expelled, and then arriving at the Dutch border to a tumultuous welcome from kindly Hollanders plying them with hot cocoa, cookies and other goodies and, especially, plenty of warm, friendly smiles.

But patently, these survivors or rather escapees were merely a handful, the lucky few. Of those who couldn't get out, but who tried and were stymied by the "paper walls," to use David Wyman's expression, erected ever higher and stronger by Breckinridge Long, no story can beat that of Otto Frank. This German-Jewish businessman did survive the horrors of a concentration camp, but not his family—and most notably his younger daughter, Anne Frank, whose unforgettable, incandescent *Diary* is now a universal classic and she herself an icon of what incipient genius the Holocaust deprived posterity.

Just suppose that Anne and her sister Margot might have come to the United States and grown up here like the Gossels brothers or the Florsheim kids, an arrangement their father tried feverishly but belatedly to accomplish in 1941. But by then, Breckinridge Long had issued his ukase of June 26, 1940, defining ever more strenuous rules for keeping persecuted foreigners out of our country on the seemingly logical but totally specious argument that the Nazis would slip in fifth columnists among the fleeing Jews.

Worse, by 1941 a new torment had been devised by the visa office. No German-Jewish or other Jewish refugee could be admitted if he or she still had relatives left in the old country.

When Otto Frank was a college student at Heidelberg in 1908, he met an American of German-Jewish background who was studying abroad.

This was Nathan Straus Jr., whose father in New York was a successful merchant. In fact, he was a co-owner of Macy's Department Store. The two young men were soon close friends, and the following year Otto accompanied Nathan to New York and was given a job at Macy's. Most likely, since he was fascinated by New York, Otto would have stayed and taken American citizenship, except that his father died in 1909, and he had to return to Germany.

On April 30, 1941, we find Otto Frank beseeching his old friend Nathan, who at the time was an important official in the Roosevelt administration, director of the Federal Housing Authority. "You are the only person I know that I can ask," he wrote from Nazi-occupied Amsterdam. "Perhaps you remember that we have two girls. It is for the sake of the children mainly that we have to care for. Our own fate is less important."[1] In order to acquire a U.S. visa, Frank needed a $5,000 deposit and was asking the well-heeled Straus to bankroll him.

The problem was that Breckinridge Long's new proviso about relatives abroad made it impossible for the two Frank girls to leave Holland without their parents, and impossible for Otto Frank go to America first with the hope of then being able to bring over the rest of his family. The meshes of the Visa Division had become so fine it was even required that deposit money be provided by a *relative* in the U.S. A mere friend, as Nathan Straus was to Otto Frank, wouldn't do.

Events caught up with poor Otto. By June 1941, the no-relative-left-behind rule was in full effect. Then, in July the Germans shut down all American consulates in their territories, retaliating for the Americans' closing of German consulates in the U.S. On July 1, 1941, Nathan Straus Jr. was writing his ex-schoolmate, "I'm afraid . . . the news is not good news."[2]

One last daring gamble was open to Otto Frank. This was an attempt to obtain a Cuban visa. These could be bought but also rescinded, as happened with the refugees in Havana harbor aboard the *St. Louis*. The Franks chose to risk applying for a single visa for Otto, again with the hope that once safely on the Caribbean island, he could manage to bring the others afterward. On December 1, 1941, the Cuban visa was sent to Holland. Whether it ever arrived is unknown. Anyway, six days later the Japanese bombed Pearl Harbor, and five days following that Germany declared war on the U.S., and the Cuban government cancelled all its visas.

In the summer of 1942, the Franks went into hiding at 267 Prinsengracht, the house on the canal, and the rest of the story is now immortalized.

Less well known is the story of the poet Yitzhak Katznelson, but just as poignant and illustrative of others lost to Lieutenant Colonel Eichmann and his efficient death machine. I have already noted the ironic coincidence that the Bermuda Conference opened on the same day as the opening shots of the Warsaw Ghetto uprising. Katznelson had participated in an earlier episode of Warsaw Jewish resistance through his membership in the *Dror* (Freedom) unit of the underground. Although born in Bielorussia, he had moved as a child with his family to Poland, where they settled in the city of Lodz, but in November 1939 fled to Warsaw. Writing in both Hebrew and Yiddish, publishing volumes of poetry and plays that were professionally staged, he became a major Jewish literary figure in prewar Eastern Europe, as well as an ardent Zionist who visited Palestine on several occasions and also made trips to other parts of Europe and to America. In April 1943, Katznelson's friends decided he had to be hidden in the non-Jewish area of Warsaw, and he and his oldest son Zvi remained in a special camouflaged bunker on Groyecka Street until mid May.

Meanwhile, the Warsaw Ghetto had been overrun and utterly destroyed, but for a brief time the Gestapo, which had gotten its hands on a number of certificates from foreign countries—especially those of Latin America—exploited this find by conferring them on Jews they hoped to trade for German prisoners of war. Thus it was that the noted littérateur Yitzhak Katznelson and his son Zvi received Honduran passports and transportation to a transit camp in the spa resort of Vittel in eastern France. So it was that Katznelson wrote *Vittel Diary*, telling of his and Zvi's experiences in the year they were held, before being shipped off to Auschwitz to join in death Katznelson's wife Chanah and two other sons who had been gassed previously.

On September 3, 1943, Katznelson stopped writing *Vittel Diary* and turned his attention to his most enduring and famous work—an epic poem, *The Song of the Murdered Jewish Nation.*

There should be a drum roll when his sad, fighting lyrics pour out upon the page. Strains of *Hatikvah* possibly, or some other stirring, dirge-like melody, accompanying the march of the naked dead, stripped of their clothing and their humanity but not of dignity, prodded straight into the crematorium. As a Nazi guard once infamously pointed out to them, their only escape from Auschwitz was up the chimney.

Here are some of Yitzhak's words, translated into English:

I long to see you all.
I want to behold you,
To behold and contemplate you all,
Oh, let me see my people,
My nation that lies murdered.
Grant me just a silent look.
Then shall I sing.
Yes, give me a harp
and I shall play a tune.

Along with that flow of "boundless love for his stricken people,"[3] the poet told how he had resisted writing anything of this sort. "Oh, Sing! Sing the Swan Song! The Song of the sole surviving Jews on Europe's soil," he then urged himself.

Yet back came the cry:
Oh, How can I sing?
How can I endure?
I am utterly alone.
The sole survivor!
Oh! Bleak desolation!

But in the end, spurred on by the haunting thoughts of his own personal loss, of his wife and two younger boys, he continued: "Oh, Chanah, my exalted one! My Muse! Oh, my Benzikel and my Benyaminkeh . . . My wonderful children! My Chanah, my Savior! Oh, my Ben Zion and Binyamin," and he extrapolated his burning internal sorrows into an external paean to the calamity suffered by his entire people.

Before Yitzhak and Zvi were taken away in the spring of 1944, the pages of *The Song of the Murdered Jewish Nation* were divided up and placed in three bottles that were buried in the park at the Vittel camp. Later, after the Katznelsons were gone, these writings and the *Diary* were smuggled out with the help of a local French laundress who kept them until the Liberation in September 1944.

One final point about this immensely creative person who failed to survive the Holocaust is the matter of his Latin American credentials. We find an interesting link here to Breckinridge Long. Katznelson opens *Vittel Diary* on May 22, 1943, with this bit of narrative:

My son Zvi and I are now in Vittel. We came with a small group of Jews, all of whom were nationals of different northern countries of South America. Zvi and I are nationals of Honduras.[4]

Long's oft-quoted memorandum of June 26, 1940, contained— in addition to his recommendations for placing "every obstacle in the way" to stop "for a temporary period of indefinite length the number of immigrants into the United States"—a specific reference to our neighbors in the Americas. In his memo's section labeled "Summing Up," Breck Long wrote:

> We can temporarily prevent the numbers of immigrants from certain localities such as Cuba, Mexico and other places of German intending immigrants by simply raising administrative obstacles.[5]

Plainly, an aspect of Breckinridge Long's World War II activities in the State Department that has not received particular attention is what he did in regard to Latin America. In the other Western Hemisphere countries, with the exception of Canada, his fears of German infiltration were far more real. Both Argentina and Brazil had large centers of German concentration, communities where in architecture and the language heard, you could think you were in Germany. Furthermore, America's restrictive immigration laws in that era did not apply to Latin America. *Hispanics* and *Brasilheiros* had no quotas assigned to them.

A rigorous study of what happened south of the border from 1941 to 1945, written by Max Paul Friedman, a professor of history at Florida State, was published in 2003 as, *Nazis and Good Neighbors; The United States Campaign Against the Germans of Latin America in World War II.*[6]

It may be remembered that besides the Visa Division and numerous other parts of the State Department, Breckinridge Long also had charge of the *Special Division*, set up in 1939 upon the outbreak of the war. Max Paul Friedman documents how in this capacity Long took control of the effort to have known Nazis deported from Latin American countries to internment camps in the U.S. On the surface, naturally, this was a good thing to do. But the implementation of the campaign left much to be desired. Favoritism was rampant. Hitlerites with the right connections remained in Latin America untouched. Among the deportees were not only anti-Nazi Germans but a not inconsiderable number of German Jews, some who had even been in concentration camps and found themselves caged cheek by jowl with rabid National Socialists. Political vendettas sent losers among the German Latin-American populations north to the prison camps, as did cases of outright theft by officials of property of the dispossessed.

In other words, elements of a scandal were reported by Friedman, and he puts Breckinridge Long right in the middle of these concatenations.

That Nazi influence in Latin America existed was incontrovertible. Breck Long had learned first-hand from Brazilian Foreign Minister Oscar Aranha of a developing Nazi threat. Likewise in Argentina, which had a very large population of Italians, many of them became admirers and imitators of Mussolini's Fascism, while from 1933 on, a good number of the German colony swore allegiance to Hitler. "Particularly after 1938, as fascist power grew in Europe, and brought forth praise from Argentine rightist admirers," wrote Ronald H. Dolkart in a book of essays called *The Argentine Right*. "Nazism became an ever more virulent issue in Argentina."[7] What was described as *"la cuestión nazi"* in political circles turned to a worry about "Nazi infiltration," and at the same time the arrival of fleeing European Jews in noticeable quantities offered opportunities for anti-Semitic propaganda. The outbreak of the Spanish Civil War in 1936 added to the mix, not only in Argentina but in most other Spanish-speaking countries. Adherents of Franco, organized as Falangists and joined by the Catholic Church, became a force. The Legión Cívica Argentina, armed and in jackboots and Brownshirt-style uniforms, sent a message in March 1938 to the German embassy in Buenos Aires of "warmest congratulations on the brilliant triumph obtained by the Führer Adolf Hitler upon annexing Austria to the great German State,"[8] Ninety miles off the Florida coast, this same conquest was being fêted at the Austrian legation in Havana with swastika pennants and tinsel and the hoisting of Austria's new Nazi flag, plus the enthusiastic support of the *Partido Nazi Cubano*, led by a journalist named Juan Prohías-Figueredo.[9]

A book about Fascists, Falangists and Nazis in Cuba, whose title, *El Fracaso de Hitler en Cuba* (translation: "Hitler's Failure in Cuba"), published under the Castro regime, propagandistically tries to emphasize the utter smashing of the Axis threat by the Cuban people. And it's true that throughout Latin America, the local fifth columnists never amounted to much but were scary at the start, especially to a nervous bureaucrat like Breckinridge Long. After all, in Cuba alone a correspondent for the *New York Tribune,* Jack O'Brien, estimated there were five to six thousand Fascists in Havana [10] and that in 1937 the Hitlerites had set up General A. D. Wilhelm Von Faupel in Franco Spain to direct Nazi activities in Latin-language countries. He soon was at work in Mexico, Chile, Argentina, Brazil and even Puerto Rico and the Philippines.[11]

Consequently, it is no surprise to find Breckinridge Long, five days after Pearl Harbor, huddling with his fellow assistant secretary of state, Adolph Berle, to answer the request of Guatemala's President Jorge Ubico who wanted U.S. help to expel Nazis of military age from his Central American country. Having decided to support Ubico, it was a no-brainer for the State Department, through Long's Special Division, to broaden the program to all the American republics and to include Germans of nonmilitary age, as well.

Panama, it goes without saying, was of special concern to the U.S. By the middle of January 1942, the Panamanian government agreed to round up its local Germans and ship them to the United States. Among this first batch of deportees were some notorious Nazis, like Herbert Jabs, head of the Nazi trade union DAF, and August Karl Westermeier, a leading Nazi, who lived in Colón, close to the Panama Canal. But also found among these internees were Max Kauffman, a Jewish refugee, Walter Wolff, a Jewish butcher, and George Karliner, yet another Jew who had been in Buchenwald, where his father had been killed. Likewise included was a non-Jewish anti-Nazi, Hans Bartsch, who had been badly beaten by the SA in 1933 and had a silver plate in his head as a result. The Panama group that would be imprisoned together contained thirty Jewish refugees and only twenty-one Nazi Party members.[12]

Given Breck Long's insistence that among the Jewish refugees let out of Germany were innumerable spies, saboteurs, fifth columnists, etc., the presence of Jews behind barbed wire in the U.S. was of no importance to him. Indeed, he strongly resisted freeing them or investigating their cases, and one of his operatives, Albert Clattenberg, was known to have told these unfortunate Jews they could either stay put or he would ship them back to Nazi Germany.

When Long released the news in June 1942 that his program, designed to rout out the "many agents" snuck in by the Axis, had removed five to six thousand of them, he was making no distinctions. If he said they were *agents*, they were *agents* (Jewish or not), and he could boast "As a result . . . the U.S. and the other American Republics as far south as Chile and Argentina will have been relieved of the presence of German agents implanted throughout the territory."[13]

Eventually, seven camps—three in Texas, one in Oklahoma, one in Tennessee, one in northern Florida, one in Louisiana—were used to house the deportees. Conditions varied; they were so bad at Stringtown,

Oklahoma, an abandoned penitentiary, that the internees there were sent to Texas. Early on, there were problems with unrepentant Nazis, who displayed swastikas and beat up Jews and anti-Nazis imprisoned with them.

In March 1942, the State Department asked the Department of Justice to take over responsibility for holding the deportees it was continuing to bring in from Latin America. The entrance upon the scene of Edward Ennis, the man in charge of the Justice Department's Alien Enemy Control Unit, was soon to make a difference. Dedicated to protecting civil liberties despite (or because of) his position, Ennis began protesting about the flimsy cases against many of the imprisoned aliens, and particularly he cited the cases of the Jewish refugees. He threatened to release them all unless the State Department provided evidence that they were dangerous.

With the State Department stubbornly continuing to oppose any releases, Ennis found an unlikely ally within their own ranks. He was James J. Keeley Jr., the *acting chief of the Special Division*, who agreed with Ennis that since enemy aliens living in the U.S. had received hearings, the enemy aliens shipped in from Latin America should, too. Keeley took the idea to his boss, Breckinridge Long, but the assistant secretary of state turned him down cold.

Not intimidated, Ennis, with the support of *his* boss, Attorney-General Francis Biddle, no friend of Breck Long's, went ahead and organized hearings for those among the deported who could prove they'd been wrongly interned, and he sent an investigating team to Latin America, led by the son of Interior Secretary Harold Ickes, another Breck Long foe, to see how the program was being run—very badly, it turned out.

In June 1943, Long received a letter from Philip Bonsal, the head of State's Latin America Division, urging that the entire program be ended, considering the Axis forces had been driven from North Africa, but especially because of the intense resentment these roundups were causing throughout the whole of Latin America. Under Secretary of State Sumner Welles, actually Breck Long's immediate boss, also chimed in that the bullying policies pursued were raising cries of Yankee imperialism and damaging the Good Neighbor policy.

When it came to bureaucratic in-fighting, though, Long was a slugger. For example, the Jews interned at Camp Forrest, Tennessee, presented an argument to have their cases heard on the grounds that since the Nazis had taken away their German citizenship, they were no longer German nationals. Long responded with what Friedman called "an exasperated memo," in which one can almost hear his haughty Ivy League snarl: "I do not see that we have to be concerned about the *citizenship* of those people." Request denied.

Now, here again, comes the question: was this flap an indication of rank anti-Semitism on Long's part? Another action of his, just as stubbornly unsympathetic, showed a more non-bigoted totalitarian streak—a "my way or the highway" mentality. It was the matter of a French national arrested in Costa Rica as a Nazi sympathizer, who was really a pro-Allied Gaullist, and had no allegations ever made against him, except that he was a "millionaire beachcomber" with eccentric habits and had refused to pay off the police chief in the capital city of San José. Breck Long said no to him, too, like he had to those American repatriates from Europe in 1940, who wanted to bring their local (and undoubtedly non-Jewish) servants with them to the U.S.

Long's wholesale rejection of all aliens resembled the stand of the American Legion at its National Convention in September 1943, when they denounced "the practice of importing into the United States aliens from other countries for detention in enemy alien relocation centers" and called for these camps to be discontinued. They weren't worried about civil liberties, either. Any aliens were taboo to them. Ipso facto, Breck Long had to be violently opposed to releasing even the most obviously innocent of these transported detainees, lest they be eligible to become legal immigrants.

One other major issue was continued with this program and these prisoners: repatriation—that is, of Germans back to Germany and of Americans held by Germans. There was similarly that small, unheralded proposal we saw in Yitzhak Katznelson's case for the exchange of Jews, given Latin American passports and then held hostage while deals were attempted to exchange them for captive Germans in America.

Vittel was only one of the sites where these hostages were kept. The main holding pen was Bergen-Belsen, better known as the death camp it ultimately became, once this swap idea was abandoned. Interestingly enough, its brief history also offers a glimpse into the workings of the Nazi bureaucracy. The impulse behind the proposed exchange of captives came from Heinrich Himmler himself, whose responsibilities, in addition to being lord high executioner of the Jewish people, also entailed bringing as many Germans as possible back to the Fatherland. Working for him towards this latter goal was another branch of the Gestapo hierarchy, Referat IV F4, headed by a Rudolf Kröning, who routinely authorized the setting aside of "exchange Jews."[14] This leniency put Kröning at sword's points with his colleague, the head of Referat IV B4, Adolf Eichmann, who insisted that all Jews, without exception, be gassed. On this issue, Eichmann was a "radical," as Hannah Arendt deemed him. No Jew was to escape Eichmann's grasp for any reason.

One might then easily draw a parallel between Breckinridge Long's behavior towards the deportees from Latin America, mirroring Eichmann's hard-nosed attitudes.

In 1942 the Justice Department had begun reviewing the cases of Jews and anti-Nazis who'd been deported as enemy aliens, and as a result they were all removed to Camp Algiers, a newly built detention center near New Orleans. In April 1943, Biddle and Ennis determined that these prisoners should be granted parole status and allowed to enter U.S. civilian life. Long fought back ferociously against the move, which might cast doubt on his vociferous claim that all these "dangerous" people had to remain behind barbed wire. Here, he plainly showed a propensity for twisting the truth that was eventually to lead him into very hot water. He stated that these "Germans" had only been sent by their countries on the condition that they (the Latin American Republics) retained jurisdiction over them, and thus only *they* could release them. Not so, documents were to prove. It was the U.S. that had requested their arrest and deportation.

Max Paul Friedman gives Breck Long very little slack on his attitudes here. *Nazis and Good Neighbors* contains statements such as:

The exaggeration of the Nazi menace [in the Americas] also contributed in a bitter irony, to the failed opportunity to rescue victims of Nazi crimes in Europe.[15]
. . .
And it was to prove fatal for thousands of Jewish holders of Latin American documents who were kept in special camps . . . pending an unconsummated trade for the very volunteers [among the Germans] the United States refused to release.[16]
. . .
The total number of Jews with Latin American papers actually saved by the single exchange finally carried out in February 1945 was 136 people.[17]

It was too late for Yitzhak and Zvi Katznelson and thousands of nameless fellow victims to be included.

Friedman does concede that Long's worries about Nazi infiltration, paranoid as they seemed, were genuine to him. The assistant secretary of state insists in one of his diary entries in 1942, writing about the bumpy reception his "Visa Procedure" had gotten, that he will weather the dissatisfactions raised and in spite of everything, "try to play it safe against any possible Fifth Column."[18]

Nevertheless, in summing up the story of this almost forgotten episode of World War II, Friedman makes note of how the policy established to combat the Axis in Latin America was tough on Jews.

Not only did they have to endure months or years of incarceration behind barbed wire in camps designed for their enemies, but they were spared a worse fate only because officials in the State Department who considered sending Jews to the Third Reich, such as Breckinridge Long and Albert Clattenburg, did not prevail over cooler heads at Justice.[19]

Chapter Twenty-Two

Breck's Boo-Boo

ON JUNE 23, 1943, WHEN Breckinridge Long wrote, "The refugee problem has died down," he may have felt life would be easier for him in the State Department from then on. He could even pat himself on the back over some additional duties given him: chairman of the Political Planning Committee—he called it "an active committee"—with responsibilities for "developing policies . . . helpful to us in prosecuting the war"; chairman of the Post-War Telecommunications Committee, whose job was devising controls on the defeated Axis powers' communications systems; chairman of the Post-War Shipping Committee, about which he was less enthusiastic; and finally the Migrations Committee chair, one he had tried to duck, since it dealt with "my other activity in connection with refugees, because it looks to their return to their homes after the war."[1]

Clearly, by the summer of 1943, the Roosevelt administration was able to start looking at a postwar world the Allies would dominate. The Axis was far from finished, but it was cracking. At the end of July, Mussolini was forced out of office. Sicily had been successfully invaded and North Africa secured. For four weeks, Breck Long vacationed at Wianno, Massachusetts, on Cape Cod, during what in retrospect could be deemed *a lull before the storm* at the State Department. On August 9, 1943, Long returned to work amid rumors (proven to be false) that the Soviet Union could be seeking a separate peace with Germany.

Twenty days later, Long's diary entry started with this terse news: "Welles is gone. He left the Department a week ago today."[2]

All at once, the dysfunctional inner workings at the Department's highest levels were exposed to the public, yet only part of the story got told. It was no secret that Under Secretary Sumner Welles, "Roosevelt's boy," was not on good terms with his boss Cordell Hull. *Time* magazine, in its August 30, 1943, issue, had hinted at the discord in a story about

U.S.-de Gaulle relations, printing the opinion of a Free French spokesman that "Mr. Cordell Hull did not get along with Mr. Sumner Welles and did not like Mr. Adolf Berle. Mr. Sumner Welles did not like Mr. Hull and Mr. Berle; and Mr. Berle liked only himself."

The following week, *Time* reported on the departure of Sumner Welles in a long article that began with a series of staccato statements:

> In factual terms, the news was brief. Under Secretary of State Sumner Welles had resigned . . . In political terms, the news was complex. When would Franklin Roosevelt cease his appeasement of Southern Democrats who had forced Welles's resignation and how would U.S. foreign policy be affected? . . . In human terms, the news was repetitious. Cordell Hull had again got his man. [Earlier, Hull had forced out Raymond Moley, another FDR plant in his organization.]

The body of this September 6, 1943, story also contained various prognostications.

> To the hubbub caused by Welles's resignation was a hubbub of speculation over his possible successor. The candidate reportedly favored by Cordell Hull—onetime ambassador to Italy Breckinridge Long—was certain to meet bitter opposition from those who think democratic aspirations are important. For Breckinridge Long, whose swank parties were attended by the fanciest members of Italian society, has won no distinction by his opposition to Fascism.

Other possible candidates the Luce publication mentioned were Breck's old pal George Messersmith, then ambassador to Mexico; Joseph C. Grew, former ambassador to Japan; and Norman Armour, who'd been ambassador to Argentina.

In Long's lengthy discussion of the resulting "hubbub" precipitated by Welles's abrupt departure, he remained quite circumspect. The press *was* mentioning him as a potential choice for the *number two* position in the Department. If his heart was going pitter-patter over the prospect, he didn't show it. But who could believe that, if only for a moment, he wouldn't have contemplated he might get his long-wished-for promotion?

Still, *Time* magazine's sarcasm about his prospects could hardly have emboldened him. His diary does tell how Assistant Secretary of State

Adolf Berle came to his office on August 25 and told him about an article in the *Washington Post* to the effect that he, Berle, had threatened to resign if Long were made Under Secretary. Berle wanted it understood he had no such intention, although it would be easy to guess he did want the job, himself.

"Welles knew he was being displaced," Long consequently wrote. "Those on the inside would know it. He knew the real reason. Those on the inside would also know that."[3] An effort to save face had been planned. The discharged under secretary would be offered a special mission to Russia; except, it so happened, while as acting secretary in the absence of Hull, Welles suddenly disappeared or rather, took off for his summer home in Bar Harbor, Maine.

While everyone within the State Department hierarchy was being coy, a sordid scandal—now three years old—had led to the downfall of Sumner Welles. Breck Long wrote he had known about the secret, since 1942. In today's climate, Welles's misbehavior would not touch the same nerve it did then. On a train ride during 1940, returning from the funeral in Alabama of Speaker of the U.S. House William B. Bankhead (Tallulah's father), Sumner Welles, who had an alcohol problem, drunkenly propositioned a Pullman porter (some versions say *two* Pullman porters) to participate in a homosexual act. The transgression was reported and made its way to the FBI, where J. Edgar Hoover, in concert with FDR, kept it quiet. But thanks to William C. Bullitt—and Cordell Hull—the story wouldn't stay buried.

William Christian Bullitt Jr.'s career in the State Department had begun about the same time as Breckinridge Long's, 1917, and at the same level, an assistant secretary of state. But this scion of a prominent Philadelphia family, a Yale man, was somehow closer to Woodrow Wilson than Princetonian Long. Soon he was on his way to an ambassadorship—first serving on a special mission to the newly established Soviet government in Russia and then as America's top envoy to Moscow. Later on, under FDR, he was ambassador to wartime France before and during its 1940 collapse. Yet Bullitt always had a way of ending up out of favor with his bosses. He broke with Wilson when the latter refused to recognize the Bolshevik regime and then—ex post facto—got his revenge by teaming up with none other than Sigmund Freud, whose patient he was, and jointly producing a hatchet-job psychoanalytic book about the late president. The break with FDR, with whom Bullitt had once been very close, was started by certain of his actions in France in 1940 but culminated with his sabotaging of Sumner Welles three years later.

The final straw was Bullitt's leaking of the Pullman porter story to key members of Congress, including Republicans, and especially Maine's none-too-scrupulous Senator Ralph Owen Brewster, who could be expected to blow the homosexual scandal wide open.

Franklin Roosevelt was absolutely livid, making it plain Bullitt's career was over, although facetiously suggesting the Philadelphian might be sent to the (then) totally hardship diplomatic post of Saudi Arabia. Sometime later, Bullitt had the temerity to ask FDR to support his run for mayor of Philadelphia. The president's response was vintage Roosevelt. "If I were the Angel Gabriel," he said to Bullitt, "and you and Sumner Welles sought admission to heaven, I would say: 'Bill Bullitt, you have defamed the name of a man who toiled for his fellow man and you can go to hell.' And that's what I tell you to do now." Without Roosevelt's help, Bullitt lost the election.

Remember that Breckinridge Long, too, hated Bill Bullitt and reserved uncommonly harsh language for him in his diary. Why this animosity, which showed up well before the Welles affair? Quite possibly, it went back to their days as junior members of the State Department under Wilson. Bullitt had a mother who was half-Jewish, but that could hardly have been a reason, and besides he was considered a WASP Brahmin and at Yale had been accepted as a member of the highly restrictive secret society, Scroll and Key.

Whatever the cause, Long definitely does seem to have played a role in this whole unseemly drama. When Welles first spoke to him about the rumored story the previous year, the under secretary said it was "a malicious lie," and Long assured Welles it was because of Bullitt's involvement. "I have known him [Bullitt] a long, long time and know him well but I have *never* had any confidence in him," he declared.[4] There then had followed frequent discussions with Cordell Hull, who was terrified the scandal would get out and besmirch the Department and the president. Prior to Long's leaving for Massachusetts on his July vacation, Hull was telling him that Welles was open to blackmail by "foreign governments who knew the story." Long insisted he merely sought to serve as a neutral go-between—"tried to calm Hull, get the two men together, hush the story, keep the boat on an even keel."[5]

But upon learning that Republicans like Owen Brewster now had this information, Long revealed how he by-passed Hull and went straight to Welles and told him that whether the story was true or not, the GOP would use it to hurt the Democrats and FDR. "I laid the cards on the table," Long admitted, telling Welles he had to do something to counteract the tale but that Welles felt helpless. "He did nothing and we never alluded to it again," Long reported.

As soon as Welles was gone and his resignation known, Long immediately advised Hull he had to move quickly and appoint someone (he didn't say it had to be himself), otherwise the press would have a field day and so would the "radicals" who hated Hull and himself and that as the facts were in the open, Welles "would be rendered useless as a public servant."

Whether Long was playing an Iago role here is a possible suspicion. No doubt in his heart of hearts he was coveting the appointment for which his name had been openly mentioned. On September 7, 1943, almost two weeks after Welles's departure, he described a talk with Hull about filling the post. Hull was quoted as saying, "It looked like the President still wanted to run the State Department." Long read this statement to mean, "The inference was rather clear that my name and others had been discussed, that no decision had been made and that the President was going to choose whom he wanted whether Hull quite agreed or not—and that Hull was not going to make an issue out of it."[6]

What Breck Long came away with from this meeting—because of a parting remark from his boss—was a sense of perplexity. Cordell Hull said in the presence of others in the room: "Breck, I want you to know I told the President you had always been in accord with me and that you and I were going to shape foreign policies in here."[7] Long was of two minds about these words of Hull. "It was either to alibi himself for any thought or suggestion he had not gone to all proper lengths to advocate my appointment—or with the the [*sic*] honest intent to let the Department know he placed just reliance on me—or—what? . . . It was just mysterious."[8]

Time magazine in its issue of September 27, 1945, reported that after a month the position of under secretary of state still was vacant. Calling it "as difficult an appointment Franklin Roosevelt has ever had to make," the writer cited the need for a skillful administrator able to deal with "power-jealous Cordell Hull." Reference was made again to Norman Armour, ambassador to Argentina, a career man who had been deemed the "perfect diplomat," but that he had been rejected because he was "too friendly with everyone." Breckinridge Long's name was still on the list, along with George Messersmith, plus three newcomers: Dean Acheson, another assistant secretary of state; James C. "Jimmy" Dunn, Hull's political advisor; and Assistant Director of the Budget Wayne Coy. *Time*'s conclusion was: "None of these would solve Franklin Roosevelt's dilemma."

As forecasted, the winner was: *None of the Above!* Even before *Time*'s story hit the newsstands, the appointee was announced and turned out to be Edward R. Stettinius Jr., a Republican businessman pal of FDR's, who at the time was running the Lend Lease program. Ed Stettinius cut an impressive figure, statuesque, movie-star good looks, distinguished but still young, and admired for his administrative skills.

On September 26, 1943, Breckinridge Long recorded in his diary, "Last night the radio announced Stettinius had been selected for Under Secretary. I did not hear it. Miss Aderton called me and told me." Next, he heard the news from Cordell Hull himself, who claimed he had urged the president to appoint Long, "but the President wanted to make his own decision." Long's reply, one might say, was *diplomatic*—that he had "no personal ambition in the complicated scheme of things and thought Stettinius better than all the others mentioned."[9]

Stettinius kept diaries, too, and they shed further light on his surprise appointment. He apparently had no idea it was in the offing, describing himself in San Francisco on September 24, when Supreme Court Justice James Byrnes contacted him in his room at the Mark Hopkins Hotel; Byrnes asked if Cordell Hull had phoned, to which the answer was no, and the justice went on to say, "I've engineered around for you. Hull wanted Armour, the President someone else but now all agree on you for Under Secretary of State. Don't tell Hull I told you."[10]

Note the discrepancy here: *Hull wanted Armour*, not Long, according to Jimmy Byrnes. If so, this would have been unwelcome news to the Missourian, even evidence of perfidy on the part of his boss. At any rate, whether Breck Long knew it or not, a discordant element was about to enter the State Department picture where he was concerned. For Stettinius had accepted the position once Hull finally reached him. General George Marshall, among others, strongly urged him to do so, telling the Lend Lease administrator: "You are an organizer."

This was a theme Long also sounded at a top-level meeting, October 4, 1943, Stettinius's first day at work. The latter's diary records:

During my visit Mr. [Breckinridge] Long [Assistant Secretary of State] was there part of the time and said unless we revamp things pretty quickly, the Department is likely to disintegrate. Long said, "Ed has the organizational experience and we can rely on him." The Secretary agreed. I said: "There are a lot of things to be revamped." The Secretary said he had thought that Welles was following the administration of the State Department, but found out he wasn't.[11]

Like he often did when defeated or thwarted, Breck Long tried to put the best face he could on the situation. On September 26, the same day he learned the news for certain of his non-appointment, he wrote, "Stettinius is an able fellow—energetic—capable—has done a good job on Lend Lease. What he knows of foreign affairs I do not know. As far as I know I like him."[12] He also imparted the information that he had worked with Ed Stettinius's father during World War I, when the latter was an assistant secretary of the treasury and connected with the Morgan investment and banking firm.

But Breck confessed he was also already reexamining his own future in the State Department. Once again, there were his complaints he was being overworked. He stated he was "filling two positions and doing the work of the counselor and that of an Assistant Secretary" and needed immediate relief from "the minutiae of executive supervision and direction." Yet left unsaid was that the under secretary's job he coveted would have probably been even more work. His wounded ego led him to mention he had served his "apprenticeship [as assistant secretary] . . . in the last war and had only accepted the offer to do it anew "reluctantly, but in a spirit of service . . . and glad to serve."

Thus at his initial meeting with Stettinius about a week later, we find Long sycophantic, praising "Ed's" organizational skills that were to save the Department from "disintegration." On Stettinius's part, he refers to Breckinridge Long in his diaries only two other times. The first of these is dated November 3, 1943, and that particular tie between them resulted from the Allied conference in Moscow in the fall of 1943. This meeting was considered so important that Cordell Hull himself attended, leaving Stettinius in Washington as acting secretary of state. The Declaration issued by the Four Power Moscow Conference was that no separate peace would be made with Germany by any of the Allied nations, but its everlasting impact was in a subordinate clause, affirming the victors would set up an *international organization* after the fighting ended, to which these countries—the United States, U.S.S.R., Great Britain, and China—would pledge their wholehearted support.

Back in DC, however, there was a political problem. The Moscow Declaration was released while the U.S. Senate was debating a resolution of a similar nature. After ten days, Breck Long, aware that a contradiction might exist between the final Senate language and the Moscow Declaration, brought the matter to Stettinius's attention.

Stettinius discussed the issue with Justice James Byrnes in a long-distance phone call and recorded the conversation.

Stettinius: "Breck Long feels that somebody should go up and talk to Tom (Senate Majority Leader Tom Connally of Texas) and hold his hand and explain the Moscow thing and find out what's on his mind for the next move. Do you have any objections?"

Byrnes: "No, I told him I had talked to Tom. I told Breck that I knew him [Connally] so well and that God alone might be able to get Tom to change a sentence in the Connally resolution . . . but I knew of no power on earth that would get him to change that resolution. If Breck can by any means get him to do it, it would be all right."

Stettinius: "I will tell Breck he can go up this morning and have a talk with Tom and see where he gets."

Byrnes: "Fine. They say the days of miracles is past, but maybe not."[13]

What Long had been asked to do was convince Senator Connally to include phrases from the Moscow Declaration in the Senate's resolution. The assistant secretary himself requested backing from the White House and the Department, that he was speaking on behalf of the administration. Given a green light, he phoned Connally, who said he would be happy to see him. Breck Long later wrote, "I emphasized that I was not there to talk to him casually and that my visit was an indication that the Department of State and the executive branch of the Government considered the situation of utmost importance from the point of view of international politics and Allied cooperation."[14]

Thus, a miracle did happen. With Connally's support secured, the resolution passed 85 to 5. Only two Democrats defected, and Breck Long gleefully recorded that one of them, Senator Robert Reynolds of North Carolina (the most outspoken anti-Semitic member of the Senate), was sure to be defeated in an upcoming Democratic primary in the Tar Heel State. The other apostate was the perennial Roosevelt-hater, Burt Wheeler of Montana.

Reminiscing in his diary, Breck Long was able to give himself a strong pat on the back. The expressed approval for an "international organization" from the very body that had helped kill the League of Nations, in Long's words, placed

both major parties in line on the great question of foreign policy which has caused so much trouble in this country and in the world since the days of Wilson. Personally, I am happy that I have kept the faith these many years—now find myself vindicated—and gratified that I had a considerable part in the maneuver . . . Now we are back at the main track—after being side-tracked and nearly wrecked in 1920.[15]

This sense of triumph notwithstanding, it could be said that Breckinridge Long had been mostly embroiled in defending his work at least since the spring of 1943. The overriding difficulty for the Missourian was the *problem* he still hadn't been able to finesse—i.e., meeting the criticism piled on the State Department—and himself—for its tepid and actually counterproductive reaction to the Nazis' Final Solution, which was now swinging into full gear.

On May 15, 1943, Long wrote to Sumner Welles, who was then still under secretary of state and his immediate boss, that they should strike back against their critics. His idea was that "the Department might instigate a story for instance in *Colliers* [magazine] which would give a picture of the activities of the Department of State in the refugee movement." And, of course, in the best sly bureaucratic tradition, the source would be masked—no hint it had originated in the Department.

> Rather, that it be presented by some independent writer . . . in order to present the refugee problem as a whole and the favorable attitude of the Department of State toward it.

Another argument offered in his memo to Welles was that the Department should stop being "close-mouthed." They'd been open to the criticism they'd received, he argued, because they hadn't said anything. "Now that the Bermuda Conference has passed and the possibility that the Intergovernmental Committee may meet, I think it may be a good time to do this." One response he solicited was a *confidential* memo from Howard Bucknell Jr. of the State Department's Division of Current Information saying he agreed and that a "very useful" article could be planted in *Colliers* "or in any other representative magazine."

It appears Breckinridge Long had already been preparing for a favorable reaction to his suggestion, producing extensive papers (of 15 pages and 13 pages) on the subject. The first was loaded with justifications for what the State Department was allegedly doing, with emphasis on those saved:

Persons known for their intense opposition to the Nazi philosophy, of persons of character and substance, of intelligence and mental vigor, authors, scientists, leaders of men—men and women worth saving from the maelstrom of death and destruction,

and adding that the Department of State acted up to the limit of its authority under the law, plus throwing in another paragraph reiterating all the kinds of people worth saving now including also

manufacturers, artisans, inventors, mechanics, bankers,

and, lo and behold, throwing in "just poor people harassed and overcome by brute strength." Included in this opus was actually a pathetic description of the desperate refugee.

They fell on their knees and begged for visas. They tried threats, bribery, trickery—any device born of desperation—to achieve their ends—even in despair attempted suicide on the spot.

But needless to say, he admonished his audience that "they all could not be given visas," and he likewise brought up his shopworn excuse that the Germans were using the refugee situation to sneak secret agents into the U.S. or blackmailing refugees with relatives left in the old country to act as spies. No statistics were ever quoted here by Long, certainly not the FBI's count of three cases at most and possibly just one instance. Meanwhile, Long was tossing around all kinds of inflated numbers about Jewish refugees saved.

The second paper prepared by him dealt with one of his pet peeves: special interest nationality groups within the U.S. lobbying for the interests of their home populations. He cited Greek-Americans attacking the U.S. in 1918–19 for not giving Macedonia to Greece and the same for Italian-Americans angry at the U.S. for not ceding Adriatic ports in Yugoslavia to their mother country. Writing of the dangers he saw in "allowing foreigners here to appeal to ethnic groups here to support the home governments," he proposed to have them [the ethnic organizations] "quietly shut down." Interestingly enough, he did not at first refer to the Jews in this vein (possibly because they didn't have a home government like the Norwegian, Dutch, German, Italian, and Greek groups that he condemned). Later, in another of his writings, he did strike out at the Bergson Group, apparently unaware he was mixing up these radical Zionists with other branches of the Zionist movement hostile to them.

In so doing, Breck Long really did go overboard. He took one of the Bergson slogans, calling for Action Not Pity, and then outrageously claimed they had copied the language from Adolf Hitler, asserting: "This slogan was first suggested by Hitler in his 1937 speech when he accused the countries [now the Allies] of 'moralizing, not acting, on the refugee problem,'" that this idea was "a favorite of the Gestapo," and that the cry had been taken up by Ben Gurion in Palestine, transplanted to England, "where certain emotionalists and impractical dreamers adopted it and shipped it on to Rabbi Wise and [Nahum] Goldmann in New York. There it was made the keynote of a mass meeting in Madison Square."[16]

Long's extraordinary rant could easily be picked apart for its inaccuracies and self-serving fantasies. For example, his conflating Rabbi Wise and Dr. Goldmann with the Bergson Group, who staged the Madison Square Garden event, and the use of the Action Not Pity slogan. These two sets of Zionists literally hated each other. By then, the Bergson group, practicing the *action* it preached, had found those friends of theirs in Congress willing to introduce resolutions for creating a separate new governmental agency, whose specific task would be trying to rescue the fast-dwindling remnant of European Jewry still awaiting Eichmann's round-up of victims for the death camps.

A key leader in the above effort was a new congressman from California with a famous name, Will Rogers Jr., who has told how he hooked up with Peter Bergson in 1943 and why he went along with him in trying to save Jews from the Holocaust. Rogers wrote,

> I was a freshman Congressman, and being a freshman, I was up on the 5th floor of the old House Office building. And somehow or other, Peter Bergson found his way up to my office, my remote office . . . I do recall sitting down there and talking to him about the Jewish position in Europe.

Rogers went on to say he was like "anybody else" in the U.S. They knew the Germans were killing the Jews . . . but what could they do about it? "I couldn't do anything about it," Rogers claimed. Yet "Peter Bergson stimulated me," he admitted.

> I began to be more interested . . . slowly it dawned on me that it was my duty to go out and speak against the destruction of the Jews.

Rogers not only spoke but *acted.* He immediately cosponsored a Resolution Providing for the Establishment by the Executive of a Commission to Effectuate the Rescue of the Jewish People of Europe. Also, as a member of the House Committee on Foreign Relations that would hear this bill, H. Res. 350, and a similar measure, H. Res. 352, he was in a key position.

Sol Bloom, the Manhattan congressman, who was Breck Long's patsy, chaired this committee and could be expected to bottle up and kill any effort to remove the rescue of Jews from the recalcitrant hands of the State Department. As a delegate to the Bermuda Conference, hand-picked by Long, Bloom had made one feeble attempt to protest all the inaction, but in no way rocked the boat of the official position essentially to do nothing.

Behind closed doors on November 26, 1943, the Bloom Committee convened and was addressed by Assistant Secretary of State Breckinridge Long. He was there to convince them that these resolutions weren't needed, and he was devilishly clever about it. The results of the Bermuda Conference had been kept classified, and so, in executive session he could reveal them to the congressmen, including what the State Department insisted was the only answer to the rescue quandary—the resuscitation of the Intergovernmental Committee on Refugees. Among the flat statements made by Long at this meeting was that 580,000 refugees had been taken into the U.S. since the advent of Hitler, his implication being that most of these people had been Jewish. Another statement Breck issued was,

> Everybody I know, everybody in the Department of State and everybody that I have come in contact with is interested and a lot of them have been active in endeavoring to save the Jewish people from the terrorism of the Nazis.[17]

When the question period started, Representative Luther Johnson, Democrat of Texas, opened with a real softball for Long, asking if the requested resolutions would not be duplications of the State Department's efforts and those of the Intergovernmental Committee that was to be reestablished. It may well have been that Johnson had been "prepped" by Long, for he then proceeded to read the *mandate* of the original Intergovernmental Committee.

Congressman John Vorys, Republican of Ohio, asked whether the purpose of these proposed resolutions was to open Palestine to the Jews and was assured by Long and also by Congressman Rogers that there was no such intent.

Posing the most questions was another Republican, South Dakota's Karl Mundt, who said he was thinking of adding amendments to cover "all refugees, not just Jews."

Long's answer was, "Something definite ought to be said about the Jews," which might seem out of character to those who have tagged him as a diehard anti-Semite. So too might his plea to the committee not to kill these resolutions, since "it would be misconstrued and might react against the Jewish people under German control."[18] Cleverly, his following suggestion that the committee simply hold the resolutions without acting on them, while seeming politically savvy, would even more cleverly have the same effect of killing them, but with everything comfortably buried behind closed doors.

The next happenstance, once the hearing was completed, seemingly had Breck Long's fingerprints all over it. Parts of his testimony were released to the press by the State Department itself. Did they, or Breck, believe he had performed so brilliantly before the lawmakers that the public would be wowed and their enemies confounded? On Saturday, December 11, 1943, on the front page of *The New York Times*, above the fold, was the headline:

580,000 REFUGEES ADMITTED TO UNITED STATES IN A DECADE
DISCLOSURE OF STATE DEPARTMENT DATA TO BLOOM'S COMMITTEE IS LINKED TO ITS OPPOSING BILLS FOR WIDER ACTION.

The story, by Frederick R. Barkeley in a "Special from DC to the *New York Times*," quoted Breckinridge Long as the source of the statement, "580,000 victims of persecution by Hitler" admitted in the past ten years, and also reported that

the release of the testimony by permission of the State Department was construed as an intimation that Mr. Long's report had swung the Committee into opposing the bills providing for executive creation of a commission to effectuate the rescue of the Jewish people of Europe.

Barkeley's story also confirmed Long had said the majority of these 580,000 refugees "were Jews," because the State Department recognized that "the Jews were the most persecuted and the object of more antipathy than others."

If Breck Long felt smug about his success in thwarting a refugee operation rivaling his, he didn't have much time to savor his "victory." Congressman Emanuel Celler would soon see to that.

Chapter Twenty-Three

The War Refugee Board Created

B Y NOW, WE KNOW "MANNY" Celler was no shrinking violet. His
particular peeve had always been the anti-immigration laws passed
by Congress, and despite being the first Democrat ever elected in his
Brooklyn-Queens district and serving his first term in 1924, he took on
the redoubtable Albert Johnson and his quota bill, aimed primarily at
keeping out Jews and Catholics. Although this freshman congressman
had a German-Catholic grandfather, he was otherwise completely
of Jewish heritage, and he bravely if futilely battled the forces of
eugenicists and nativists, who were pushing to keep the U.S. as Anglo-
Saxon and Nordic as possible. Celler was to say of his maiden fight on
the issue,

> Thanks to the ill-considered and improvident Johnson Bill . . .
> race is set against race and class against class.

The advent of Hitler and the mounting plight of the Jews of Europe
had brought Manny back on the attack, and although a strong follower
of FDR, he did not shy away from lambasting the Roosevelt State
Department for its "cold and cruel" policies and "glacier-like attitude" in
addressing the Nazi massacres, especially of the Jews.

In *You Never Leave Brooklyn*, Celler tells of the visit to his office,
once the exterminations had become common knowledge, of Rav
Kalmanowitz, an aged rabbi and "noted sage," who came to plead the
case of the Jews of Europe awaiting death in late 1943. Celler described
his unforgettable visitor in vivid terms.

> Everything about him, his hat which he didn't remove, his long
> black coat and patriarchal beard, the veined hands clutching
> a cane, these stand before me, even to this day. Trembling and

enfeebled, he had traveled from Brooklyn to Washington to talk to his Congressman. Not once did he seem conscious of his tears as he pleaded: "Don't you see; can't you see; won't you see that there are millions being killed? Can't we save some of them? Can't you, Mr. Congressman, do something?"

And Celler then added: "I dreamed about him that night. The old rabbi stood on a rock in the ocean and hordes of people fought through the water to get to that rock."

On December 12, 1943, the day after the front page *New York Times* story about Breckinridge Long's testimony, Celler had his riposte in the press. The headline in the *Times* was:

JEWS DEBARRED, CELLER DECLARES

and below was: New York Congressman Says Long Shed Crocodile Tears Over Refugees. It was a special to *The New York Times*, but without a byline, and incidentally was on page 8, the only column of print on a page otherwise devoted to jewelry and girdle ads.

Celler went after Long on a number of accounts, disputing the assistant secretary of state's claim, "the Government had done everything to permit the immigration of victims of Nazi tyranny and that the majority of these had been Jews," and added:

I would like to ask him how many Jews were admitted during the last three years in comparison with the number seeking entrance to preserve life and dignity. It is not a proud record.

He also dismissed Long's excuse of a *lack of shipping* to accommodate refugees, by pointing out there now were "bridges of ships reaching to all parts of the world and they come back void of passengers."

But what proved to be the Celler's knockout punch was his debunking of Long's figure of 580,000 people saved in a decade and his insinuation that most of them were Jews. Celler insisted the 580,000 were "in the main ordinary quota immigrants coming in from all countries and the majority were not Jews."

To defend himself, Breck Long might have attributed Manny Celler's attack to overwrought Jewish emotionalism, but as we know, other even more formidable enemies were organizing against him in the Treasury: the three Protestant young men, Randolph Paul, Josiah Du Bois, and

John Pehle, with Lend Lease's Oscar Cox in the background, pushing Henry Morgenthau Jr. to confront FDR.

In his diary on New Year's Day, 1944, Long was candid, admitting his figures were inaccurate, but excusing himself. Referring to the House Foreign Affairs Committee meeting, where he'd been treated royally, as a "four-hour inquisition," he pleaded that he had spoken "without notes from a memory of four years, without preparation and on a day's notice." Gratuitously, he added: "It is remarkable I did not make more inaccurate statements."

Conceivably, the shock of realizing what a blunder he had made brought out a vituperative strain in his writing. Along with tweaking the figures he had presented and admitting they were only of *authorized visas*, he claimed that he had been "pilloried as an enemy of the Jews" because of this miscommunication (no indication that he had led the Bloom Committee to believe that more than half a million Jews had been saved by the State Department). His snarling conclusion:

> The Jewish agitation depends on attacking some individual. Otherwise they would have no publicity. So for the time being, I am the bull's eye.[1]

A week and a half later, he again began venting on the subject. Still feigning nonchalance but perhaps already recognizing his battle was lost, he now claimed he *wanted* to "relinquish jurisdiction over the refugee problem." In his January 11, 1944, diary entry, Long stated that he had been working with a Rabbi Willes (otherwise unidentified) and a colleague of his to send "a message to Switzerland" to encourage an ongoing escape of Jews from Poland into Hungary.

Long then followed up with a disquisition on the status of the Jewish groups in the U.S. and their rivalries, alleging that they were "all divided and in controversies of their own." Once more he reiterated, "But it will be only a few days now before I relinquish jurisdiction in connection with refugees and let somebody else have the fun."[2]

The *final straw* leading to the stormy meeting in the Oval Office on January 16, 1944, which caused Breck Long to lose his monopoly of the refugee question, concerned a bungled chance to rescue 70,000 Rumanian Jews.

Rumania, allied with Nazi Germany, was no less anti-Semitic, and indeed its fascistic Iron Guard had perpetrated one of the most hideous atrocities of the entire war—killing a group of Jews in a Bucharest slaughterhouse as if they were cattle. But Rumania's dictator, Marshal Ion Antonescu, by 1943 had seen the writing on the wall. The Soviets were advancing into his country. So he offered to bring back the 70,000 local Jews he had interned in a region called Transnistria and let them live, if food, clothing, and medicine were provided.

Gerhart Riegner in Switzerland had a plan to accomplish this Rumanian exchange. Jewish organizations would lend the money—a total of about $600,000 (or $8.50 per human being). But first Riegner would need earnest money of $25,000 from the World Jewish Congress as an opening installment, and here's where the hang-up came.

Under U.S. wartime regulations, both the State Department and Treasury would jointly have to agree to issue a license to Riegner before money could be sent overseas. Treasury was not a problem. Its Division of Foreign Funds Control under John Pehle quickly granted approval. Contrarily, the State Department's intentional snag started with a memo from one of Breckinridge Long's underlings—R. Borden Reams— telling his boss he shouldn't sign off because it was a matter for the Intergovernmental Committee on Refugees to handle. Reams, who had been Long's man at the Bermuda Conference, knew full well that the reactivation of this bureaucratic operation would take months to accomplish.

And so it was that months went by. The Riegner initiative might have died altogether had it not been for Dr. Herbert Feis, the State Department's economic advisor and one of the few Jews in a position of importance there. Even then, objections from the British government caused another six months to pass before U.S. minister Leland Harrison cabled DC for specific instructions.

Once again, Borden Reams protested, saying the Jews were *enemy aliens* who would be getting preferential treatment and that the British would be "incensed" at not being consulted (as well as upset by the prospect of more Jews they would have to keep out of Palestine). Breck Long, ever the politician, did eventually agree to approve the license, even chiding Reams for his remark about Jews as "enemy aliens." Still, the message sent to Minister Harrison in Bern was so equivocal that more delay was incurred, while Secretary of State Cordell Hull's approval of the transfer of funds months earlier continued to be ignored. By then, the British Foreign Office had also forcefully added they could not deal with 70,000 rescued Jewish refugees.

After a showdown meeting between Morgenthau, John Pehle, Hull, and Breckinridge Long, Harrison in Switzerland was finally ordered to issue the money transfer license to Riegner. Eight months had gone by, and about Christmas time 1943 the $25,000 arrived. Of the 70,000 Rumanian Jews who had been alive at the start, only 48,000 returned from Transnistria. The State Department's stalling in this case had cost 22,000 lives.

Another complaint made against Breckinridge Long and the State Department during that climactic Sunday in FDR's office went back to the 1942 news from Gerhart Riegner about the extermination policy the Nazis had put into effect. There were accusations of how State Department personnel had deliberately sought to keep the news of the Final Solution buried. The Treasury's criticism centered on a certain Cable 354, which ordered Minister Harrison not to allow any further reports "to private persons in the U.S." Morgenthau and his boys claimed this wire "was designed to countermand . . . specific requests for information on Hitler's plans to exterminate the Jews." Breck Long's connection to the notorious Cable 354 was that, when ordered by Hull to furnish Treasury with a copy, he *doctored* the original language, making the message appear innocuous. His trickery, which happened after a December 20, 1943, meeting, was fresh in the minds of the Treasury group in the Oval Office the following January, and they angrily charged that Cable 354 "stopped the obtaining of information concerning the murder of the Jews" and that "State Department officials have even attempted concealment and misrepresentation within the government."

The crucial January 1944 meeting, we're aware, ended with FDR saying, "We'll do it," in regard to creating the War Refugee Board and taking the handling of refugees away from Breckinridge Long.

The doings of the War Refugee Board, once it was up and running, could furnish material for a dozen thriller movies. In the matter of approximately a year and a half, it did save several hundred thousand lives, 90 percent of them Jewish. Its most famous operator was Raoul Wallenberg, the martyred Swedish diplomat who worked in Hungary, where a large Jewish population still existed in 1944 and was being deported by Eichmann to the death camps. Many people do not know that Wallenberg worked for the War Refugee Board, but then again, a lot more have probably never heard of the War Refugee Board. Wallenberg's Wikipedia biography states: "In spring 1944, US President Franklin D. Roosevelt sent Iver Olsen to Stockholm as the official representative of the War Refugee Board"[3] and that Olsen recruited Wallenberg, the son of a very wealthy, distinguished Swedish family. In the guise of the first secretary of his country's legation in Budapest, Wallenberg began his heroic effort to save as many Hungarian Jews and non-Jewish anti-Nazis as he could. He began by handing out "passports" to intended victims of the Hitlerites and the Hungarian Arrow Cross fascists, which gave them the status of Swedish citizens. Once he was even so bold as to leap onto a packed train destined for Auschwitz, climb up on the roof and hand down these passes, despite loudly shouted orders from the German guards to desist and shots fired at him by the Hungarian militia, which perhaps deliberately were aimed too high. The Jews, waving their Swedish documents, were then allowed to detrain and soon sped away in waiting automobiles stationed by Wallenberg. His role with the War Refugee Board may have led to his mysterious demise, for as soon as the Red Army captured Budapest, he was arrested by the Soviets, who deemed him an American spy, and he apparently died in a Russian prison in the summer of 1947.

That the War Refugee Board had the successes it did could well never have occurred had not it been for a series of happy coincidences.

The first hurdle was the structure decided for it and spelled out in FDR's Executive Order 9417. The leadership of the operation was to be shared equally in troika fashion by the secretary of the treasury, the secretary of state, and the secretary of war. There is some speculation that this awkward arrangement was devised by Breckinridge Long and spelled out in a memo he'd been asked to prepare by Cordell Hull. Needless to say, if all three secretaries—Morgenthau, Hull, and Henry L. Stimson—had had their fingers in the pie, the delay in getting the WRB up and running could have been monumental. Writing about this episode, Professor Jeffrey S. Gurock of Yeshiva University in his book *America, American Jews and the Holocaust*, states the unexpected outcome succinctly: "The latter two [Hull and Stimson] accepted these responsibilities reluctantly and, in effect, the new agency was Morgenthau's."[4]

Furthermore, one of "Morgenthau's boys," John W. Pehle, was put in charge as director of the WRB.

There was also the problem of insufficient funding to overcome. Roosevelt had only allowed it a budget of $1 million. In order to accomplish its tasks, money had to be raised from private sources— mostly Jewish—who contributed another $17 million.

Parenthetically, Professor Gurock does mention Breck Long's role in this whole affair. He asserts that "Breckinridge Long, the State Department official primarily responsible for refugee matters believed that making refugee policy meant protecting the security of the United

States." Then he discusses "Long's counterpart in the British Foreign Office," one Alex Randall,

> who was not so afraid of mythic dangers as he was on protecting Britain's Palestine policy. When the War Refugee Board was created, the British initially assumed that the Roosevelt action was mere "eyewash." Their concern that this was not the case was evident by April.[5]

For this reason, Randall proposed to his colleagues in London that they offer to set up a camp jointly with the U.S. in Tripolitania (Libya) for Jewish escapees, so as to keep these survivors of the Final Solution out of Palestine.

Numerous other instances of Wallenberg-style derring-do accompanied the widespread work of the WRB. Its out-front agents, established in neutral countries like Spain, Switzerland, and Turkey, were backed by underground operatives and couriers in German-occupied cities like Budapest, Bratislava, Bucharest, Prague, and Vienna.

Breckinridge Long's prediction that the WRB would not be able to do any better than he had done in saving Jews was obviously considerably off-base. The estimated 200,000 Jews rescued, while not a huge number compared to the overall more than 6 million targeted for death, was a significant accomplishment, carried out in what had to be record time.

In the immediate aftermath of the president's decision to create the War Refugee Board, Breckinridge Long still temporarily had a role to play vis-à-vis refugees. On January 25, 1944, Long met with Cordell Hull, ostensibly to talk about the memo he'd been asked to draft on the structure of the War Refugee Board. Also, verbally, he warned his boss not to get involved personally with this new outfit but let Under Secretary Stettinius front for him. That done, Breck switched gears, already pointing himself and his career, it seemed, in a fresh direction where he hoped to shine.

During the rest of the hour the two men were closeted, they mostly conversed about the Roosevelt administration's intent to create an "international political organization" (the future United Nations). This was an area where Long had definite credentials, dating back to the League of Nations. He hoped to ensure himself attendance at the birth of the League's successor. The main preoccupation brainstormed by Hull and Long that day was how to shepherd a resolution through the

U.S. Senate supporting the idea. After all, it was in the U.S. Senate that the League of Nations had been mortally wounded.

So Breck Long remained in the State Department, albeit with his wings somewhat clipped, but finding lots of other work to do, especially on the United Nations project. Occasionally, the "Jewish matter" even crept into his bailiwick. At the end of February 1944, resolutions were introduced in both branches of Congress favoring a Jewish "commonwealth" in Palestine. In his diary, you almost could hear him groan as he wrote,

> Just when our negotiations with King Ibn Saud of concessions to American companies was under consideration. That would all be jeopardized by injecting the Palestine issue.[6]

Wearing his congressional-liaison hat, Long at once sent letters to Secretaries Hull and Stimson, advising them to oppose these Palestine resolutions, which the secretary of war answered by saying they shouldn't even be discussed. "But as a consequence," Long summed up in a sort of mock peevishness, "I now have the whole politics of the region and the whole of the oil question crossing my desk."[7]

As the year 1944 advanced, Long's major concern, as evidenced in his diary entries, was more and more involved with bringing the new international organization into being. Initially it was slow going, and we find Breck Long on March 3, 1944, complaining that the "post-war studies" were moving too slowly into recommendations and conclusions. He actually blamed one of his colleagues, Leo Pasvolsky, a Czarist Russian émigré and personal assistant to Secretary Hull (his "one-man think tank"), who was in charge of producing the first draft plan for the future UN. Long wrote that "part of the delay is due to the failing of Pasvolsky to let anyone peek at the work."[8] A month previously, Hull had told the rotund Russian, who had come to the State Department from the Brookings Institution, to give Long access to his papers on the issue, but he hadn't done so. Weekly reminders since had been just as futile. Breckinridge Long, master of creating bureaucratic inertia, was getting back a bit of his own medicine.

About a week later into March, Long learned that the president was hoping to convene a meeting by June. In his discussions with Secretary Hull, Breck suggested that the *general principles* behind the proposed world organization be vetted with members of the U.S. Senate—from both parties—who would eventually be called on to ratify it. Simultaneously, the other three founding countries involved, Great Britain, China, and the Soviet Union, would be briefed and, hopefully, would agree. On March 15, 1944, the finished study for what Long called "the new League of Nations" was received—a two-year effort that the Missourian pronounced "pretty good—but a little unbalanced as to powers between the Council and the Assembly." Specifically, he felt there was too much power in the Security Council and not enough in the General Assembly.

We are now on the cusp of the deliberations that have gone down in history as the Dumbarton Oaks Conference. The four nations previously cited met at this estate in the Georgetown section of Washington, DC and literally laid out the framework for a world government. The bulk of the planning, as well as the primary impetus for the project, came from the United States and was the work of a team at the State Department. Franklin Roosevelt, it should be added, was bound and determined that the end of World War II would not be followed as World War I had been by a "peace conference" between the warring parties. His druthers were that after the "unconditional surrender of the Axis powers, the victors were to set up a mechanism—a body of countries—aimed at preventing such wholesale catastrophes from ever happening again."

On May 1, 1944, Breck Long was writing, "The International Organization to secure the Peace is the thing just now receiving the topside attention." Here, the "bone of contention," he reported, was "the use of force—by what authority, how and when." The U.S. Senate had formed a committee of four Democrats and four Republicans to work with the State Department. On the GOP side of this Committee of Eight, the leading figure was Senator Arthur Vandenberg of Michigan. Long was leery of him, saying, "He hates Roosevelt," but Vandenberg was to prove extraordinarily useful in forging a bipartisan approach to these postwar challenges. Vandenberg himself in discussing his reaction to the State Department's plans for a UN-type organization, remarked on his surprise that it was "so conservative." He stated: "This is anything but a wild-eyed internationalist dream of a world State," and how it provided a "framework to which he could heartily subscribe."[9]

The Senate's Committee of Eight went on to endorse the idea of having the U.S. begin preliminary conversations with Great Britain, Russia, and China—which as the Big Four, constituted the final makeup of the Dumbarton Oaks Conference that opened on August 21, 1944, and continued until October 9, 1944.

The name Dumbarton Oaks has a certain lasting resonance to this day, sometimes linked with Bretton Woods, a resort in New Hampshire where an international financial policy was earlier worked out under the leadership of the Treasury Department. It was said that Breckinridge Long was responsible for suggesting the Georgetown site. It had been the home of a former State Department official, Robert Woods Bliss, ex-ambassador to Argentina, who had donated it in 1940 to his alma mater, Harvard University, as a center for the study of Byzantine art.

In a gated setting of spacious gardens and within a rambling, elegant red-brick mansion, Dumbarton Oaks provided a perfect retreat amid the nation's bustling capital city for sensitive talks away from prying eyes and ears, including those of the press. Long was also credited with having justified such secrecy, since he had written a book on the U.S. Constitutional Convention and its deliberations that were kept from the public at the time. The one instance when this privacy was threatened likewise drew in Breck Long, who had been appointed a member of the U.S. delegation. He was given the job of dealing with a would-be interloper, the notorious American fascist and anti-Semite Gerald L. K. Smith, now making a nuisance of himself by demanding that a "nationalist" be allowed to participate in the talks. The two such nationalists Smith proposed were Democratic Senator Robert Reynolds, the well-known bigot, and the archconservative isolationist Colonel Robert McCormick, the publisher of the *Chicago Tribune*.

Long conveyed the message that Smith was welcome to present his views in writing to the State Department. But this rabble-rouser rejected the idea and kept bombarding Long's secretary Winifred Aderton with nasty phone calls, and finally on August 25 he appeared at the mansion's gate and tried to enter. By the time Breckinridge Long, sent to intervene, arrived at the guard post, Smith had left the scene. One of the British delegates, the noted professor and author Isaiah Berlin, declared himself *astounded* that Long had even bothered with this "notorious fascist demagogue in the first place" and that the assistant secretary of state had been instructed to stay in touch with Gerald L. K. Smith.

The presence of Breckinridge Long in the U.S. delegation may have been due in part to his now exclusive State Department position of congressional liaison. Besides, starting as early as 1940, he had been on several advisory groups to the secretary of state, formulating plans for a world organization. If not really an expert like Pasvolsky in structuring governmental organizations, he had experience enough, plus the cachet of a faithful League of Nations supporter.

Because of political protocol, the conference was divided into two parts. Since the Soviet Union, while fighting Germany and Italy, was not at war with Japan, and China was, it had been decided that those two nations would have to meet with the U.S. and the U.K. separately, and so they did. This first phase, which included the U.S.S.R. lasted from August 21 to September 28, and when the Soviets departed, the Chinese moved in on September 28.

The way had been paved for the Chinese *inclusion* among the Big Four, much desired by FDR, when Congressman Magnuson's *exclusion* repeal act had been signed into law almost a year earlier. It had had the complete approbation of Senator Vandenberg, the Republican guru on foreign policy, who had declared it would be "the best counter propaganda to the Japanese Co-Prosperity Sphere."[10]

Britain had wanted France to participate at Dumbarton Oaks, too, but De Gaulle was still anathema to the State Department and FDR. Breck Long, in his best Machiavellian mode, suggested the U.S. also propose Brazil but be willing to drop the South Americans in return for the British abandoning France. So it worked out. China alone would constitute the fourth power, although in a somewhat junior manner.

The Chinese, led by their noted diplomat Wellington Koo, were left waiting for weeks in DC's summer heat, while the Russo-American-Anglo talks continued in the tree-shaded coolness of Dumbarton Oaks, which also contained a swimming pool. Only a week remained until the cutoff deadline of October 9, established by Chairman Stettinius, before the Chinese were admitted to a separate tripartite negotiation with the U.S. and U.K. Koo, a graduate of Columbia University, flawless in English, a former ambassador to the U.S. and now ambassador in London, was experienced enough not to rock the boat. He explained to Breckinridge Long, an old friend of his, that he "had no disposition to quibble about any details . . . the important thing was to agree to something," and he was sure the U.S. proposals "would be fair and without self-interest."[11]

Consequently, the bulk of the Dumbarton Oaks recommendations was the work of the Big Three—the U.S., Great Britain, and the U.S.S.R.—headed respectively by Edward Stettinius, Sir Alexander Cadogan, and Andrei Gromyko. The elaborate intricacies of these intense discussions have been spelled out by several authors and need not be repeated here. Suffice it to say that a few loose ends were left, the veto question in particular and the last-minute Soviet demand that all sixteen of their "republics" be recognized as individual countries. On the veto question, the American delegation had actually split. During the heated internal debate that resulted, Breckinridge Long acted quite out of character. Having always tended to be sycophantic in relation to his superiors, he suddenly openly exhibited stubborn argumentative opposition to Cordell Hull. Robert C. Hillenbrand, in his diligent study of the Dumbarton Conference,[12] reports that Long, stressing that the original American position had been to support the veto, told Hull of his fear the Russians would exit if the U.S. held to its new position that the veto had to be limited. Stettinius, whose relationship with Long had never been too good, told the assistant secretary not to "get in a lather"—that a compromise was in the works.[13]

Hillenbrand writes, "The excitable Long did not give up, however." During an all-day meeting of the American delegation on September 18, 1944, he claimed vociferously that the U.S. Senate would not ratify an agreement that could hamstring American policy and that without full great-power support, the proposed organization would fail. The military members of the delegation strongly backed Breckinridge Long. General Stanley Embick, the ranking officer, spoke for the Joint Chiefs of Staff and their overriding desire to have the Soviet Union declare war on Japan. Also, they feared that an international organization which did not include Soviets would end up as toothless as the League of Nations had been.

Other members of the delegation did not support Long and the military. Hull and Stettinius joined them, and Hull was said to have been especially irked with Long and his argument the U.S. had once supported an unfettered veto. Hull shot back that he, as secretary of state, "had never made up his mind on that question" and Under Secretary Stettinius claimed Long's allies, "the admirals and generals" plus "some of our political advisors, have lost their grip . . . are not thinking straight about this thing [and have become] a little bit hysterical."[14]

At the end of the day in Dumbarton Oaks, it was decided that a final decision on the veto question and the Soviet demand for sixteen additional votes would be put off until the final San Francisco meeting. On October 9, 1944, this Washington conclave was adjourned on schedule, pleased that it had produced a *framework agreement*, to which contentious decisions could later be attached. As it turned out, in San Francisco Breck Long's position on the veto was upheld and the big powers given the right to exercise it, even when parties to the dispute; in addition, a compromise settled the quarrel over representation for the Soviet republics by allowing two of them, the Ukraine and Byelorussia, additional seats in the General Assembly.

One pet proposal of FDR's, on which he would have liked to insist, never even got discussed. It concerned a permanent location for the world organization, once it came into being. The president wasn't thinking of New York City or any other metropolis. On the contrary, his notion was that the site should be totally isolated, and he proposed two small islands—one in the Atlantic and one in the Pacific—between which sessions of the UN would be rotated. These two pinpoints in the ocean were the island of Flores, one of the smallest components of the Portuguese-held Azores, and the tiny island of Niihau in what was then the U.S. territory of Hawaii. Niihau, at the time the privately owned property of a single family, still has the same status today and is kept in pristine condition, off-limits to visitors, where the inhabitants all speak to each other in Hawaiian and voted en masse against having Hawaii join the United States of America.

Secretary of State Cordell Hull wisely never bothered to present this quirky idea to the Dumbarton Oaks conference for its consideration.

Chapter Twenty-Four

The War's Ending

THE WAR—ESPECIALLY THE WAR in Europe—was trending towards a conclusion in the fall of 1944. Germany was besieged from east and west—the Russians continuing their push towards Berlin—and the Americans, British, Canadians, French, etc. closing in from the other side. While the Dumbarton Oaks conference was still formulating a blueprint for postwar means of keeping the peace, others in the U.S. government were proposing schemes for dealing with Germany's unconditional surrender, which soon might be in the offing.

Breckinridge Long, in the end pages of his wartime diary, posted an entry on September 26, 1944, almost two weeks before the Dumbarton Oaks meetings concluded, and it dealt with yet another interference by Treasury Secretary Henry Morgenthau Jr. in the State Department's handling of foreign affairs.

"Yesterday and today, the Secretary [Hull] talked to me under suppressed nervous excitement and a great emotional strain."[1] Thus did the subject of the "Morgenthau Plan" arise—a draconian measure guaranteed to keep postwar Germany disarmed, dismembered and essentially turned into a non-developed rural backwater. Cordell Hull seemed especially wroth, because the president had taken Morgenthau with him to Quebec City for a high-level gathering between the U.S., the U.K., and Canada, where the treasury secretary's ideas were accepted. Long described its potential results as follows.

> Under the Morgenthau proposal to take over the Ruhr and the Rhineland . . . this segregated area is given to England . . . it would in its drastic extreme destroy all the manufacturing facilities and turn the country into an agricultural area with the probable exception that the mines and other sources of natural wealth would be under the control of England for an indefinite period, perhaps in perpetuity.[2]

It was bad enough that Treasury had already taken the refugee rescue situation away from the State Department. Now, because the Quebec meeting had also accorded Great Britain $6.5 billion in Lend Lease during the first year after the war ended, Long saw Morgenthau grabbing Lend Lease as well.

The disconcerting effect of these maneuvers on Cordell Hull was described by Long.

> He is in the worst humor I have ever seen him in. He is worried sick and has not slept for two or three nights and finds it impossible to get this off his mind. He feels that it is a repudiation . . . He feels that a rift between him and the President has become real and that his position under these circumstances may not long be tenable.

As it turned out, the Morgenthau Plan for Germany engendered too much opposition and was dropped, but also that Cordell Hull's reign at the State Department would soon be coming to a close. On October 1, 1944, the venerable Democrat from Tennessee developed a fever and had to stay in bed and break off an appointment with FDR. Later, when he did see the president, he said he wanted to resign but would hold off until the November election, in which Roosevelt was running for a fourth term. Allegedly, the secretary of state bared all his feelings about the attempts made by certain individuals to usurp his position as the head of the State Department—assaults by people like Sumner Welles, Henry Morgenthau, Raymond Moley, George Peek, Vice President Henry Wallace . . . Hull complained he "was tired of intrigue . . . of being bypassed . . . of being relied upon in public and ignored in private."[3]

Breck's conclusion was: "It will not be long till there is a successor to Hull," He further surmised that if the position were only to be held until January 20, 1945 (the inaugural date), Stettinius would hold it until then. For a longer term, he predicted ex-Vice President Henry Wallace or Donald Nelson (head of the War Production Board) or Frank Walker (director of the National Emergency Council), with ex-Ambassador Bill Phillips as a dark horse.

By mid October 1944, the political campaign was heating up. Thomas E. Dewey appeared to be a strong candidate for the Republicans. Among his positions was a dedicated commitment to cooperate with Congress in putting the Dumbarton Oaks plans into effect. Cordell Hull issued a statement supporting the president's reelection, and Long reported he had had a hand in revising the original draft.

In this same diary entry of October 26, 1944, the assistant secretary of state also recorded his sense of estrangement from Ed Stettinius. "It is always difficult for me to talk with him except over the phone," he wrote, "and when that happens there is a record made—surreptitiously—on his end. So I do *not* talk with him on the phone, unless he calls me and then I am guarded."[4]

On November 7, 1944, Franklin D. Roosevelt handily defeated Thomas E. Dewey, and the Democrats retained control of the Senate and the House. Breck Long does not seem to have played a prominent role in the election, although he did attend the Chicago Convention, where he was "an interested spectator" and a "behind the scenes contact on the foreign policy aspects of the Democratic platform." He was there for three days and joined in the fight to have Harry Truman replace Henry Wallace on the ticket for vice president.

"I was glad to help Truman—a fellow Missourian," he wrote and then added,

> in spite of the opposition his crowd [the Pendergast group] afforded me in my entire political activity in Missouri. He is a product of machine politics but he is entirely honest, has his feet on the ground, is bright and capable . . . We have been friends for years and he has frequently told me how sorry he was of the vicious treatment his gang bestowed upon me years ago.[5]

Normally, Long did not allow himself any gush of emotional feeling in print, but at this 1944 convention, he did let go. Or at least he wrote the confession below that could be seen as a coda to his political career.

> Some moments during the Convention moved me very much. The platform about foreign relations and references by the different speakers to the struggles of the Wilson era several times brought me an urge to cry. A quarter of a century ago I made a hard fight for the League of Nations . . . I gave all I had in that fight. I emerged after seven years a political derelict. I knew I was right. I saw America abstain—and weaken the League . . . I saw the League suffer, decline and collapse.[6]

Yet he finished his spate of rueful nostalgia with an upbeat prognostication.

For years I have been working to rebuild a world almost destroyed by the violence of a war which still rages but which should never have been allowed to start. And now I see my party espouse the cause I fought for and believed in and see the opposing party generally endorse the idea. And it is but natural I feel happy, gratified. Perhaps I will soon feel compensated for myself, confident of peace for my grandchildren.[7]

There were intimations that already, prior to the Chicago Democratic Convention and this self-delivered pat on the back, Long had begun feeling more than a little sorry for himself. "My loyalty is to Roosevelt—just as it once was to Wilson," he declared.

I once had Roosevelt's confidence. That seems to have been withdrawn. Passing me over for appointment on two different occasions—once under unfortunate circumstances—has been a definite announcement to say the least. Yet I have stuck to a duty as a soldier . . . On the first of those occasions I felt terribly hurt—possibly should have resigned then.[8]

That he kept silent as to what incidents he had in mind, particularly the one where he was "terribly hurt," seems characteristic of his gentlemanly upbringing. His demotion, as such, from his iron-clad control of the Visa Division was hinted at in an extensive if veiled outburst, where he claimed he had been

thrown to the wolves and took the brunt of the worst attack made against *any* officer of this government and which raged in the press and on the radio for a full year—ending only last winter—and without help of any kind from *any* quarter—when my attackers included other persons in responsible positions in other departments in the Government as well as slanderers and Jack-a-napes on the floor of the Congress.[9]

Another complaint of his was that people like James Forrestal had been promoted from under secretary of the Navy to secretary of the Navy, and an assistant secretary of the Navy, Ralph Bard, had been made under secretary, underlining the hope Breckinridge Long no doubt had nourished that he would follow a similar route in the State Department. He felt put out that he had not been asked to meet important visitors to DC, like Winston Churchill, Madame Chiang Kai-shek, and General Charles de Gaulle—and finally, despite his *unwavering loyalty* to Franklin Delano Roosevelt, he sensed an estrangement, hadn't seen him for two years, except for "a formal occasion and at a distance," and for more than three years had not been invited to the White House to talk to him. All this subdued crybabying took place in the summer of 1944, before FDR had even been nominated for a fourth term, and Breck Long has begun contemplating that if his chief is reelected, he will offer his resignation, as he had done in 1940, when it had been rejected.

Roosevelt was a candidate late in August 1944, when the two men did meet face to face again. This time, Breckinridge Long *was* invited to the White House, not on his own account, however, but as a participant in the Dumbarton Oaks conference. Long had been a bit dicey about going to see the president after such a long hiatus, not sure FDR wanted him there or even knew he was a member of the American delegation. It happened that after the three leaders, Stettinius, Cadogan, and Gromyko, went in first, followed by the Russian and British delegations, Long led in the Americans. He expressed his shock immediately upon seeing FDR, who looked as if he'd lost 50 to 60 pounds and "aged years."

He thought Roosevelt might have had the same reaction to him—to his "whitening hairs," deeply lined face and scrawny 122-pound frame. At first, the president regarded him with an inscrutable expression. Long smiled. Then Roosevelt smiled. They shook hands. The president said: "Mr. Long"—and that was all. The assistant secretary of state commented, "As far as my recollection goes, it is the only time in my memory he has called me anything but 'Breck.'"

To ease the pain of this apparent putdown, "Breck" wrote that he saw it as ambiguous. It could be the president was being facetious—or in earnest—he couldn't tell which.

But next there followed three paragraphs of soul-searching. If he had incurred FDR's "displeasure," should he resign? Or, like a good soldier in wartime, should he keep on swallowing his pride and stay in service? Admitting he couldn't *evaluate* the president's reactions upon his looking him in the eye, Breck went on to say,

What difference does it make? I have given my all in the war effort. My work has been exactly and effectively done for five long years. The war is being won—rapidly now . . . The effort for a security organization [the future UN] has had the benefit of all I could contribute toward it.[10]

And so on and so on. His final wrap-up was:

> In the light of it all, the experience today was enigmatic—the
> querulous expression, the moment of incredulity, the kindly
> smile, the "Mr. Long"—without being able to label it as formal or
> facetious—and my own saddening reaction at his appearance—
> But I am still sure I have followed the right course and that my
> deletion from the White House list is not attributable to him
> personally.[11]

The "today" of that revelation was August 23, 1944. Like the "good
soldier" he felt he was, Breckinridge Long returned to his labors at the
Dumbarton Oaks estate, where the plenary meetings were held in a
large, transformed music room, and planning sessions and negotiations
continued for another month and a half.

When Roosevelt was reelected to his fourth term on November 7,
1944, there was no immediate sign on Breck Long's part—as a good
lifelong Democrat—of anything but elation. Still, it seems obvious he'd
been stewing inwardly since his possible snub by FDR in August, although
no rancor had shown up in his diary entries. The possible exception
occurred shortly before Election Day, when Frank Walker told Long the
president had wanted Stettinius to back him publicly for reelection and
that Stettinius, still a Republican, had said no. Now, needing help, FDR
was turning to Long to "speak to" Stettinius. When Long demurred,
stating he "could not direct" his superiors, Walker said the president
expected him to get Stettinius to do something.

Whether Long succeeded in doing so, he doesn't record, only that
he failed to reach the under secretary by phone and hoped to meet with
him in person.

It was soon to be obvious that Ed Stettinius had become Long's big
problem. Even before November 27, 1944, when the news broke that an
ill and infirm Cordell Hull had resigned as secretary of state and Stettinius
would replace him, Long had already been talking about resigning.

On November 28, Long reported his own resignation had been *accepted
de facto* because he'd been offered the post of ambassador to Mexico in
a phone call from Harry Hopkins, FDR's personal aide. Told that FDR,
before leaving for Warm Springs, had asked Hopkins to ask Long if
he'd take the Mexico City job, Long answered no, due to the altitude and
his lack of Spanish. Hopkins suggested he write the president directly,
stating his objections. In response, a "long telegram purporting to be

from the President," came back, now offering Long the ambassadorship to Cuba, instead of Mexico. His reaction was to write in his diary in Italian *"mi non piaci"* [*sic*] (I don't like it).[12]

A phone conversation with Stettinius firmly established that Long's resignation was not just pro forma, as happened after every presidential election among high-ranking non-civil service officials. It was for *real*, Long insisted.

And so, at age 63, Breckinridge Long ended his government service. He declared:

> My record in the Department speaks for itself. I am satisfied and happy . . . I do not consider myself a scholar—rather a man of action.

Plus, finally, perhaps the nub of the reason behind his departure:

> And Stettinius is certainly no scholar, and is definitely a man of action—but his methods, background and lack of experience grated on me. There is no alternative in such cases but separation.[13]

His wartime diary ends with the pithy statement: "And we have arrived at the end of *that* chapter."[14]

What the *next chapter* might have been seems obscure. Breckinridge Long lived for another fourteen years. He never held another government position. The postscript in the published diaries that Fred L. Israel edited affirms that on July 28, 1945, Long sat in the U.S. Senate gallery and listened to the lawmakers debate and in an historic roll-call vote, ratify the United Nations Charter. The ex-assistant secretary of state remarked,

> This has been the motivating thought of my political life for about thirty years . . . The faith of Woodrow Wilson has been vindicated. Civilization has a better chance to survive—but the will to make it work will be a continuing necessity.[15]

In ringing down the curtain on Breckinridge Long's public career, a summing up is obviously appropriate. Wikipedia reports that in his retirement he went on raising and running his racehorses, luxuriating at his elegant home, Montpelier Manor, in Laurel, Maryland, collecting antiques and ship models, fox-hunting, fishing, sailing, and spending time in other locations where he had vacation property, like Nantucket and

Palm Beach, Florida. His Wikipedia page also cites his interactions with Jews, especially linked to those crippling visa regulations he fashioned, as well as his reputation, stoutly denied by him in an exchange with Treasury Secretary Henry Morgenthau Jr., that he was a diehard anti-Semite.

Where is the truth? Am I really going too far in mentioning him in the same breath as Adolph Eichmann? This courtly Missourian in his photos has a distinctly Southern air about him, thin and wiry, and no doubt mannerly and perhaps intense inside, while at the same time suave on the exterior. It *is* hard to connect him to the death camps—but not so difficult to think of him exemplifying the banality of evil.

Chapter Twenty-Five

In Retirement

W HEN BRECKINRIDGE LONG LEFT U.S. government service for good
in early December 1944, World War II in Europe had about six
more months to run. Despite Hitler's mad fantasies about the Third
Reich's preordained victory, some high-ranking Nazis were already
thinking about ways to save their skins. Not so Adolf Eichmann, who
kept on applying his own fanaticism to the work of Bureau IV B4 and its
task of transporting Jews to the death camps. Even after his top superior
Heinrich Himmler closed the gas chambers and ordered the deportations
to cease, Eichmann deliberately disobeyed and continued rounding
up the last untouched concentrations of Jews in Europe, especially in
Hungary, where he went in person to direct the operations. Furthermore,
he tried to set up a gas chamber at Theresienstadt in Czechoslovakia, a
camp where there never had been one since its inception.

It was to be Eichmann's plea at his trial in Jerusalem sixteen years
afterward that he was only "following orders." He himself, he claimed,
had never killed or molested a single Jew. He was not an anti-Semite, he
insisted. Naturally, he didn't explain why he'd ignored Himmler's order
to leave the Jews alone and had maintained his deadly transports, and he
displayed full knowledge of the fate awaiting the people he'd dispatched
by his emphasizing that others—not he—had done the killing.

His odyssey is now in the history books: How Eichmann made it to
Juan Perón's Argentina, where he assumed the alias of Ricardo Klement
and lived a humble, low-income, factory-worker life with his spouse and
children in an undeveloped suburb of the sprawling city of Buenos Aires,
and how Jewish avengers found him a decade later, daringly abducted
him and put him on trial.

The Israeli capture of Eichmann continues its reverberations to this
day. The arch war criminal's trial and execution is still being talked about
and dissected in our twenty-first century. Thus it seems appropriate at

this point to examine my instinctive question that remains unanswered: Was Breckinridge Long an American Eichmann?

Undertaking a biography of a person as thoroughly castigated for his actions as Breckinridge Long offers an immediate invitation to demonize the subject. Perhaps, given my Jewish background, that was my subliminal intent. Warring against this instinct was sheer curiosity: Who really was this person and what led him to commit the harm he did?

Furthermore, what message is there in his story, linked to the greatest crime ever committed on this planet, that might elucidate a genuine truth about the capabilities of our species to participate in as well as promulgate basic evil?

Hannah Arendt has been roundly roasted for coining the term, "the banality of evil." I myself have been hectored for having associated—even in question marks—this rather minor figure in the U.S. State Department with the archfiend of the Holocaust, Adolf Eichmann. Frankly, I have to argue that I think Hannah Arendt had it right. The *banality* she cited was in the outward ordinariness with which wholesale murder was treated under the Nazi regime. On our side of the Atlantic, Breckinridge Long went to work each day in an office a figurative stone's throw from the White House and literally in effect handed out death sentences to countless unseen victims in Europe, while happily convincing himself he was protecting our country from deadly if theoretical enemy agents.

Similar mindsets were also honed on ideologies of "superiority-inferiority," flagrantly so in the case of Nazi Germany, and very much alive not only in the Southern United States but also in the entire fabric of a "Protestant ascendancy" America, feeling itself under siege from newcomers who were different and deemed inferior. Economic depressions certainly intensify and unleash the tribal genetics within us all, as we see so clearly now in the U.S. with its current wave of immigration demagoguery that has surfaced yet again. Breckinridge Long wasn't alone in setting his face against "aliens" coming into the U.S. Polls in the 1930s and early '40s showed overwhelming opposition to any change in the country's Anglo-Nordic-Teuton-slanted quotas. Franklin Roosevelt himself could share his friend Breck's paranoia about Axis fifth columnists and complacently allow the building of "paper walls" to keep them out, just as he could acquiesce, too, in real barbed-wire fences to pen in Japanese-Americans, whose loyalties hysterically and unjustly were suspect.

Götterdämmerung—the "twilight of the gods"—hardly enters into the drama of these two bureaucrats. There is nothing operatic, nothing tragic, nothing larger-than-life about either of them. They illustrate the unfortunate truth that the most heinous of villainies can be the handiwork of energetic, unthinking second-raters.

Were both these men virulent anti-Semites?

Squirm as he might in Jerusalem, Eichmann had no defense on that score. A story told about him concerned his reaction to an incident when a German soldier tried in vain to save a young Jewish boy from death because he was as blond and blue-eyed as any Aryan Teuton was supposed to be. Eichmann had listened to the tale, shrugged and commented, "But he was a Jew, wasn't he?"

Regarding Breck Long, the jury seemingly remains still out. An unabashed defender of his, one Sikeli Neil Ratu, author of a thesis written at the University of Sydney, Australia, with the title, *Anti-Semitism and American Refugee Immigration Policy During the Holocaust: A Reassessment*, declared that Long's actions were primarily driven by *bureaucratic empire building*,[1] especially when he went before the House Appropriations Committee to argue for budget increases. Sikeli Neil Ratu posits that the "natural constricting and retarding effects" were mistakenly seen by certain scholars as a mere façade hiding anti-Semitic attitudes."[2] Specifically mentioned on this score was David Wyman in his book, *Paper Walls*.

Ironically, Wyman himself has expressed doubts about the anti-Semitic label so frequently attached to Breckinridge Long and his activities. In another of his volumes, *The Abandonment of the Jews*,[3] Wyman plainly wrote,

> Whether Long was actually anti-Semitic is not clear. The record does not show him to be overtly negative toward Jews simply because they were Jews. He appears to have had good relations with the more conservative Jewish leaders—that is, the ones who did not rankle him or openly criticize him.[4]

Other chroniclers of this period, such as Richard Breitman and Alan M. Kraut, are equally cautious. In their book, *American Refugee Policy*,[5] they have included statements like, "But any portrait of the suspicious, misanthropic Long as using his position to exercise a special anti-Semitism by deliberately barring Jews from the United States is overly simplistic,"[6] and "Appointed by a president known for his close personal and political ties to prominent American Jews, Breckinridge Long's reputation as an anti-Semite is gradually being revised by historians," and these historians are finding it "increasingly difficult to answer the question [of Long's anti-Semitism] with certainty."[7]

Even Henry Feingold, the author of *The Politics of Rescue*, who had unequivocally dubbed Long an anti-Semite, was also saying that his feelings were a matter of "gentility and class," rather than ethnic, religious, or racial animosity.

Indeed, the closeness of Breckinridge Long's relationship to Bernard Baruch, who never made any attempt to disguise his Jewishness, entered into that category of *gentility* and *class*, which Long's associate Bernie exuded as the epitome of a Southern aristocrat. Breckinridge Long often was a guest at Baruch's South Carolina plantation, the manorial Hobcaw Barony, and on one occasion when Baruch couldn't be there to greet him, the financier had his daughter do the honors until he could arrive. A series of letters between the two men in April 1947 gives a sense of their relationship as it continued after Long left the State Department. "My dear Breck," Baruch began, "Thank you so much for your letter of April 17th. Have you any winners in the stable? As ever . . ." To which, three days later, Long responded, "No winners. No losers. No runners . . ." But he had "two great prospects coming on and ended with: "Someday we will go to the races."[8] Two years after this, they were trying to get together in New York City. Long had written to "Dear Bernie" that he hoped they could meet and talk about world affairs and "renew an association which has been a treasured one with me."[9] Baruch offered several dates once he had returned to his Long Island estate from South Carolina and expressed a hope, "You will be able to fit in some time with me in New York. As ever . . . Devotedly yours . . ." And finally, there is Christine Long's handwritten appendage to the thank-you note sent after her husband's funeral in 1958: "Dear Mr. Baruch. Thank you so much for your lovely letter. Breck was always extremely fond of you. Sincerely yours . . ."[10]

Other upper-crust Jews appear in Long's writings. There are diary entries like, "Dinner at the Seligmans," "Bridge at the Seligmans"—which Seligman family isn't identified, but Seligmans were certainly the cream of German-Jewish society in America. Breck's role in raising money for the Democrats had him working in lockstep with Henry Morgenthau Sr., and even when Breck's pejorative term of "Frankfurter's boys" is cited as an example of anti-Jewish feeling, there remains that diary entry describing his awed respect in encountering the Supreme Court justice and being admonished for not calling him Felix, as he had apparently done in the old days.

Laurence Steinhardt, the top Jewish diplomat in the State Department at the time, won Long's praise as "an able man" with "decisiveness and courage," although arguably for his sharing similar views with Breck on immigration and not being afraid to liken some of his coreligionists (while he was ambassador to the Soviet Union) as akin to "the criminal Jews who crowd our police dockets in New York." Steinhardt, who was the nephew of super-lawyer Samuel Untermyer, FDR's close friend and an ardent Zionist, later on somewhat redeemed himself, when ambassador to Turkey, by significantly helping the War Refugee Board's rescue efforts.

Let us now also throw into the pot an entirely different dimension of Breckinridge Long's behavior, as presented by a British author, Charles Higham, in a book of his called *Trading With The Enemy*.[11] The title means exactly what it implies—that the work is a study of a high-powered group of international businessmen, primarily American, who worked with the Nazis before and *even during* World War II. Breck Long is variously mentioned in the course of Higham's exhaustive investigations into the hush-hush activities of a bloc of companies he refers to as "The Fraternity."

The assistant secretary of state's name first appears on page 99 as the recipient of a memorandum from a State Department lawyer named R. T. Yingling. The date on the missive was February 26, 1942. What Yingling revealed to Long was that American-owned ITT (International Telephone and Telegraph Corporation) was doing business with the enemy and "with the concurrence of the Department of State." But Yingling was no whistleblower. He was writing to Long for "some insurance it [ITT] will not be prosecuted for such activities." According to author Higham, ITT went ahead anyway, and with the backing of the State and Justice Departments continued in its ways.

On several occasions cited by Higham, while dealing with two countries not unfriendly to the Axis, Argentina and Chile, Breckinridge Long seemed very much like a gung-ho American patriot. But there's another episode in Higham's book that involves the Missourian in a much less favorable star-spangled light.

The Ford Motor Company was the culprit in this instance. It seems that Henry Ford Sr., despite publicly repenting his open anti-Semitism, had never entirely shaken off his attachment to the Nazis, even once the U.S. went to war against Germany. Previously, in 1940, he had refused to make aircraft engines for the British, when they were fighting alone for western civilization's survival. The situation in which Breckinridge Long found himself entangled occurred during the rule in Detroit of Henry's successor, his son Edsel. The Ford Company had a factory in France producing military vehicles for the Wehrmacht, which it could do legally after the fall of France, until December 1941. But the moment the U.S. was at war with Germany, the Trading With The Enemy Act kicked in, and even any communication between the truck plant near Paris and Ford headquarters in Dearborn, Michigan, would be a violation of the law.

Breck Long's involvement began early in 1942, when Edsel Ford paid him a visit at his DC office. Their discussion apparently led to a joint decision by the two men that letters could be sent surreptitiously to the U.S. from German-controlled territory via Vichy or through Lisbon. To be on the safe side, those compromising letters that detailed Ford's continuing aid to the Nazis would have to go by courier, and an assistant at Ford's European facility named George Lesto was given the job. Conceivably, Breck Long's willingness to stick his neck out may have had to do with the State Department's (and his boss Cordell Hull's) predilection for the Pétain regime. But November 1942 saw the Allied invasion of French North Africa and the end of the quasi-independent Vichy government. Also, the pesky Treasury Department was investigating the auto company's arguably treasonous activities, when on May 26, 1943, Edsel Ford died suddenly, and pursuit of the case was subsequently dropped.

More on the comic-opera side, was Charles Higham's ultimate allusion to Breckinridge Long. Sensing the Missourian's straight-arrow, if not puritan demeanor, this tale is hard to believe—centering on an Austrian or Hungarian adventuress, the Princess Stephanie von Hohenlohe, admired by Hitler, made an Honorary Aryan by Himmler (since she was half-Jewish), and arrested in the U.S. as a Nazi spy, a day after the Pearl Harbor attack. Higham quotes an FBI report dated January 15, 1942, revealing that the princess had

a very influential friend in the State Department whose mistress she had been and the Princess had stated that this friend had the authority to permit Axis aliens to enter the country and to keep anti-Axis aliens out of the country.

Higham goes on to write, "The name to this day has been blacked out in the report." But he postulates: "the reference presumably is to Breckinridge Long."[12]

If so, there is some acute irony at work. Nazi agents *were* infiltrating our nation—however, not in the guise of Jewish or other alien refugees. Breck Long's much-feared fifth column wasn't just a figment of his fertile and self-deceiving imagination. These furtive exchanges were important to major U.S. companies doing business clandestinely with the enemy, and it might well have been that Breckinridge Long, sycophantic careerist as always, knowingly or unknowingly abetted the exact opposite of what he was preaching in regard to legitimate asylum seekers desperately trying to flee certain death.

By 1944 time had begun running out for the Nazis. Adolf Eichmann was up to his murderous tricks, right until the very end. Late in the year, he still rounded up Jews in Hungary, but attempted—shall we say—to soften his image by offering the Allies to trade the lives of these remaining Jews for ten thousand heavy-duty military trucks—a Devil's bargain that never took place. After a stint hiding out in Austria, Eichmann made his way with the help of the Nazi underground to Argentina. His surreptitious capture there and removal to Israel caused a worldwide sensation. Possibly the rather tepid response of the Argentine authorities to this flagrant violation of their sovereignty was due to embarrassment that such a wanted mass murderer of all time had been harbored in their midst.

Two events, the creation of the United Nations and its creation in turn of the state of Israel, had made Eichmann's capture and the trial that followed possible. Breckinridge Long had a connection to both these happenings—directly through his work on fashioning the United Nations and indirectly, in that Israel would never have come into being without the United Nations vote of approval it received. Maybe, if Long hadn't helped create a system in which uprooted European Jews could find no safety, the Zionist idea would never have garnered the support it did and result in a homeland where Jews' citizenship could not be arbitrarily stripped from them as it had been by Germany.

The Israeli writer Hanna Yablonka made a similar point in her 2004 book, *The State of Israel vs. Adolf Eichmann*, stating that

> At the same time the "lessons of the Holocaust" drove home to the Jews the need for a sovereign state and a military force of their own.[13]

Cordell Hull's *Memoirs* (in two volumes) were published in 1948, the year Israel proclaimed its independence and fought back a multination Arab thrust to crush its existence and most likely inflict a second Holocaust. It is instructive to dig out Hull's reaction to the refugee question, from within his 1700-plus pages. He is as self-congratulatory and myopic as was Breck Long in treating this matter, stressing the "strenuous efforts" he claimed the State Department had made to save Jews. In 1942, learning of the Final Solution, Hull swore they "exhausted all efforts authorized by law to grant visas" and that he and the president "had many conferences on the subject of Hitler's attempts to exterminate the Jews." The creation of the War Refugee Board in 1944 was drily noted by the Tennessean with no indication that in its short life it had rescued 200,000 Jews. Furthermore, Hull took another swipe at Treasury Secretary Morgenthau, "who found grievous fault with the State Department and especially with every official handling the refugee problem," and his final argument was: "President Roosevelt at no time complained to me that the Department had not done enough."[14]

Both Cordell Hull and Breckinridge Long exhibit the mindset and language tone of careful bureaucrats whose world is one of slippery maneuvers within a web of rules, laws, protocols, and often a stasis that resembles paralysis.

In a speech given at Tel Aviv University after the establishment of Israel, Rabbi Herbert Rosenblum of Wilkes Barre, Pennsylvania, lecturing about the War Refugee Board, used another expression for such institutional foot-dragging as it applied to the Holocaust. *Official silence* was his term, and he applied it not just to entities like Breckinridge Long's Visa Division or Cordell Hull's State Department but in relation to "the mass murder of the Jews of Europe," even indicting organizations like the International Red Cross and the Vatican. Rosenblum also saw the connection I have sensed when he told his audience at the Shazar Institute,

> This collective silence, both governmental and organizational, had been just as bureaucratically perpetuated as had the energy and thoroughness of the Nazi governmental machine in its methodical mass murder process.[15]

Another way of expressing the same idea comes from a book by the founding president of Brandeis University, the highly distinguished Dr. Abram L. Sachar. In his *The Redemption of the Unwanted,* there is this striking definition of a new type of mass killer, the man who exercises his bloody craft as a faceless bureaucrat. A new word was coined to describe the role of all the Eichmanns of the soulless hierarchies, *Schreibtischmörder*—the murderer at the desk.[16]

Here it strikes me we must reenter the realm of Hannah Arendt's arresting conundrum—the "banality of evil." The fury she aroused by that phrase centered on her implication that the mousy figure inside the glass booth in Jerusalem was not the *Devil's own superman of atrocity* but a second-rate human, a hate-twisted twerp, who ended up in a position to inflict unprecedented horror. Some of the anger flung at Ms. Arendt I have felt directed at myself, for having had the *chutzpah*—in the words of an outraged reader of this manuscript: "To compare a pathetic careerist with hopeless designs of higher public office to a cunning desk murderer complicit in the mass murder of hundreds of thousands of Jews is ludicrous to say the least." Sorry, I do see a connection.

Had Breckinridge Long been shunted off to another diplomatic post in 1939 and never taken up the reins of America's visa policy, would more of the Jews of Europe have escaped to the U.S.? Conceivably his energy and ingenuity in the erection of ever more impenetrable paper walls would have made a difference by its absence. His oft-quoted internal memo of June 1940—that

> We can delay and effectively stop for a temporary period of indefinite length the number of immigrants entering into the U.S . . . by simply advising our consuls to put every obstacle in the way and resort to various administrative devices which would postpone and postpone

is an argument for his fanaticism in strengthening a restrictive intent already being asserted. It found no opposition in the State Department of that time. Nor did his friend Franklin Roosevelt object, which encouraged Long all the more. His frenzied behavior during the *Quanza* incident, when a few dozen Jewish refugees made it into our country without his blessing, seemingly mirrored the admittedly far more deadly spectacle of Eichmann's frantic dashing from country to country in German-occupied Europe, to keep any remaining Jews from flopping out of his net, even after he'd been ordered to stop. Both men bewailed their frustrated ambitions. Long dreamed in vain of becoming secretary of state. Eichmann told his Israeli interrogator that if he'd been allowed to go fight on the Russian front, he might have made general. Both were high-level bootlickers.

In the hundreds upon hundreds of pages in diaries, letters, etc. left by Breck Long to the Library of Congress, there is not one word of self-awareness—never mind regret—of how his actions impacted and facilitated the unspeakable nightmare of the Holocaust. If that is not *evil*, the "murderer at the desk," I don't know what it is. And the daily grind of office work, even within his cushy State Department quarters, certainly you can label that *banality*. Eichmann himself—despite protesting "there is no blood on my hands" and calling it "journalistic rubbish" that a newspaper story had deemed him "a bureaucrat of murder"—managed to express a momentary hint of insight. He told his interrogator, Israeli Captain Avner Less, "I am prepared as an example and deterrent to all the anti-Semites of the earth, to hang myself in public." Of course, the sly boots then asked for time to write a book that would serve "as a warning and example for the young people of the present and future."[17] Such penny-ante conniving also connotes banality, I feel.

At the end of his Wartime Diaries, Breckinridge Long is left wondering why he fell out of favor with President Roosevelt. His alleged joy at having been relieved of his visa and refugee duties was nothing if not hypocritical sour grapes. What he wouldn't or couldn't realize was that times had changed for him by 1944. No president was as attuned to the public pulse as FDR. Thanks to Peter Bergson and others, the horror of the Holocaust was finally penetrating the American consciousness. The threat of an Axis fifth column in the United States no longer seemed credible. It was hardly a problem for Roosevelt to switch gears, distance himself from his loyal Breck, and try something else. Left to dangle in his stripped-down State Department post, Long could carry on as if nothing had happened, and so he did. More banality at work, except the worst damage already had been done.

Chapter Twenty-Six

Last Year and Death

THE BRECKINRIDGE LONG COLLECTION AT the Library of Congress does not end with his sudden resignation from the State Department in November 1944. Material exists throughout 1945 and 1946, even a few pieces dated 1947 and 1948, and there essentially the trail terminates.

What emerges from these immediate post-State Department years is the picture of a man who hadn't yet given up on continuing his career in government. Perhaps with a new president, a new administration. But first, understandably, at the beginning of 1945, with FDR still in office and World War II still raging, he sought to improve his health, seemingly worn down by all his bureaucratic exertions, by taking an extended vacation in a pleasant climate.

Thus, undoubtedly due to the fact that daughter Teenie, her husband Arnold Willcox, and their two children were living in California, Breck and Christine joined them at the upscale seaside resort of La Jolla near San Diego, where they stayed for at least three months.

It was a time for reflection, and Long's thoughts were tinged with barely concealed bitterness.

I am out of office—and a free man again—free to rest a little, readjust my life and plan for the future at the age of 63 and a half,

he wrote in early December 1944.[1] Then, on Christmas Day, he gave vent to his growing unhappiness, stating: "I am depressed at the very thought of my enforced idleness,"[2] and called it "enforced" in the belief that if he hadn't offered his resignation, he would have been fired.

Ensconced in La Jolla, he listened by radio to FDR's fourth inaugural on January 20, 1945, and was openly upset. A whole range of petty slights at previous Rooseveltian inaugurals welled up in him.

The first time I was given seats on the outer circumference of
the stand in front of the Capitol—and not invited to the large
luncheon to which all the other members of the campaign
company were asked.

All this despite his help on presidential speeches and having given
"more money to the [campaign] funds than I could afford."[3] Wallowing in
his hurt from this latest perceived snub, he called himself "the forgotten
man of 1932" and believed he had not even received an invitation to
the 1945 inauguration. As it turned out, tickets had been sent to him in
Washington, but his faithful secretary Miss Aderton had returned them,
since he was on the West Coast.

In that diary complaint was also soul-searching about his estrangement
from the White House, and he ended by putting it all down to the "sub-
surface hostility" towards him from Harry Hopkins, whom he had always
considered too liberal.

During this period in California, the DC world did reach out to
Breck Long, although hardly on the scale to which he was accustomed.
A letter arrived at 7718 Lookout Drive, La Jolla, from his old friend,
former Attorney-General Homer S. Cummings, inviting him to be the
commencement speaker at Lincoln Memorial University in Harrowgate,
Tennessee, "near Cumberland Gap." When at first Long declined, it was
due to the condition of his health, not the diminutive size of this little-
known rural campus. Cummings, although disappointed, commiserated:
"I think you are quite right. Nothing but a long uninterrupted rest will
do the trick."[4] Yet somehow it turned out that Long *was* able to speak
and also receive an honorary Doctor of Laws degree from the school.
Consequently, he found himself in Tennessee on the morning of June 4,
1945, delivering an address entitled, "Opportunity and Responsibility of
Youth in the Post-War World."

One section did reflect his attitude towards the war, which still had
several months to run in the Pacific, while the Axis surrender already had
been sealed in Europe.

Influenced possibly by the revelation of the concentration camp
atrocities, Long touched upon this horrific aspect of World War II,
without specific reference to the mass murders that later became known
as the Holocaust. He said:

Whole populations were deprived of the rights of human beings.
Millions were uprooted and transported by the Nazi armies to

work as slaves to produce the weapons by which their fellows would be destroyed. Those who demurred were persecuted with fiendish cruelty.[5]

Note: Long's exclusive emphasis on forced labor, no mention of gas chambers or premeditated, wholesale extermination, or even of Jews, although by then the ghastly newsreels of what our troops discovered in the liberated camps had been widely shown.

Proud of his efforts, Breck Long had copies made of these thoughts of his and sent them to friends who were college presidents, such as Isaiah Bowman of Johns Hopkins and Harold Dodds of Princeton.

It was, one could argue, a means of *keeping his hand in*, if not advertising his availability for public service.

Homer Cummings, whose DC law firm handled Long's affairs, also helped by connecting the Missourian to a set of influential political figures invited by him to the Homer S. Cummings Golf Tournament, held twice a year at Pinehurst, North Carolina. In 1945, the first outing was scheduled for April 27–29, and Bill Stanley, one of the partners, writing on March 9 to Breck in La Jolla, facetiously assured his client that their playing golf and carousing at the Carolina Hotel would not hurt the war effort. Later, Breck was invited for another round in early November 1945, well after the end of all hostilities overseas.

Those intervening months had witnessed a series of highly dramatic events—the sudden death of Franklin D. Roosevelt in April, Hitler's suicide, the German surrender in May, and the Japanese capitulation in August.

On April 12, 1945, Breckinridge Long sent a telegram of condolences to Eleanor Roosevelt at the White House: "Please accept this humble expression of my deepest sympathy." Twelve days afterward, a black-edged printed card came back, stating: "Mrs. Roosevelt and her family thank you very much for your condolences and appreciate your kind thoughts." It had been sent to him at the State Department. In truth, Long had never been close to the president's wife. Unbeknownst to him, she had, in connection with his refugee work, labeled him "a Fascist" during a discussion with FDR and been upbraided by her husband, who had defended his appointee to the State Department.

On the same April 12, Long had also sent a telegram to Harry Truman: "In the middle of sadness, I send this message of entire confidence and deep personal respect . . . Breckinridge Long." A thank-you was sent back to him by Harry H. Vaughan, the new president's military aide.

Earlier in the year, while Long was still recuperating in La Jolla, the then vice president had sent him a letter that read, "Dear Breck. Thanks for your note of congratulation the 22nd [of January, 1945, following the Roosevelt-Truman Inaugural on January 20]. I appreciate it very much. Sincerely, Harry." Then a P.S.: "Hope to see you when you're in the neighborhood of Capitol Hill."[6]

No doubt this friendly postscript triggered memories that went into his diary; to wit, how at the 1944 Democratic National Convention "There was a fight, short and somewhat acrimonious over the Vice Presidential ballot," that he did not want to see Vice President Henry A. Wallace re-nominated, "and when I was free of Presidential restraint, I did what I could for Truman." Hopefully his fellow Missourian was aware of that, Long must have thought, when he sent those congratulations to now President Truman on April 12, 1945.

Concurrently, the jolt of FDR's sudden death opened another floodgate of reminiscences for Breckinridge Long.

Roosevelt died this afternoon. Harry Truman becomes President . . . I have lost a friend of long standing—nearly 30 years. True, the last few years have not seen any close personal contacts.

Soon Breck's mind was off to the early Wilson days in 1917:

His office and mine were close together in the east corridor of the old "State, War and Navy Building" in World War I when he was Assistant Secretary of the Navy and I of State. From time to time, we would meet on the way to lunch or somewhere out at dinner. Or I would meet him in the locker room of the Chevy Chase Club, he usually after tennis and I after golf.[7]

In 1920, when Roosevelt was the Democratic vice-presidential candidate, Long campaigned with him in Missouri. "I joined his train, rode with him and introduced him to local audiences," in what was a losing race for their party when Warren Harding handily defeated James Cox. The following year, 1921, FDR contracted polio, and it looked very much like the end of his political career. Long wrote: "I saw him several times in his New York home, flat on his back, unable to move from his waist down." But two years later, it could be reported that FDR was able to go "with a strong body servant" to a New York City office, "and I visited him there." By 1924, Roosevelt could move "with two crutches and drag his legs behind him." At the Democratic Convention that year in Madison Square Garden, FDR was the floor leader for Al Smith and Breck Long for William Gibbs McAdoo, the only occasion on which the two ever opposed each other. Neither of their candidates was successful, by the way.

During the 1928 campaign, Long got sent from the Smith campaign (this year, Al Smith *had won* the Democratic nomination) to visit FDR at Hyde Park and coordinate plans for Roosevelt, who was running for governor of New York, to assist the Democratic presidential hopeful. They met on a side veranda of Roosevelt's "comfortable home overlooking the Hudson" one September afternoon. Roosevelt was sure he'd be elected governor, but was not at all certain Smith could even carry his home state.

In 1930, after Roosevelt was reelected governor, Long felt convinced that his friend should be the Democrats' 1932 candidate. He claimed that he and Nevada Senator Key Pittman were "pioneers" in the effort to nominate Roosevelt. Long stated he operated for FDR as he had for McAdoo, "but with better success." He then described himself at Warm Springs, Georgia, with his friend Admiral Cary Grayson, swimming with FDR in his pool. The president showed some strength in his legs, but he never did walk unaided. Long put that fact down to FDR's being too busy in office for regular exercise.

The last chapter of this nostalgia included a reference to his final moment with FDR at the White House reception for the Dumbarton Oaks delegation. Noticeably absent was any mention of the slight he felt when Roosevelt merely addressed him as "Mr. Long," instead of "Breck." After the president's fourth victory in November 1944, Long sent him "a line of congratulations and received from him a friendly little note signed FDR in his own handwriting." However, when Long shortly afterward sent in his resignation, he got back a letter he was sure had not been signed by FDR.

While Frank Roosevelt was still alive in these early months of 1945, his old friend Breck was keeping an eye on current events and commenting on them for his own benefit, if no one else's, and keeping *his own benefit* in mind as he did. For example, the fate of the proposed United Nations was of keen interest to him and not only because he had had a hand in formulating its structure. The Veto Question had not been settled at Dumbarton Oaks, and adding that the dispute had been "the cause of my outburst one day," Long expressed confidence that this issue would be "in all probability settled with FDR, Churchill and Stalin" at their impending meeting in Yalta. Furthermore, he could not resist expressing his wish to be called upon to help in obtaining Senate ratification of the treaty needed to create the new body—an actual lobbying job, in other words.

Three months later, his March 10, 1945, diary entry written in La Jolla noted that "the missing link of Dumbarton Oaks"—an agreement on a Security Council veto—had been accepted by the Big Three at the Crimean meeting. Whereupon Long turned his ire on Ed Stettinius for having blocked a veto decision at Dumbarton Oaks, which resulted in FDR's now being attacked for having sold out to Stalin at Yalta.

More months passed until on May 8, 1945, Long exultingly recorded: "V-E Day, Victory in Europe. Truman proclaimed it this morning but was post-climactic." Having the new president in mind, he wistfully added, "If I can be of any use until Victory-in-Asia Day, I am ready."

By July 1, 1945, his phone still hadn't rung, but there was satisfying news to report that day: "Stettinius is out and Byrnes is going in as Secretary of State."

At the end of July, Long's phone did ring. However, he was invited not as he once had hoped to lobby for the United Nations treaty but to *attend* the Senate session where it would be voted on. His help, it seemed, had never been needed. Accompanied by Frank Thompson, he sat in the visitors' gallery and observed the lopsided roll call. The senators were voting on a resolution: "consenting to ratification of the United Nations Charter"—89 in favor and 2 opposed. "The faith of Woodrow Wilson has been vindicated," Breckinridge Long declared.

Were all doors now closed to him for a spot in the Truman administration? Occasionally this subject would be brought up by others. One person who did was Herbert Bayard Swope, a Pulitzer Prize-winning newsman, who was considered the dean of American journalists and worked for the *New York World*. Swope had written for the *St. Louis Post-Dispatch*, was born in St. Louis about the same time as Breck Long, and possibly they had known each other as boys. A number of things connected them. Gambling, for example. Swope was considered one of the best poker players in the United States and had served as chairman of the New York Horse Racing Commission for a decade. Bernard Baruch was another tie. Swope had become his assistant at the War Industries Board in 1917. Swope's parents, incidentally, were German-Jewish emigrants, and his older brother, Gerard, was chairman of General Electric for many years.

Breck and Herbert seemed on very warm terms. Swope's letter

announcing his retirement from the Racing Commission was signed, "Faithfully across the years." In June 1945, Long was writing to "My Dear Herbert" that he had "talked to Bernie on the telephone" and that he, himself, was headed to California for a few months' rest and hoped to see him (Baruch) in the spring.

In April, Swope lent Breck a copy of the *World Almanac* he'd requested, adding this P.S.: "If your health is good, why should not the new President ask you to do something for him? You are old friends, aren't you?"[8]

Well, not exactly, Breck might have honestly replied.

A more serious stab at getting Breckinridge Long a position with Truman was tried by a friend of Long's—possibly a fraternity brother— one Tom L. Gibson, living in Mississippi, who wrote to Missouri State Senator Michael J. Kinney for assistance in the effort. His thesis was: "Senator Mike McKinney of St. Louis made Bob Hannegan a member of the National Democratic Committee and Bob made Truman Vice President." From this happenstance, Gibson extrapolated:

The thought occurs to me that there might be a vacancy in the Secretary of State office—would not our old friend, Breck Long, fit in very nicely? His long experience as Ambassador and Assistant to Cordell Hull along with his ability makes him excellent timber. How about taking this up with Bob and have him take it up with Truman?[9]

Replying from the Missouri Senate, McKinney stated: "I agree with you on Breck Long and will do all I can," however, with this caveat, "but think Breck is not on the list."[10]

Sometime in the early fall of 1945, Breck Long wrote in his diary, "About a year has passed since I left the Department. At first I thought I needed a perfect and innocuous rest. I tried it and it palled on me. I was restless, nervous, dissatisfied. I went through one month of it and decided I could not stand *that*." By the time he returned home to Maryland in April, he decided he would extract his Rome diaries and put them together as a book, covering international political developments from 1933 to '36.

By December 1945, he had a manuscript ready to show. Despite the efforts of powerful journalist friends like Arthur Krock, the Washington Bureau Chief for *The New York Times*, and Anne O'Hare McCormick, the nationally known *New York Times* columnist, it was tough going to find a publisher. *Reader's Digest* declined to give it an advance review. Long sent a typed copy to Leslie Biffle, the secretary of the Senate, and asked him to get it to President Truman. Biffle never responded. Rewrites were done. The title was changed to *And The War Came.* But finally the rejection slips won out, and the project was abandoned.

Later, Long revealed he was contemplating an autobiography. No sign of that, either.

In the spring of 1946, Breck Long may have been making one final fling towards influencing the Washington elite by throwing a big garden party at Montpelier. His list of invitees included lawmakers, media stars, White House intimates, and even a Supreme Court justice. The senators and congressmen were chosen on a bipartisan basis and included Democrats Speaker of the House Sam Rayburn, Congressman Sol Bloom, Senators Alben Barkley and Tom Connally, and Republican Senators Arthur Vandenberg and Warren Austin. Most sent their regrets. Among the prominent press, Arthur Krock said yes, Walter Lippmann replied he wasn't sure, and Eugene Meyer, owner of the *Washington Post,* said he couldn't come. Despite his silence on Breck's book, Leslie Biddle came. So did Steve Early, who had been FDR's press secretary and stayed on with Truman. Justice Stanley Reed, a family friend, was also on hand for this elegant affair at that beautiful setting in Laurel, Maryland.

During these last fourteen years of Breck Long's life, Montpelier assumed far more of a role for him than in the days when he was commuting back and forth to the State Department. He had bought the estate in 1928 with 600 acres of land for $80,000 and was to write Frank Thompson back in St. Louis, "We are living in the country, about 20 miles from town. Everybody here thinks we are crazy because nobody lives in the country. Everyone else lives huddled up around the narrow side streets of Washington, which is more or less one big outdoor garage."[11]

The property had first come to his attention in 1926, and he had gone out to see it with Cary Grayson. Throughout 1927, he had fretted, waiting to hear if his offer for it would be accepted, which it was a year later. More than a decade after the Longs took occupancy, a description of their magnificent eighteenth-century, red-brick Georgian home overlooking the Patuxent River was printed in the *Washington Times-Herald* in 1939, shortly before the newcomer Maryland squire started his second stint as an assistant secretary of state. The article, written by social columnist Martha Blair, following a lunch she had at Montpelier, gave a quick snapshot of the backdrop for what were to become Breckinridge Long's most turbulent years, and out of which he earned, because of his refugee actions, a reputation so bad in some quarters that he could even be named a "war criminal."

The tranquil luxurious counterpoint of Montpelier's ambience is well recorded in the Blair piece. "Never have I seen such boxwood of varying ages," she began.

> There are literally high walls of it . . . In the huge white stable, with its red clay floorings, we saw a brand new baby percheron colt . . . two days old and ready to go and Mr. Long says it gains 10 pounds a day . . . The house is a museum. All of the floors are bare and very beautiful . . . Among other treasures in the library is an unfinished portrait of Andrew Jackson. (Mr. L inherited it from Francis Blair) . . . China collection immense . . . An enchanting view across polo fields to Maryland hills wooded and joyous in their fresh soft greens . . . An entire household of dachshunds, a beagle, lots of sheep and baby lambs and two fillies about whom Mr. Long had high hopes for next year's racing.

The manor house was called a "depository for Mrs. Long's antiques" and she had snuff boxes by the thousands along with her immense array of china.

It was here in 1937 that daughter Teenie told her father she wanted to marry Arnold Augur Willcox, and Breck said he and Christine had no objection to the Yale Engineering School graduate.

Within four weeks, Teenie and Arnold were wed at Montpelier. FDR and Eleanor Roosevelt had been on the invitation list, but obviously didn't come. If they had, Breck would have crowed about it. Known to have attended was Mrs. Henry Morgenthau Jr., whose husband was to play such a key role in Long's career. Among the presents—a touch of irony—were gold spoons that had once belonged to Emperor Haile Selassie of Ethiopia, who had been driven from his throne by Mussolini while Long was ambassador to Italy.

Montpelier and its upkeep were frequently discussed in Breck Long's diaries. Even while in Italy, he was writing to his manager William Crawford about six locust trees that had blown down in a storm and the need to remove a cedar struck by lightning, and that Admiral Grayson "might do anything he wants with the horses on the place." Instructions were also conveyed to Crawford that he was to ship twelve large jars of Baker's Instantaneous Silver Polish to Rome, using the diplomatic pouch, with detailed directions on wrapping the jars into four parcels; otherwise, they'd be too bulky for the pouch.

The staff at Montpelier included, besides the manager, butlers, cooks, chauffeur, grooms for the horses, even a farmer. Following Pearl Harbor, the scarcity of labor became a constant problem, particularly after a "civil war" between the chauffeur and the farmer, with the former withholding gasoline from the farmer and the latter refusing the chauffeur any milk.

Immediately post-war, the human resources situation seemed just as precarious. He had to employ several not-yet-repatriated Italian war prisoners for tending his grounds.

One description of Long at this time can be found in Dean Acheson's autobiography, *Present at the Creation*. He wrote:

> My fellow secretaries were a mixed bag. The senior of them was Breckinridge Long, formerly of Missouri but in 1941 the owner of one of Maryland's most beautiful colonial houses, Montpelier near Laurel. Like Mr. Hull, he was a gentleman of the old school—spare, courteous, and soft-spoken. As his house and his wife Christine's distinguished collection of silverware indicated, he was well off. Thoroughbreds graced the pastures surrounding Montpelier destined for the track, their promise always seemed to exceed their performance. Genial and popular at the Metropolitan and Alibi Clubs, retired Breckinridge Long took life easily and enjoyed it.[12]

Certainly, Breck Long was a joiner. At the Metropolitan, still today one of Washington's most prestigious private clubs, he was on the Board of Governors. He was president of the Washington, DC Princeton Club. He ran the Democrat bigwigs Jefferson Island Club. Add memberships at the Burning Tree Golf Club, the Chevy Chase Country Club in Maryland, and the Jockey Club in Baltimore, Princeton trustee, vice-president of the Jefferson Memorial Foundation, trustee of the Corcoran Art Gallery, and the list goes on.

Although the Longs had other homes—in Palm Beach, Florida (where they were members of the Everglades Club, and the Bath and Tennis Club) and on Nantucket Island (he was commodore of the Nantucket Yacht Club), it was at Montpelier where his retirement life remained centered. It was there on September 26, 1958, that Breckinridge Long died.

His funeral, curiously enough, was held at the National Cathedral in Washington, DC—and the puzzlement is due to his often-expressed fervent attachment to the Presbyterian Church, with which his family had always been active. Conversely, the National Cathedral, the sixth largest church structure in the world, is Episcopalian, as the American branch of the Anglican Church of England is called.

It may have been his wife Christine's doing that the Cathedral was chosen. She died less than four months later, and they are both interred in the vaults of this massive, gothic edifice.

Officiating at Breck's funeral was Dean Francis B. Sayre, the grandson of Woodrow Wilson—an appropriate connection. Also, in the interment section of the Cathedral, which is called a columbarium (holding the ashes of the dead), are to be found the remains of Woodrow Wilson himself and Cordell Hull. Almost adjacent to the Longs is the crypt that holds Helen Keller and her teacher Annie Sullivan.

In 1959 the Long's collection of art and antiques was put on the auction block and took in at least one million dollars. The china alone fetched $100,000.

After the estate lay vacant for several years, Teenie donated it to the Maryland-National Capital Park Commission's Department of Parks and Recreation. It has been designated a National Historical Landmark and with the addition of an art center and school is open to the public. The interior has been restored to a period well before its ownership by the Longs.

Postscript

Questions Answered

S O THERE YOU HAVE THE story of Samuel Miller Breckinridge Long, much of it in his own words. Still, some final thoughts are appropriate.

First of all, immigration into the United States and refugee policy is as much a red-hot topic now as it was in Breck Long's day. For those rednecks and America-Firsters and Madison Grant eugenicists who railed against the non-eugenic "hordes" they felt were overwhelming them, how apoplectic they would be now to see the folks who have since come here *legally*—Somalis and Ethiopians, Vietnamese and Hmong, Dominicans and Haitians, Israelis, Egyptians, Iraqis—until even in an out-of-the-way place like Maine there are forty different languages spoken in the biggest city's high school. The people they had then deemed "unassimilable"—European Jews, Italians, Slavs, Greeks—are now thoroughly Americanized, and loud mouths with surnames like Tancredo and Arpaio are leading anti-immigrant voices.

There has always been a question of, when is the United States saturated. Breck Long was forever saying, "but we can't take them all." And he was right, politically speaking at the time—although we have taken in millions during the years since, from a paltry 250,000 in the 1930s to 2.5 million in the 1950s and onward to an astounding 7.3 million in the 1980s and 10 million in the 1990s. A Wikipedia offering on the subject asserted that "By high margins, 'Americans are telling polls it was a very good thing that Poles, Italians and Jews emigrated to America'"[1]— the very ethnic groups that the State Department gang was straining so hard to keep out. One awaits the future's verdict on the contributions of today's immigrants, which will probably be no less valuable.

I believe that Breckinridge Long was only an anti-Semite in the "but some of my best friends are Jewish" sense. He lived in a high-end WASP world. He was not averse to making the acquaintance of those members of the Hebrew persuasion who had advanced enough in wealth and prestige, or even cultivating and accepting their friendship. And his single-mindedness in barring "aliens" was not levied solely against Jews. A case in point was his huffy admonishment to Americans evacuating Europe to leave their servants—assuredly not Jews—back across the Atlantic. Above all, behind his paper walls, Breck Long could enjoy the bureaucrat's greatest delight—he could play God with people's lives.

There is a decided irony in one of his interventions. In 1940 and 1941, after he had slammed the visa gate tightly shut, Breckinridge Long was essentially acting as a one-man appeals board, and he did go to bat for certain select Jewish individuals. In a paper of his dated February 7, 1941, we find the name again of the well-known Schneersohn family—specifically the Rabbi Menachem Mendel Schneersohn. This Orthodox leader, born in the Ukraine, eventually to be renowned worldwide in Jewish circles as the Rebbe, had moved to Paris in 1931, and then found a tenuous asylum in Vichy after the German triumph of 1940. Needless to say, he was anxious to get to the United States and had applied for a visa, but a snafu had arisen. His application had inadvertently been transferred from Nice to Marseilles, and Breck was well aware that immense complications and insufferable delays could occur. Hadn't he arranged the system to do just that? With a word from him, the red tape was immediately snipped and Rabbi Mendel Schneersohn was even advanced from waiting on an outside-the-quota list and given the coveted immigration visa that made possible his finding a haven in the Crown Heights section of Brooklyn. The irony here could be said to follow from the fact that the Rebbe, now deceased, is revered particularly among the fast-growing Lubavitcher section of the Orthodox as the *Mosaiach* (the Messiah) something of a God in his own right.

None of the other individual Jews that Breckinridge Long allowed himself to help were in that exalted category, but some had important American Jews pleading for them. Supreme Court Justice Felix Frankfurter wasn't bashful. He periodically handed lists to Breck of persons he wanted him to assist and, on one occasion, got the assistant secretary of state to overrule a consul in Zürich who was refusing to give visitor visas to children whose parents were in the U.S. Benjamin Cohen, of FDR's "Brain Trust," asked Long if he could intercede for the parents of Dr. Witold Hurewicz, a distinguished mathematician teaching at the University of North Carolina, and a note went out to the head of the Visa Division requesting that he accommodate Ben Cohen. Abe Lowenhaupt, a St. Louis lawyer, came to Breck Long in October 1940 with the case of Sigmund and Anna Gusdorf, of Worms in Germany.

They had two sons in the U.S., yet had been turned down on the ground there was no evidence of enough financial support for them. Breck shot back to the consulate: "I have known Mr. Lowenhaupt for a great many years and know him to have a lucrative law business in St. Louis and to be financially able to be responsible for the applicants." The case of a Robert Katz, a concentration camp inmate who would be freed if given a visa, was also forwarded to the administrator of the Visa Division. Long's secretary had added a P.S. that "Mr. Forney (who had written on Katz's behalf) is an old friend and classmate of Mr. Long's."

Not everyone passed muster in these rounds of cronyism. Roger Baldwin, director of the American Civil Liberties Union, whom Breck had known in St. Louis, was turned down cold when he tried to get visas for the widow and grandson of Leon Trotsky. Long replied that he hoped Baldwin would "give me an easier one to deal with." It's doubtful that his negative response had anything to do with Trotsky's Jewish origin—rather, because the Russian was the world's most rabid Bolshevik. A thumbs-down was also given to an Ernst Knopfmacher and his wife, who had been recommended by Rabbi Stephen Wise, a man whom Long disliked intensely. He was wont to associate him with "Radical Jews like Peter Bergson," either unaware or unimpressed that these two Zionists had such enmity towards each other that Wise was trying to have Bergson deported back to Palestine. In the matter of Herr and Frau Knopfmacher, Breck merely reported that he had discussed the case with FDR, and "the President expressed his thorough agreement with the policy which would resolve all doubts in favor of the U.S. and which in its application would deny the issue of visas to these people."

For the record, it should be mentioned that whenever in these diaries and papers Breckinridge Long badmouthed Jews (and these outbursts were very infrequent in print) the adjective "radical" was always was part of the slur. Good Jew. Bad Jew. The M.O. of the "but some of my best friends are Jewish" syndrome is clearly at play, as indeed one hears stories, apocryphal perhaps, of even Nazi leaders—including Göring and, astonishingly, Hitler—who had lists of favored Jews they ordered their satraps to leave alone.

Certainly, Adolf Eichmann wasn't in that category. One of his main pitches to his jailers in Jerusalem was that he had always worked so well with Jewish community leaders. Of course the truth was that as long as they helped him fill his transportation quotas, he tolerated their continued existence, yet when their usefulness ended, in they went to the cattle cars. This man *was* a diehard anti-Semite. His claim that he himself had never killed or physically harmed a single Jew was refuted by a camp survivor who saw him shoot a Jewish boy, but for him to be prosecuted under Israeli law, there had to be a second witness, and there was none. His morbid fascination with things Jewish—claiming even that he had learned Hebrew—was, in my experience, the hallmark of an obsessed Jew-hater. I'd known guys like that at my high school in Massachusetts during the 1940s. A story was told that Eichmann in Linz, Austria, where he grew up, led a gang that attacked Jewish schoolboys. Another story from his past referred to his somewhat Semitic looks—especially his hooked nose—and how he'd been teased about being a Yid, so to prove himself an Aryan he had to become the ultimate anti-Semite.

In this regard, no parallel behavior can be found on the part of Breckinridge Long. Chalk up one vote on the "no" side of my question marks.

How did Eichmann view himself? On trial for his life, he was offering a defense that resembled "but some of my best friends are Jewish," or at least citing instances where he had attempted to assist this Jew or that one, usually without success. Not surprisingly, he sought to shrink any importance he had in the Nazi hierarchy as best he could. "Who is a little man like me to trouble his head about it? [The Holocaust.] I got orders from my superiors and I look right and left," he stated during his interrogation.[2] That he knew what was going on at the death camps, he readily admitted, confessing to having observed scenes that made him sick to his stomach.

Did Breck Long have as clear a view of the consequences of his actions? How much time did it take him to overcome—if he ever did—his immediate post-World War I prejudice in favor of Hugh Gibson's dictum that the Jews of Poland were exaggerating their torments? One could argue he knew full well after Riegner's telegram in the summer of 1942 that extermination was a Nazi option. Disbelief still lingered but assuredly had to be dispelled by 1943, following the spotlight that Bergson had thrown on the as-yet-unnamed super-atrocity known as the Holocaust. Breck Long's post-World War II remarks at Lincoln Memorial University still had him incorporating the Nazi camouflage that deportations to the east were for forced labor purposes, except he had to have known the fate of those—Jews in particular—he had helped keep in Hitler's grasp. The argument he made—to himself and others—was that nothing could be done about it so late in the game.

The energy Breck Long expended in trying to prevent anyone one else in the U.S. government from doing anything about it could be likened to

Eichmann's fanaticism at the end of the war—not just obeying orders, as he claimed—but disobeying them in order to maintain the deportations. The stubbornness of both men placed them high in the order of the *Schreibtischmörder*. In that regard, Breckinridge Long does present an example of a killer bureaucrat much harder to pinpoint than the much more seemingly flamboyant figure of Eichmann, but still with us behind the scenes during the genocides erupting worldwide ever since the end of World War II. There are persons of this ilk walking around in Rwanda, Yugoslavia, Cambodia, Darfur, whose names we will never know.

Susan Neiman, a professor of Philosophy at Yale and Tel Aviv University, put her finger on the uproar over Hannah Arendt's "banality of evil" thesis, asserting that

> Arendt sought a formulation of the nature of evil that resists all images of 'Satanic greatness,' and combats all impulses to mythologize the horrible.[3]

Perhaps the deprivation of that comfort zone goes against the grain of human nature and produces the anger I myself have elicited for even suggesting a comparison between Eichmann and Long.

Evil is committed on this planet by human beings. Satan is a human construct and to bring him into the act is, in a sense, to do the perpetrators a favor.

I seem to have come to the point where my question marks regarding Breckinridge Long's culpability can be answered with a yes. There is still a contrast, though, in the "final solution" to both men's tenure on earth: Adolf Eichmann in his glass booth, on the gallows, his ashes strewn into eternal anonymity over the Mediterranean; and Breckinridge Long, strolling amid his boxwood hedges, supping in the Metropolitan Club, or at Laurel Park raceway, cheering on his thoroughbreds, his ashes permanently secured inside one of the storage vaults of an elegant cathedral that rises above the high-rent district of Washington, DC.

Afterword

The extent of Breckinridge Long's insidious efforts to impede immigration to safe harbor in the U.S.A. for Jews and gentiles alike is painted by Mr. Rolde with deft strokes and brought into the light of day in this detailed and intriguing account.

Mr. Rolde takes us through the story using Long's personal diary to provide insights into Long's motivations. Rolde makes convincing and powerful assertions that Long, heartless and uncharitable, played by the book with devastating consequences, actions that parallel those of his peers in Hitler's Third Reich.

My grandmother, Frances Perkins, worked to open the doors wider, while authority for immigration was under the Department of Labor, where it resided when she took office. In May of 1940, partly because of her resistance to stemming the tide of immigrants, Long was successful in moving authority for immigration to the Department of Justice, effectively removing her from that role. Yet she remained one of the voices in the FDR administration that encouraged Jewish immigration and continued to do all that she could to help. This book reveals the behind-the-scenes machinations of a political operative who may well be responsible, albeit indirectly, for the death of many Jews in Nazi Germany.

Tomlin Perkins Coggeshall, grandson of
Frances Perkins, Secretary of Labor, 1933–1945

Acknowledgments

As always, books, especially nonfiction, are not the work of the author alone. Thanks are to be given by me even to people whose names I never learned. The staff at the Library of Congress's manuscript collection were always unfailingly helpful. The same was true at the library of the Missouri Historical Society in Saint Louis, Breckinridge Long's hometown. At Long's estate, Montpelier in Laurel, Maryland, the director, Mary Jurkiewicz, and her staff gave me plentifully their time and assistance.

Individuals who helped include Charles Stanhope, then a high official at the Library of Congress, now back in his home state of Maine, and especially Chris Breiseth, Rabbi David Gordis, and Tomlin Coggeshall, for not only reading my manuscript but also providing comments for the final, printed copy, and Charles Ferguson, prof emeritus, Colby College, who read with extreme care, amending my mistakes, particularly punctuation. Jennifer Bunting at Tilbury House Publishers in Gardiner, Maine, also read the manuscript and gave me sage advice, as she always does.

To my publishers Paul Cornell du Houx and his wife Ramona du Houx at Polar Bear & Company, it has been a pleasure working with you. Finally, to Seymour Kurtz of Elmhurst, New York, who encouraged me to write about Breckinridge Long, even if he eventually didn't like the approach I took. And the great prodder, my wife Carla, deserves my appreciation as well.

Notes

PREFACE

1. *Los Angeles Daily News,* January 21, 2008, article by Bridget Johnson, columnist.
2. Wistrich, Robert S. *Anti-Semitism: The Longest Hatred.* New York: Schoken Books, 1991, page 119; Long's *Mein Kampf* quote: Urofsky, Melvin J., *We Are One! American Jewry and Israel,* New York, 1978.
3. Henzel, Ian. "Another Chilling Episode in American History," Amazon.com customer review of *America & The Holocaust,* April 6, 2003.
4. Friedlander, Saul. *The Years of Execution.* New York: Harper Collins, 2007, page 85.
5. Rosen, Robert N. *Saving The Jews: Franklin Roosevelt and the Holocaust.* New York: Thunder's Mouth Press, 2006, page 499, Afterword by Alan M. Dershowitz.

CHAPTER ONE

1. Celler, Emanuel. *You Never Leave Brooklyn.* New York: J. Day Company, 1953.
2. Jackson, Robert H. *That Man: An Insider 's Portrait of Franklin D. Roosevelt.* Oxford: Oxford University Press, 2003, page 29.
3. Ibid., pages 112–13.
4. Feingold, Henry. *The Politics of Rescue: The Roosevelt Administration and the Holocaust,* 1938–1945. New York: Holocaust Library, 1970.
5. Ibid., page 14.
6. Hull, Cordell. *The Memoirs of Cordell Hull,* Volume I. New York: The Macmillan Company, 1948, page 471.
7. *The New York Times,* December 12, 1943, page 8.
8. *The American Experience: America and the Holocaust.* John Pehle on establishing the War Refugee Board. PBS, http://www.pbs.org/wgbh/amex/holocaust/.
9. John Pehle, Memo for Secretary Morgenthau's files, January 16, 1944.
10. Hull, Volume II, page 1539.
11. Ibid., pages 1539–40.
12. Breitman, Richard and Kraut, Alan. *American Refugee Policy and European Jewry, 1933–1945,* Bloomington, IN: University of Indiana Press, 1987, page 192.
13. Israel, Fred L. *The War Diaries of Breckinridge Long: 1939–1944.* Lincoln, NE: University of Nebraska Press, 1966, page 336.
14. Ibid., pages 336–7.
15. Ibid., page 337.

CHAPTER TWO

1. Heidler, David S. and Heidler, Jeanne T. (Editors). *Encyclopedia of the American Civil War: A Political, Social and Military History,* Volume 1. Santa Barbara, CA: ABC-Clio, 2000, page 277.

2. Another James Webb, in the 21st century, has written a history of the Scots-Irish immigrants to the U.S. It is called *Born Fighting: How the Scots-Irish Shaped America*, and the author is now a Democratic U.S. senator from Virginia, after having won the Navy Cross and other medals with the Marine Corps in Vietnam and having been secretary of the Navy and assistant secretary of defense in the Reagan administration.

3. Blame, James G. *Twenty Years of Congress*, Vol. 1. Norwich, CT: The Henry Bill Publishing Company, 1886, page 507. Also, in a previous piece of writing Blame described a scene in Paris, France, where he was visiting in 1867, connected to another relation of the Breckinridge Long family. "At the *Théâtre de l'Impératrice* last night, I saw John [Cabell] Breckinridge and his wife. They sat but a very few boxes from us and were very intently gazing at our party the whole evening. They look sad, downcast and dispirited. He is in Paris *without money*. What situation could be more deplorable?"

4. Greeley, Horace. *The American Conflict: A History of the Great Rebel War in the United States of America, 1860–1864*, Vol. 1. Hartford, CT: O. D. Case and Company, 1884, pages 489–90.

5. Container 8, "Papers of Breckinridge Long," Library of Congress, Manuscript Collection, Madison Building.

6. Stevens, Walter B. *History of Saint Louis, the Fourth City, 1764–1909*, Vol. 2, page 704.

7. Ibid.

8. Container 10, "Papers of Breckinridge Long."

9. *St. Louis Post Dispatch*, January 25, 1917.

CHAPTER THREE

1. Garraty, John A. (Editor). *Dictionary of American Biography*, Supplement Six, 1956–60. New York, NY: Charles Scribner's Sons, 1980, page 387.

2. Ibid.

3. McCombs, William F. and Lang, Louis Jay. *Making Woodrow Wilson President*, New York, NY: Fairview Publishing Company, 1921.

4. Clark, Champ. *My Quarter Century of American Politics*, Vol. 2. New York, NY: Harper & Brothers, 1920, page 392.

5. Ibid., page 398.

6. Long, Breckinridge. Diary 1. Library of Congress, Manuscript Division, Madison Building, Washington, D.C.

7. Actually St. Louis had hosted Democratic National Conventions before, in 1876, 1888, and 1904. Since this one in 1916, the Democrats have never gone back there.

8. Link, Arthur S. *The Road To The White House*. Princeton, NJ: Princeton University Press, 1947.

9. Long. Diary 1.

10. Long. Diary 2.

11. Ibid.

CHAPTER FOUR

1. Long. Diary 2.
2. Gilbert, Clinton W. (the alleged author) with Kirby, John and cartoons by Cesare, Oscar Edward. *The Mirrors of Washington,* New York, NY: OP Putnam and Sons, 1921.
3. Diary of William Phillips, pages 23, 26, 28, Phillips Papers, Houghton Library, Harvard College, Cambridge, MA.
4. Long. Diary 3.
5. David R. Francis Collection, Missouri Historical Society Library, St. Louis, MO.
6. Ibid.
7. Long. Diary 3.
8. Ibid.

CHAPTER FIVE

1. Long. Diary 5.
2. Ibid.
3. Ibid.
4. Long. Diary 6.
5. Long. Diary 5.
6. Long. Diary 6.
7. Ibid.
8. Ibid.
9. Ibid.
10. Long. Diary 8.
11. Ibid.
12. Ibid.
13. Francis to Martha Slaughter, March 1, 1919. David R. Francis Collection, Missouri Historical Society Library, St. Louis, MO.
14. Francis to Lenore, March 1, 1919. Francis Collection, September 17, 1919.

CHAPTER SIX

1. Francis Collection, September 17, 1919.
2. Long. Diary 8.
3. Miller, Robert Moats. *Harry Emerson Fosdick,* Oxford, UK: Oxford University Press, 1985, page 192.
4. *The New York Times,* June 17,1919.
5. *The New York Times,* June 11, 1919.
6. Kapiszewski, Andrzej. Article, "Controversial Reports on the Situation of Jews in Poland in the Aftermath of World War I," etc. Studio Judaica, 2004, page 275.
7. Ibid., pages 276–7.
8. Ibid., page 302.
9. Long to Gibson, December 30, 1919. "Papers of Breckinridge Long," Library of Congress, Manuscript Collection, Madison Building.

10. Long. Diary 8.
11. Ibid.
12. Ibid.
13. Ibid.
14. Ibid.

CHAPTER SEVEN

1. Long. Diary 10.
2. Ibid.
3. Ibid.
4. *The New York Times*, June 11, 1920, page 16, column 2.
5. *The New York Times*, July 2, 1920.
6. Editorial by H. L. Mencken, *American Mercury*, April 1929.
7. Long. Diary 10.
8. Long. Diary 8.
9. Long. Diary 10.

CHAPTER EIGHT

1. Long. Diary 11.
2. Ibid.
3. Hinton, Harold B. *Cordell Hull*. Garden City, New York: Doubleday, Doran and Company, 1942, page 166.
4. Ibid., page 167.
5. All letters quoted are from the Charles Martin Hay papers at the Western Historical Manuscript Collection, Columbia, MO.
6. Webster, Noah. *New Universal Unabridged Dictionary*. New York, NY: Simon and Schuster, 1983, page 1103.
7. Reprinted in *Time Magazine*, September 19, 1927.
8. *The New York Times*, April 27, 1922, page 8, column 2.
9. *Time Magazine*, September 13, 1926.
10. *The New York Times*, August 3, 1922, page 12, column 2.
11. Ibid., August 6, 1922, page 5, column 3.
12. *St. Louis Globe Democrat*, April 21, 1933.
13. March, David D. *The History of Missouri*, New York, NY, and West Palm Beach, FL: Lewis Historical Publishing Company, Volume II.

CHAPTER NINE

1. Long. Diary 12, October 15, 1922.
2. Long. Diary 12.
3. Ibid.
4. Klein, Jonas. *Beloved Island: Franklin & Eleanor and The Legacy of Campobello*. Forest Dale, VT: Paul S. Eriksson Publisher, 2000, page 119.
5. Long. Diary 12.

6. Ibid.

7. Ibid.

8. Wallace, Max. *The American Axis: Henry Ford, Charles Lindbergh and the Rise of the Third Reich.* New York, NY: St. Martin's Press, 2003, page 64.

9. Higham, John. *Strangers in the Land.* New York, NY: Atheneum, 1981, page 177.

10. Daniels, Roger and Graham, Otis C. *Debating American Immigration, 1882–Present.* Lanham, MD: Rowman and Littlefield Publishers, Inc., 2001.

11. Roberts, Kenneth. *Why Europe Leaves Home*, New York, NY: The Bobbs-Merrill Co., 1922, page 50.

12. Ibid.

13. Roberts, Kenneth. *I Wanted To Write.* Garden City, NY: Doubleday and Co., 1949, page 144.

CHAPTER TEN

1. Long. Diary 13, May 23, 1923.

2. Long. Diary 14, February 6, 1924.

3. Wilson to Long, March 28, 1922. "Papers of Breckinridge Long," Library of Congress, Manuscript Collection, Madison Building.

4. Long. Diary 14, July 15, 1924.

5. Ibid.

6. Long. Diary 14, September 19, 1924.

7. Long. Diary 14, 1924.

8. Long. 1926 Diary, February 14, 1926.

9. Long. 1926 Diary, February 14 and February 27, 1926.

10. Long. 1926 Diary, February 10, 1926.

11. Long. 1926 Diary, March 17, 1926.

12. Long. Diary 17, January 20, 1927.

13. Ibid.

CHAPTER ELEVEN

1. Long to Meredith, October 23, 1925. "Papers of Breckinridge Long," Library of Congress, Manuscript Collection, Madison Building.

2. Ibid.

3. Long to Meredith, February 19, 1926.

4. Long to Meredith, November 24, 1924.

5. Roosevelt, Elliott and Brough, James. *The Untold Story: The Roosevelts of Hyde Park.* New York, NY: G. P. Putnam's Sons, 1973, page 246.

6. Long. Diary 18, June 30, 1928.

7. Long. Diary 18, August 24, 1928.

8. Long. Diary 18, October 15, 1928.

9. Slayton, Robert A. *Empire Statesman: The Rise and Redemption of Al Smith.* New York, NY: The Free Press, a division of Simon and Schuster, Inc., 2001, page 276.

10. Ibid., page xiv, Prologue.

11. Ibid., page x, Prologue.
12. *Time Magazine,* October 1, 1928.
13. Ibid.
14. Ibid.
15. Long. Diary 18, October 21, 1928.
16. Long. Diary 18, November 5, 1928.
17. Management Audit of Kentucky Horse Racing Authority, December 2006.
18. Long. Diary 18, December 30, 1928.
19. Slayton, page 355.

CHAPTER TWELVE

1. Long to Senator Key Pittman, July 5, 1932, Pittman Papers. Library of Congress, Manuscript Collection, Madison Building.
2. Ibid.
3. Roosevelt, Elliott and Brough, James. Pages 287–8
4. Ibid., page 285.
5. Ibid., page 294.
6. Nash, George H. *The Life of Herbert Hoover: Master of Emergencies, 1917–1918.* New York, NY: W. W. Norton & Company, 1996, page 222.
7. *Atlanta Constitution,* October 25, 1932.
8. Morgan, Thomas B. *Speaking of Cardinals.* New York, NY: G. P. Putnam's Sons, 1946.
9. Ibid., page 27.
10. Ibid.
11. Breckinridge Long to FDR, May 31, 1933. "Papers of Breckinridge Long," Library of Congress, Manuscript Collection, Madison Building.
12. FDR to Breckinridge Long, June 16, 1933. "Papers of Breckinridge Long."

CHAPTER THIRTEEN

1. Long to FDR, June 27, 1933. "Papers of Breckinridge Long," Library of Congress, Manuscript Collection, Madison Building.
2. Feingold, Henry, *The Politics of Rescue.* New York, NY: Holocaust Library, 1970, page 133.
3. Marks, Frederick W. III. *Wind Over Sand.* Athens, GA: Georgia University Press, 1988, page 5.
4. Pearson, Drew and Allen Robed S.: *Washington Merry-Go-Round.* New York, NY: Blue Ribbon Books, 1931, pages 137–8.
5. Ibid., page 139.
6. Modem History Sourcebook. *Benito Mussolini.* Article for the definition of Fascism for the Italian encyclopedia, 1932.
7. Long. 1935 Diary, March 7, 1935.
8. Long. 1935 Diary, March 6, 1935.
9. Long. 1935 Diary, September 17, 1935.
10. Ibid.

11. Ibid.
12. Ibid.
13. Ibid.
14. Nixon, Edgar B. (editor) *Franklin Roosevelt and Foreign Affairs,* Volume III. Cambridge, MA: The Belknap Press of Harvard University Press, 1969, Louis Howe to FDR, October 18, 1935, page 28.
15. Long. 1936 Diary, January 4, 1936.
16. Ibid.
17. Ibid., March 10, 1936.
18. Ibid.
19. Ibid.
20. Ibid., March 13, 1936.
21. Nixon (ed), page 324.
22. Ibid., page 330.
23. Ibid.

CHAPTER FOURTEEN

1. Long. Diary 20, October 1936.
2. Long. Diary, January 24, 1937.
3. Long. Diary, January 25, 1937.
4. Long. Diary, 1938.
5. Long. Diary, February 18, 1938.
6. Wallace. Pages 157, 158.
7. Long. Diary, February 18, 1938.
8. Ibid.

CHAPTER FIFTEEN

1. Long. Diary, 1938
2. Ibid.
3. Ibid.
4. Arad, Gulie Ne'eman. *America: Its Jews and the Rise of Nazism.* Bloomington, IN: University of Indiana Press, 2008, page 135.
5. *Frances Perkins and the German Jewish Refugees.* American Jewish History, March 2001.
6. Ibid.
7. Habe, Hans. *The Mission,* New York, NY: Coward-McCann, 1965.
8. Habe, page 251.
9. Ibid., page 280.
10. McDonald, James G. *Refugees and Rescue*, Volume II, edited by Richard Breitman, Barbara McDonald Stewart and Severin Hochberg. Bloomington, IN: University of Indiana Press and U.S. Holocaust Museum, page 178.
11. Ibid.
12. *Time Magazine*, June 17, 1966.

CHAPTER SIXTEEN

1. Long. Diary, 1939.
2. Ibid.
3. Ibid.
4. Ibid.
5. Ibid.
6. Ibid.
7. Long. Diary, October 30, 1939.
8. Stiller, Jesse. *George S. Messersmith: Diplomat of Democracy.* Chapel Hill, NC: University of North Carolina Press, 1987.
9. Ibid., page 144.
10. Ibid., page 51.
11. Ibid., page 55.
12. Long. Diary, 1939.
13. Ibid.
14. Ibid.
15. McDonald, James G. *Advocate For the Doomed: The Diaries and Papers of James G. McDonald, 1932–1935,* Vol. I, edited by Richard Breitman, Barbara McDonald Stewart and Severin Hochberg. Bloomington, IN: Indiana University Press, 2007, page 803.

CHAPTER SEVENTEEN

1. Israel, Fred L. *The War Diaries of Breckinridge Long.* Lincoln, NE: University of Nebraska Press, 1966.
2. Ibid., page 88.
3. Ibid.
4. Ibid., page 91.
5. Long. Diaries, 1940.
6. Ibid.
7. Ibid.
8. Israel, page 92.
9. Downey, Kirstin. *The Woman Behind the New Deal: The Life of Frances Perkins.* New York, NY: Doubleday, page 296.
10. *The American Experience: America and the Holocaust.* Margaret E. Jones on the visa situation in Vienna. PBS, http://www.pbs.org/wgbh/amex/holocaust/.
11. Ibid.
12. Long. Diaries, 1940.
13. Israel, page 114.
14. Ibid., pages 113–14.
15. Long. Diaries, 1940.
16. Ibid.
17. Ibid.
18. McDonald, James G. *Refugees and Rescue,* Volume II, edited by Richard Breitman, Barbara McDonald Stewart and Severin Hochberg. Bloomington, IN:

University of Indiana Press and U.S. Holocaust Museum, page 209.
19. Ibid.

CHAPTER EIGHTEEN

1. Long. Diary, November 13, 1940.
2. Ibid.
3. Ibid.
4. Ibid.
5. Ibid., November 20, 1940.
6. Ibid.
7. Ibid., November 25, 1940.
8. Ibid., December 12, 1940.
9. Mayer, Arno. *Why Did the Heavens Not Darken?* New York, NY: Pantheon Books, 1988, page 234.
10. Ibid., page 235.
11. Ibid.
12. Wyman, David S. *The Abandonment of the Jews.* New York, NY: The New Press, reprint 2007 of 1984 original, page 4.
13. Israel. *The War Diaries of Breckinridge Long.* Lincoln, NE: University of Nebraska Press, 1966, page 169.
14. Ibid., page 173.
15. Ibid., page 174.
16. Ibid., page 205.
17. Ibid., page 178.
18. Ibid., page 182.
19. Ibid., page 197.
20. Ibid., pages 206–7
21. Ibid., page 215.
22. Ibid., page 216.
23. Ibid.

CHAPTER NINETEEN

1. Mayer, Arno. *Why Did the Heavens Not Darken?* New York, NY: Pantheon Books, 1988, page 291.
2. Private communication from Seymour Kurtz of Elmhurst, New York, NY.
3. Wyman. *The Abandonment of the Jews,* New York, NY: The New Press, 2007.
4. Ibid., page 3.
5. Arendt, Hannah. *Eichman in Jerusalem: A Report on the Banality of Evil.* New York, NY: Penguin Books, 1963.
6. *The New York Times,* November 9, 2009, pages C1 and C.
7. Arendt, page 287.
8. Long. Diary, January 13, 1942.
9. Lehrer, Steven. *Wannsee House and the Holocaust.* Jefferson, NC: McFarland & Company, Inc., 2000, Appendix C, pages 146–153.

10. Wise, Stephen S. *The Challenging Years: The Autobiography of Stephen Wise.* New York, NY: G. P. Putnam's Sons, 1949.
11. Israel, page 282.
12. Ibid., page 283.
13. Ibid.

CHAPTER TWENTY

1. Israel. *The War Diaries of Breckinridge Long.* Lincoln, NE: University of Nebraska Press, 1966, page 306.
2. Notes of the Meeting at the Harmonie Club, April 10, 1943.
3. Ibid.
4. Israel, page 307.
5. McDonald. *Refugees and Rescue,* Volume II. Bloomington, IN: University of Indiana Press and U.S. Holocaust Museum, page 311.
6. *The New York Times,* May 25, 1943.
7. *The New York Times,* May 24, 1943.
8. *The New York Times,* May 23, 1943.
9. Israel, page 309.
10. Ibid., page 316.
11. Ibid.

CHAPTER TWENTY-ONE

1. *The New York Times,* February 15, 2007, page A1.
2. Ibid., page A25.
3. Katznelson, Yitzhak. *Vittel Diary.* Tel Aviv: Ghetto Fighters House, page 30 of the biographical note.
4. Ibid., page 43.
5. *The American Experience: America and the Holocaust.* PBS, http://www.pbs.org/wgbh/amex/holocaust/.
6. Friedman, Max Paul. *Nazis and Good Neighbors.* Cambridge, UK: Cambridge University Press, 2003.
7. Deutsch, Sandra McGee and Dolkart, Ronald H. *The Argentine Right.* Wilmington DE: SR Books, 1993, page 87.
8. Ibid., page 88.
9. Chongo Leiva, Juan. *El Fracaso de Hitler En Cuba.* Havana: Editorial Letras Cubanas, 1989, page 23.
10. Ibid., page 17.
11. Ibid., page 43.
12. Friedman, page 110.
13. Ibid., page 118.
14. Ibid., page 211.
15. Ibid., page 193.
16. Ibid., page 209.
17. Ibid., page 213.

18. Long. Diary, August 30, 1942.
19. Friedman, page 232.

CHAPTER TWENTY-TWO

1. Israel. *The War Diaries of Breckinridge Long.* Lincoln, NE: University of Nebraska Press, 1966, page 315.
2. Ibid., page 322.
3. Ibid., page 323.
4. Ibid., page 324.
5. Ibid.
6. Ibid., page 328.
7. Ibid.
8. Ibid., page 328.
9. Ibid., page 330.
10. Stettinius, Edward R. Jr. *The Diaries of Edward R. Stettinius Jr.*, edited by Thomas M. Campbell and George C. Herring. New York, NY: New Viewpoints, 1975, page 5.
11. Ibid., page 9.
12. Israel, page 331.
13. Stettinius, page 13.
14. Israel, page 332.
15. Ibid., page 333.
16. Long. Papers on Refugees, May 7, 1943.
17. Printed Record of the Hearings Before the House Foreign Relations Committee, November 26, 1943, page 31.
18. Ibid.

CHAPTER TWENTY-THREE

1. Israel. *The War Diaries of Breckinridge Long.* Lincoln, NE: University of Nebraska Press, 1966, pages 334–5.
2. Israel, pages 335–6.
3. *Wikipedia*, biography of Raoul Gustav Wallenberg, http://en.wikipedia.org/wiki/Raoul_Wallenberg
4. Gurock, Jeffrey S. *America, American Jews and the Holocaust.* London, UK: Taylor and Francis Group, 1998, page 304.
5. Ibid. page 307.
6. Israel, pages 337–8.
7. Ibid., page 338.
8. Ibid.
9. Vandenberg, Arthur. *The Papers of Senator Vandenberg,* edited by Arthur H. Vandenberg Jr. with the collaboration of Joe Alex Moses. Boston, MA: Houghton Mifflin Company, 1952, page 96.
10. Vandenberg, "Statement by Senator Vandenberg," page 51.
11. Hoopes, Townsend and Brinkley, Douglas. *FDR and the Creation of the UN,* New

Haven, CT: Yale University Press, 1997, page 156.

12. Hillenbrand, Robert C. *Dumbarton Oaks: The Origins of the United Nations and the Search for Postwar Security.* Chapel Hill, NC: University of North Carolina Press, 2001.
13. Ibid., page 218.
14. Hoopes and Brinkley, page 154.

CHAPTER TWENTY-FOUR

1. Israel. *The War Diaries of Breckinridge Long.* Lincoln, NE: University of Nebraska Press, 1966, page 382.
2. Ibid.
3. Ibid., page 388.
4. Ibid.
5. Ibid., page 389.
6. Ibid., page 369.
7. Ibid.
8. Ibid., page 370.
9. Ibid., page 366.
10. Ibid.
11. Ibid., page 374.
12. Ibid., page 391.
13. Ibid.
14. Ibid.
15. Ibid., page 392.

CHAPTER TWENTY-FIVE

1. Sikeli Neil Ratu Thesis, page 44.
2. Ibid.
3. Wyman. *The Abandonment of the Jews.* New York, NY: The New Press, reprint 2007.
4. Ibid., page 191.
5. Breitman, Richard and Kraut, Man. *American Refugee Policy and European Jewry, 1933–1945.*
6. Ibid., page 121.
7. Ibid., page 126.
8. Bernard M. Baruch Papers. Baruch-Long, April 25, 1847; Long-Baruch, April 28, 1947. Seeley G. Mudd Manuscript Library, Princeton University.
9. Ibid., Long-Baruch, April 17, 1949; Baruch-Long, April 14, 1949.
10. Ibid.
11. Higham, Charles. *Trading With The Enemy.* Lincoln, NE: iUniverse, Inc., 2007.
12. Ibid., page 203.
13. Yablonka, Hatma. *The State of Israel vs. Adolf Eichmann.* New York, NY: Schoken Books, 2004, page 233.
14. Hull. *The Memoirs of Cordell Hull*, Volume I. New York: The Macmillan Company, 1948, pages 1539–40.

15. Speech by Rabbi Herbert Rosenblum, Tel Aviv, May 7, 1980, entitled *The US. Government, the Jewish Organizations and the War Refugee Board During The Holocaust* (originally in Hebrew, translated by the lecturer, September 25, 2004).
16. Sachar, Abram L. *The Redemption of the Unwanted*, New York, NY: St. Martins/ Marek, 1983, page 143.
17. Von Lang, Jochen, in collaboration with Sibyll, Claus. *Eichmann Interrogated.* New York, NY: Vintage Books, 1984, pages 291–2.

CHAPTER TWENTY-SIX

1. Long. Diary, December 4, 1944.
2. Long. Diary, December 25, 1944.
3. Long. Diary, January 20, 1945.
4. Long Papers. Letters, 1945. Homer Cummings to Long, March 12, 1945.
5. Long Commencement speech, Lincoln Memorial University, Harrowgate, TN, June 4, 1945.
6. Vice President Harry S. Truman to Long, January 26, 1945. "Papers of Breckinridge Long," Library of Congress, Manuscript Collection, Madison Building.
7. "Papers of Breckinridge Long." Container 5, page 509.
8. Herbert Bayard Swope to Long, April 20, 1945. "Papers of Breckinridge Long."
9. Long Papers. Container 158, Tom L. Gibson to Missouri Senator Michael McKinney, April 20, 1945.
10. Ibid., McKinney to Gibson, May 4, 1945.
11. Long to Frank Thompson, January 20, 1930, from Long Papers at Montpelier Mansion.
12. Acheson, Dean. *Present at the Creation.* New York, NY: W. W. Norton, 1969.

POSTSCRIPT

1. "Immigration to the United States." *Wikipedia*, http://en.wikipedia.org/wiki/ Immigration_to_the_United_States
2. Von Lang, Jochen (editor, in collaboration with Claus Sibyll). *Eichmann Interrogated: Transcripts from the Archives of the Israeli Police.* New York, NY: Random House, Vintage Books, 1984, page 158.
3. Aschheim, Steven E. (editor). *Hannah Arendt in Jerusalem.* Essay by Niemen, Susan, "Theodicy in Jerusalem," pages 65–90. Berkeley, CA: University of California, 2001, pages 89–90.

In addition to his many publications, Neil Rolde (1931-2017) was a long-time public servant, philanthropist, Renaissance man, and gentleman. The renowned Maine historian grew up in Brookline, Massachusetts. He earned a BA at Yale and a master's in journalism at Columbia University. He worked as a film scriptwriter before moving to Maine with his wife, Carlotta Florsheim, to raise their family. In York they brought up four children and enjoyed family visits with their eight grandchildren.

Photo Ramona du Houx

The author won book awards from the Maine Historical Society, the Maine Humanities Council, and the Maine Writers & Publishers Alliance. Most of Neil Rolde's books involve the history of his beloved Maine and its people. With a wealth of historical knowledge about politics, the author turned his skill and wit to blogging current political incidents in a historical context.

Rolde's public service included six years as assistant to Maine's Governor Kenneth M. Curtis and sixteen years as representative in the Maine State Legislature. He was the Democratic candidate for U.S. Senate in 1990. The author served on many state boards and commissions, including the Maine Health Care Reform Commission, the Maine Historic Preservation Commission, the Maine Humanities Council, and the Maine Arts Commission.

www.ingramcontent.com/pod-product-compliance
Lightning Source LLC
Chambersburg PA
CBHW022005080426
42733CB00007B/475